"*The Principles of Pleasure* lays out an inclus
health that empowers both professionals a
serve. For every professional—teacher, soci
professional—who has ever faced the over
difficulties in the U.S. and thought, *there m*
fessional who has struggled to explain to th. ....gues (or funders) why pleasure
must be integrated into their practice, Laura Rademacher and Lindsey Hoskins have
written a playbook. This book is essential reading for anyone who takes seriously the
life-changing work of preventing sexually transmitted infections, unwanted pregnancy, sexual violence, and the sexual distress that can end marriages."

—**Emily Nagoski, PhD,** author, *Come As You Are:*
the surprising new science that will transform your sex life

"Laura Rademacher breaks the silence about promoting sexual pleasure as part of
sexual education and therapy! While we focus so much on amelioration pain, disease, and dysfunction, pleasure is one of the most essential elements of sexual health.
Yet is it the part that too many people are uncomfortable talking about. This book is
an essential guide for mental health professionals and sexuality educators to put the
P back into sex, sexuality and sexual health!"

—**Eli Coleman, PhD,** professor and director,
Academic Chair in Sexual Health, Program in Human Sexuality,
University of Minnesota Medical School

"*The Principles of Pleasure* is an excellent, sex-positive, evidence-based guide for sexuality professionals who are invested in helping their clients explore and experience
pleasurable aspects to their sexualities. Highly recommended!"

—**Debby Herbenick, PhD,** associate professor,
Indiana University; author, *Because It Feels Good*

"Laura Rademacher and Lindsey Hoskins have put pleasure in its proper place—as
one of the cornerstones to developing healthy sexuality. *The Principles of Pleasure*
understands that pleasure is a creative and life affirming force, not a problematic or
destructive one. This is a powerful and much-needed message!"

—**Al Vernacchio, MSEd,** sexuality educator; author,
For Goodness Sex: Changing the Way We Talk to Teens
About Sexuality, Values, and Health

"I would like to give high praise to Rademacher and Hoskins for delivering a
comprehensive menu of accessible sexual health treatment interventions. Packed
full of information that can be easily integrated in to a variety of clinical settings. Research studies report clients and patients want their health providers to be
comfortable in discussing the "taboo" topic of sexuality. This book provides clear
instructions and accurate information to support the difficult and challenging topics related to sexuality. *Principals of Pleasure* is a reliable resource for both professional
and personal development."

—**Heather Raznick MSW, LCSW,** AASECT certified sex therapist;
clinical training and supervision by
Dr. William Masters (Masters and Johnson Institute)

The Principles of Pleasure

There are tremendous benefits to discussing the subject of sexual and emotional pleasure with clients, and this book addresses the challenges and misconceptions of doing just that. Laura Rademacher and Lindsey Hoskins teach the skills necessary for mental health professionals and sex educators to build competence in this work with their clients. Readers get techniques to implement in therapeutic, clinical, and educational settings, and learn how to examine pleasure in ways that are currently lacking from academic work on sexual health. This book covers skills for working with populations of all orientations and gender expressions. Language and phrasing for addressing pleasure issues in a wide variety of educational or therapeutic settings is also provided. Information about sexual lubrication and sex toys that is rarely taught in professional training programs is included, as well as how to appropriately incorporate information about these important sexual tools into your work. Issues such as abstinence, sexual orientation, couple therapy, and sexual education will be discussed outside of the standard medical model of sex therapy. *The Principles of Pleasure* will help you feel relaxed and confident while moving clients and students closer to their pleasure goals, and provides the evidence to back up the importance of talking and teaching about pleasure, should you need to justify this work.

Laura Rademacher, MA, LMFT, CST, has more than 12 years of experience working with pleasure issues in professional settings. While currently working as a Certified Sex Therapist in Minnesota, she also teaches and provides trainings nationally. Her workshop with Lindsey Hoskins, Teaching Pleasure: Best Practices, was awarded the 2014 Schiller Prize from AASECT (American Association of Sex Educators, Counselors, and Therapists).

Lindsey Hoskins is a sex ed nerd devoted to helping people of all ages take pride in their sexuality and find pleasure in their bodies in the ways that are right for them. She is the Director of Health Education at Family Tree Clinic, an innovative sexual health care center in Minnesota. Lindsey is a tireless advocate for sex-positive sex education and believes that access to safe and shame-free sexuality is a lifelong human right.

The Principles of Pleasure

Working with the Good Stuff as
Sex Therapists and Educators

Laura Rademacher, MA, LMFT, CST
With Lindsey Hoskins

Illustrations by Hannah Jorden

Routledge
Taylor & Francis Group

NEW YORK AND LONDON

First published 2017
by Routledge
711 Third Avenue, New York, NY 10017

and by Routledge
2 Park Square, Milton Park, Abingdon, Oxon, OX14 4RN

Routledge is an imprint of the Taylor & Francis Group, an informa business

Library of Congress Cataloging-in-Publication Data
A catalog record for this book has been requested

ISBN: 978-1-138-88483-0 (hbk)
ISBN: 978-1-138-88482-3 (pbk)
ISBN: 978-1-315-71587-2 (ebk)

Typeset in Bembo
by Apex CoVantage, LLC

Contents

Preface

Hi, I'm Laura Rademacher and I love to talk about pleasure. I began my career in sex therapy and education through a somewhat nontraditional route: selling sex toys.

Sex toy salespeople are not always considered sexual health professionals. Stereotypes about sex toy salespeople cast them as frivolous at best, smutty or uneducated at worst. I worry that this is because of their focus on pleasure, their willingness to talk about the good stuff: orgasms, lube, dildos and yes, if you must, even dongs. Devaluing the work of sex toy salespeople especially bothers me because selling vibrators was how I developed skills I now use daily as a sex therapist.

Working at a progressive sex toy store with a strong focus on education gave me an experience that many sexual health professionals do not get: permission to focus on the important topic of pleasure. Talking to nervous people about the basics of harnesses or lube gave me skills that were never covered in my academic study or therapeutic training, as important as that academic study and therapeutic training was. I know I am not alone in that experience. In general, professionals specializing in sexual health do not receive much formal training about pleasure issues. In the small amount of training that professionals in the fields of mental health, medical health, or education receive about sexuality, the topics most frequently covered tend to be dysfunction, diagnosis, risk prevention, or Sexually Transmitted Infections (STIs): so much talk of how bodies and relationships can go wrong, so little talk about what happens when they go so very right.

Sex therapists and other professionals are taught not to work outside of our "scope of practice." So what happens when we are never taught how to work with clients around pleasure issues? Naturally we worry that we are not equipped to handle the topic. We've never been trained for this and we don't have standard interventions: Is it even ethical to address these issues in that case? We care about our commitment to do our professional best and, sadly, sometimes as professionals we feel the best we can do is avoid the topic.

When professionals do not receive training on how to work with pleasure issues it is easy to be nervous about asking clients important questions: "Are you happy with your sex life?" "Are you having orgasms?" "What do you enjoy about your body?" "What does pleasure mean to you?" Direct questions about sexual pleasure can seem invasive or worse, perverted. These fears often cause professionals, even sexual health professionals, to avoid the topic of pleasure. Unfortunately, this ends up creating a difficult catch 22: When we don't learn how to address pleasure in a professional way we avoid the topic, and when as professionals we avoid the topic, we create the impression that pleasure itself is an unprofessional subject.

One of the many times I witnessed the direct effect of professional silence around pleasure was while teaching an educational sex toy party. You may have heard about toy parties: A salesperson (who hopefully has been trained as an educator) comes to a person's home, talks about products and how they are used, and then customers place orders, usually in a separate room to provide some privacy. At this particular party, a woman who looked to be in the third trimester of her pregnancy came into the ordering room and carefully sat down. I smiled and said "Hi," expecting the usual slight embarrassment that would dissolve as we had time to chat. Instead, she started to cry. She said, "Please, I need help." Trying to stay calm while nervously scanning the room for tissues, I said, "OK, what's going on that you need help with?" She told me that she and her husband had never had pleasurable sexual experiences together. She talked about how they had expected sex would improve as their marriage went on, but it hadn't. She told me they had tried seeking help but her doctor hadn't really known what to say and she ended up embarrassed that she had even brought up the subject. She told me they were devoutly religious and they had consulted their clergy person hoping for guidance. Their clergy person, while kind about the question, told them he didn't know how to help. She said to me, "I don't know what to do. I'm so embarrassed. We've tried so hard and now with the baby coming . . . I just don't know if we will ever be able to do this."

In that moment I felt scared and out of my depth. This was clearly such an important issue for this woman, what if I said something wrong? What if I was the next person in the line of professionals to come up empty-handed for her and make her feel embarrassed for asking? But what else was there to do but talk with her about it? So we talked about the clitoris as a place to start. We covered some basic pleasure anatomy information that seemed new for her and I suggested maybe she could call a therapist to work on some of the relationship issues she mentioned. Most of all, I validated her desire for a happy sexual relationship and told her how wonderful it was that she was still pursuing pleasure even after some embarrassing experiences seeking information. I told her, "These are questions you are absolutely right to ask. I hope you keep asking until you get all the information you need, and keep looking until you find professionals who help you reach your goals."

My experience with this woman, and so many others with situations like hers, helped me to understand the importance of pleasure in people's lives and how difficult it can be for people to find professional help in this area. As I continued in my work as a sex educator, people told me over and over, "No one will talk with me about this." Even now, as a sex therapist, my clients are surprised when I ask them open and professional questions about pleasure. Many say, "I've never said this out loud before. I always thought these concerns were dirty, frivolous, something I was supposed to figure out on my own." *The Principles of Pleasure: Working With the Good Stuff as Sex Therapists and Educators* aims to convey skills I have learned while working as a sex toy educator, a sex-positive sex educator, and a sex therapist. While I share stories, please know that names and identifying details have been changed to preserve confidentiality for my students and clients. In many cases, situations have been mashed together in order to further ensure privacy and to encapsulate themes that I see frequently in my work. And since we all get stronger with a little help from our friends . . .

Lindsey Says

Hi, I'm Lindsey Hoskins. I am the Director of Health Education at Family Tree Clinic, an amazing nonprofit sexual and reproductive health clinic in St. Paul, Minnesota. I love to talk about pleasure! I've been doing this work for about 15 years, and I get to work with groups of all ages, in just about every setting you could imagine (in schools and out). It has been my experience that no matter the type of group I am with, there is consistently a huge desire for honest and open discussion about the topic of pleasure. All people need is to be given a green light to venture into this territory, and then the fun and learning begin. My main focus is typically on healthy relationships, family planning, and disease prevention, but I see clearly how adding in concepts of pleasure brings enthusiasm and relevance to a topic that may otherwise be a bit of a downer or even just kind of dry.

I often walk into a group for the first time and hear "Awww, man, why do we have to do this? I already know this stuff. I hate sex ed." Eyes are rolling, arms are crossed. I get the sense that these people have been burned before—by sex ed that was boring, irrelevant, overly simplistic, shaming, paternalistic, or all gloom and doom. It always takes a while for the group to warm up, but once I demonstrate that I am taking a different approach—a sex-positive one in which the concept of pleasure is included—suddenly everyone is participating! Next time I return to this group, there is excitement buzzing in the air and people can't wait to get started and dive in with their questions.

I know I am not the first one to realize this. I am lucky enough to work in a vibrant community of awesome and collaborative sex educators. For a long time, our community had been wanting to explore the concept of how to teach pleasure appropriately in a way that supports our work in public health. There was a lot of energy around this, but no real training. Somehow, a sense of "taboo" lingered, even for those of us who had dedicated our careers to healthy sexuality. Laura and I decided to dig in and use our combined experience with education and therapy, youth and adults to get the ball rolling, and the conversation hasn't stopped since. We are so excited to witness how work in this area is taking off across the country, and we know that sexuality professionals will continue to innovate, learn, and develop strategies at a breakneck pace. Please, take our ideas, make them better, make them your own.

Together, Lindsey and I aim to provide a big-picture view of how to work with pleasure issues in a variety of professional settings and with people of all ages. Our work has shown us that when people are given permission to value pleasure, it is a life-changing experience. There is always a factual and appropriate way to talk about pleasure. So let's start talking about talking about it.

Part I

The Principles of Pleasure

Chapter 1

The Importance of Pleasure in the Work of Sex Therapists and Educators

Pleasure: The Unspoken Goal

Sexual health professionals work with people whose end goals almost certainly involve pleasure, but we don't often frame it that way. The people we work with care about pleasure, even when they are dealing with other struggles. Of course, a person experiencing genital pain during sex wants the pain to stop. But beyond that, they are probably striving for pleasurable sexual experiences. A student who asks questions about condoms might want to know how to prevent STI transmission, but ultimately they aren't looking for information on how to have frustrating, uncomfortable safer sexual experiences. They want to know how to have pleasurable safer sexual experiences with their partner(s). Couples may want to increase their sexual frequency, but they probably aren't trying to have lots more boring, yawn-worthy sex. They want more pleasure together. So often, sexual health professionals aim for the goal of pleasure without naming it directly; so the objective becomes cessation of pain, lower rate of STI transmission, or increasing intimacy. The general assumption seems to be that pleasure should be self-explanatory or will "just happen naturally." However, in many people's lives it doesn't happen easily. Like many important experiences in life, pleasure often takes some time to figure out.

The sexual health field has painstakingly edited manuals detailing sexual dysfunction or STI symptoms. Pleasure, however, is often left a nebulous concept. Important opportunities are missed when we do not study, discuss, and define pleasure. It is just as important to have a clear idea of the outcome we would like to achieve as the issues that are hindering our progress. More concerning, when sexual health professionals frame the majority of conversations about sexuality as avoiding pain and illness, the people we work with get the unspoken message that the goal of sexual expression is not pleasure, fulfillment, and fun but rather avoiding missteps and keeping safe from this activity that apparently holds much danger.

Pleasure is an incredibly important reason to be sexual. If people aren't having sex for pleasure (for physical, emotional, mental or relational pleasure), then why are they having it? Maybe to make someone else happy, to keep a relationship, because it is scary or dangerous to say no, because they need to trade sex for other things (a place to stay, money, or food). There are a wide variety of reasons people choose to be sexual: No one should be shamed for the decisions they make to have consensual sex, whatever the reason or circumstance. People can decide to have sex for transactional reasons rather than pleasure reasons and be happy with that decision. But wouldn't it be amazing if we could help people have more pleasure in a wider variety of circumstances? At the very least, professionals must work to associate sex with pleasure so people are not putting up with unpleasant or painful sex because they think this is "just the way it is."

Pleasure is teachable. Pleasure skills can be learned and positive sexual experiences can be increased. Pleasure deserves a central position when professionals talk about sex.

Fear and Silence Around Pleasure

There are very legitimate reasons why sexual health professionals might sometimes be afraid to talk about pleasure. Pleasure is controversial. Educators may fear that they will lose their job or their program will lose funding, even if the information they are including is medically accurate. Medical professionals may be concerned they will be accused of sexual harassment if they ask patients about pleasure, despite the fact that capacity for pleasure is a key component of health and changes in sexual functioning can be a warning sign for other medical issues (Basson & Schultz, 2007). Couples therapists sometimes feel it is "not their business" to ask how sex is going and that their clients may be offended if they do. Those working with young people may especially fear getting into trouble. Meanwhile, clients, patients, and students experience the silence around these issues and feel that perhaps sexual pleasure concerns are inappropriate subjects to bring to their professionals.

Many professionals feel unqualified to address pleasure issues because they haven't had specific training to do so. The lack of professional information and trainings around pleasure is a serious problem in various fields. Sometimes it may feel embarrassing or unprofessional to talk about pleasure. For people who have never heard pleasure concerns addressed in a professional way, it can be hard to imagine talking about these issues without blushing, giggling, or referencing one's own personal experiences.

However, the silence around pleasure that results from this lack of training disadvantages the people we work with. Pleasure needs to be talked about. Learning about pleasure helps the people we work with to improve their lives; increase physical, mental, emotional, and relational health; increase happiness and connection; fight oppression and discrimination; better understand their bodies; heal from traumatic experiences; and deepen their understanding of what sexual consent looks like. Knowing how to work professionally with pleasure will mean you are better able help your clients, patients, and students. Avoiding directly working with pleasure reinforces a silence that makes the topic feel taboo and leaves people unsure of where to turn for information. After all, if you can't talk to your therapist, sex educator, or medical professional about it, who can you talk to?

While this book focuses on the work of sex educators and sex therapists, it also pertains to helping professionals in many different fields: counselors, medical professionals, couple's therapists, family therapists, pelvic-floor physical therapists, and more. While our work might differ in some ways, it is united in that our clients, students, and patients all have questions and concerns about pleasure.

Working Professionally With Pleasure: What Is Pleasure Education?

What exactly does "pleasure education" mean? There are infinite possibilities for how pleasure education might look. You don't have to consider yourself an educator to convey information to the people you work with. Pleasure education does not necessarily mean a whole class or workshop devoted to pleasure (although those are very important classes), but can and should be worked into just about any sexual health topic you can think of. Pleasure education belongs in a wide variety of settings and should be the work of a wide variety of professionals. Of course, what is appropriate will vary based on the situation, your audience, the topic, and what role you are in; but there is always an appropriate and factual way to educate about pleasure. Here are some of the situations in which Lindsey and I have taught about pleasure as well as why we view them as pleasure education.

At Community Centers

In Sex-Positive Parenting classes, parents want to learn how to talk with their kids about sex in a way that makes them feel happy, healthy, good in their bodies, and help them understand good boundaries. These are all pleasure education issues.

In Mental Health Settings

Pleasure education includes talking to adults in sober houses and substance abuse treatment centers about how to have great sex while sober. By receiving pleasure education people are less likely to think they need to choose between sobriety and having a great sex life.

Therapy groups for adults who are healing from sexual abuse or assault can easily incorporate pleasure education. This might include teaching that physical arousal is not the same as consent and suggesting that finding pleasure in your body can be a path to healing.

Training on "healthy sexuality" for professionals who work with sex offenders is pleasure education. Connecting the dots between pleasure and consent means they can help their clients find ways to have pleasure in life without violating the boundaries of others.

With Adults

Pleasure education frequently occurs through sex toy stores, which often teach adults about a wide variety of topics. Many sex toy stores have been on the forefront of the movement to normalize and value pleasure. Every class I have taught at a sex toy store has also included information about sexual anatomy, function, relationship dynamics, consent issues, and diversity of sexual expression. Pleasure education incorporates all of these topics.

Classes about BDSM or kink issues that teach about boundaries, consent, checking in with partners, sexual negotiation, and sensation play are all elements of pleasure education.

Teaching Sex Toys 101 to college students is pleasure education. Helping young adults normalize pleasure will empower them to advocate for pleasurable experiences in relationships and seek out help if they find sex to be painful or unwanted.

With Young People in Schools or Clinics

Classes for people choosing abstinence are a great place for pleasure education. Pleasure can be included by helping people discover ways to feel good and satisfy emotional and physical needs for intimacy while sticking with their plan to be abstinent.

When STI prevention classes in high schools include ways to confidently use safer-sex materials, discuss safer sex with a partner, and help students figure out which sexual activities are fun and also safe, they are providing pleasure education. By covering these important pleasure topics they are increasing the chances that young people will have safer sex.

Within birth control education classes for teens, pleasure education might include finding the birth control method that works best with the ways they are most likely to be sexual. If they tend to be spontaneous but pick a method that requires planning, chances are it won't be a good fit for them or be very effective. This is also an example of how valuing pleasure can result in better health outcomes.

Peer education training for LGBTQ teens might include pleasure education by teaching about safer sex while centering sexual practices that are relevant to the group rather than covering heterocentric behaviors only. This promotes confidence in advocating for safety while seeking out pleasurable activities.

With All Kinds of People in All Kinds of Situations

An STI prevention class for blind adults could include pleasure education by passing out dildos and lube so participants get experience with using lubricant and how to properly put on a condom. Pleasure education values sex toys and lube as helpful teaching tools where appropriate, and encourages a positive, empowered attitude toward condoms.

Pleasure education includes classes for people who are pregnant, postpartum, peri- or postmenopausal, or are experiencing changes in erections, because people value pleasure throughout the many body changes they may go through in life.

Pleasure education might take place at a private, in-home class about enjoying sex after ovarian cancer. Valuing pleasure as a way to heal from the trauma of illness and teaching people how to have pleasure with themselves and others in various stages of wellness, health, and recovery is pleasure education.

After reading these lists, maybe you are thinking about the ways you already provide pleasure education, or the ways you could. Even if you don't consider yourself an educator, there are helpful ways to incorporate pleasure education in your work. Medical professionals often explain how bodies work. Describing sexual norms of bodies to patients can absolutely be pleasure education if it helps patients understand themselves, their partner(s), and better enjoy their body's capabilities. Mental health professionals frequently find themselves doing psycho-education with clients around issues like anxiety and depression. Providing psycho-education about pleasure issues can increase their clients' happiness, self-esteem, and relationship satisfaction.

Beyond Education: Pleasure as a Lens for Your Work

I have come to see pleasure not just as a topic, but as the lens through which I view all of my work as a therapist and educator. I see the ability to create pleasure as a form of empowerment and a possible way to connect with self and others. Better understanding and increasing ability to create pleasure is an incredibly helpful experience for the people I work with. This is not to say that my ultimate goal is to increase pleasure with every client or student, or that I value pleasure over other possible goals. I am not the pleasure pusher. It is always up to my clients or students to decide what pleasure means to them and how important of a goal it is currently in their lives. Many times it is not their primary goal—but even then, pleasure may still play an important supporting role.

Being clear about your willingness to work with pleasure up front can be a great way to incorporate pleasure into your professional work. I advertise myself as a "sex-positive sex therapist and educator," and when people choose to come see me it is often because they feel reassured that I will be able to address their concerns about sex and pleasure. Pleasure positivity and sex positivity are schools of thought that deepen each other. I ascribe to Dr. Charlie Glickman's definition: "Sex-positivity is the view that the only relevant measure of a sexual act, practice, or experience is the consent, pleasure, and well-being of the people engaged in it or the people affected by it" (Glickman, n.d.). Adopting this stance means that I strive for my work to be as non-stigmatizing, non-judgmental, and as celebratory as possible. It also means I want my work to prioritize and legitimize pleasure, again, not as the one and only measure of well-being, but as an important way for people to gain positive feelings in their own bodies and with others.

So what does this actually look like? I bring up the topic of pleasure with students and clients: I don't shy away from asking about it; I feel confident having conversations about it; and I find ways to help the people I work with feel more comfortable talking to me about it. I ask about their beliefs about pleasure and how they feel about pleasure in general. I want to know what pleasure would look like for them and their partner(s) rather than tell them what I think it should be. I validate questions about pleasure as important. I tell them I see pleasure as fulfilling and meaningful goal rather than selfish or trite. I encourage the people I work with to develop their own value systems around sex and pleasure and use these to stand firm in their own pleasure goals. If they can articulate why they believe pleasure is valuable and worthy, then they will be better able to stand firm in the face of a sex-negative world that says they should be ashamed and fearful if they value pleasure in their lives. I strive to give the information that will be most helpful to them in trying to meet their goals. I don't see pleasure as a separate, secret, or superlative aspect of life, but rather as intertwined with many other aspects. I ask what they think an appropriate balance of pleasure in their lives would look like.

But that is just me: You get to decide the place that pleasure holds in your professional life. No matter what role pleasure plays, this book will address skills to help you tackle the subject factually and appropriately. If you are a professional in a situation where you need to justify the importance of working with pleasure—whether that is to your employer, funders, or your clients/students/patients—you will find this book provides evidence to help you do so.

What Is Pleasure?

Pleasure is a complex topic. Experiences of pleasure are different for everyone and we are seldom encouraged to focus in and really examine them. The dictionary definition is fairly straightforward: "a feeling of happiness, enjoyment, or satisfaction." However, this does not address some of the most compelling questions about pleasure: Is pleasure physical or emotional? Can we learn to experience more pleasure, or does pleasure "just happen"? Could a taste of pleasure cause us to become out of control and ruin our decision-making abilities? Could pleasure possibly improve health and self-esteem?

The Experience of Pleasure: Physical, Mental, Emotional, Relational

People can experience pleasure in a variety of ways: physical, mental, emotional, relational, and more. Pleasure is often physical, meaning that it is felt in the body like warmth on the first sunny day of spring or the coziness of curling up in a comfy bed at the end of a long day. What one finds physically pleasurable is not a universal experience, however. One person feels great after their morning jog, while another hates the too-warm, sweaty feeling. Pleasure can be brought on by emotions—the way it feels to hold a loved one's hand or seeing our child smile. We experience mental pleasure every time we have a fun fantasy (sexual or nonsexual). Pleasure can also be a transactional or relational experience. Someone may derive pleasure purely from giving pleasure to another: Say, in a couple where one person gets bored giving massages, but enjoys their partner's enjoyment. Pleasure is often a mix of physical, emotional, mental, and relational aspects that can be difficult to separate. When I ask people about their experiences of pleasure, most of the time their answers amount to, "It's complex."

"Good" and "Bad" Pleasure

Here in the United States, pleasure is often categorized as "good" or "bad." Sexual pleasure is often viewed as "bad" unless it is achieved in a certain specific set of circumstances prescribed by society, religion, or upbringing. Emotional pleasure is often deemed "good" unless a person experiences too much of it—and then they are assumed to be losing touch with reality or getting carried away. Relational pleasure is good, as long as it is done "for the right reasons" and not in a "codependent" way. Pleasure in the body that is nonsexual is often considered "good" only if a person has worked for it. For example, feeling great after a hard workout is "good"; feeling great after a day spent on the couch is "bad." However, pleasure is often much more nuanced than "good" and "bad" can accurately describe.

Just like the distinction between "good" and "bad" pleasure, creating a line between sexual and nonsexual pleasure is somewhat artificial. Pleasure that feels platonic to one person may be erotic to another, and the point where pleasure becomes sexual or nonsexual can be difficult to decipher. A massage between lovers might be sexy but a massage from a masseuse is supposed to be purely professional. A foot rub means different things to different people. The hormones released in bodies after exercise, during orgasm, or during breastfeeding have significant similarities and yet we assign different meanings to all of these feelings. The ways we interpret our experiences of pleasure are subjective and are based on culture, experience, and personal beliefs.

You may be noticing that none of this helps to narrow our definition. Pleasure's complexity is a good thing. Broadening the parameters of pleasure is valuable because all pleasures are a part of the same family of experiences. Identifying and acknowledging nonsexual pleasure is an important step in increasing sexual pleasure. Many times, the more easily people welcome and acknowledge general pleasure, the more easily they will identify and increase sexual pleasure. When people come to me reporting low desire or lack of arousal I often ask about what they find pleasurable in their daily lives. Gardening? Curling up with a blanket and a good book? Their morning cup of coffee? Those good sensual (in the five-senses kind of way) experiences are times they feel good being present in their bodies. Positive sexual experiences are not all that different.

Sexual Pleasure

Sexual pleasure may involve all the aspects mentioned so far: engorgement of genitals and changes in breathing (physical), arousing fantasy or thoughts (mental), the electric awareness of a romantic partner's fingers brushing your skin (emotional, relational), and, perhaps, the over-the-top feeling of orgasm.

While people often think of sexual pleasure as being focused on bodily sensation, the mental, emotional, and relational aspects of sexual pleasure are just as important. The presence or thought of a sexual partner can turn an ordinary experience into a sexually exciting one. Being caught in a storm with a broken umbrella can be arousing with a person we find attractive but less sexy when we are alone in the cold, socks squishing with rainwater. The presence of un-arousing mental or emotional elements can deflate a sexy situation, such as when a partner says something hurtful and suddenly no one is turned on anymore. Emotional, mental, and relational factors change the way we interpret situations and so, of course, they influence our perceptions of sexual pleasure.

Helping People Define Pleasure Differently: Physical Arousal Is Not the Measure of Pleasure

An important part of pleasure education is teaching that physical signs of arousal do not always mean a person is experiencing sexual pleasure. People with penises have probably had the puzzling experience of having an erection without pleasurable feelings accompanying it. People with vulvas likely have experienced engorgement or lubrication without feeling pleasure. Physical sensations that are pleasurable in erotic contexts can be annoying without desire; attempting to hide that random erection while browsing at the bookstore or realizing your nipples are showing through your shirt during that work presentation. Bodies often just do what they do. While these situations are common, they can also be confusing for people if they feel their physical arousal always indicates they should experience pleasure or desire. Or, more dangerously, these situations can be used to justify unwanted sexual contact. This issue will be covered further in Chapter 3.

It can be problematic and even dangerous to use genital arousal as the sole measure of sexual pleasure. People experiencing Persistent Genital Arousal Disorder (PGAD) struggle with constant, unrelenting, and/or spontaneous physical arousal unrelated to mental, emotional, or relational stimuli. While we generally correlate arousal with pleasure and pleasure with arousal, PGAD is a situation where this constant physical arousal is painful and unwanted. People who have experienced arousal or orgasms during acts of sexual violence often feel betrayed and confused by their own bodies' response since the sexual contact was not wanted or pleasurable. While this is a physical response of arousal, these instances certainly do not constitute pleasure.

When physical arousal is given primacy and ultimate focus, people sometimes get the message that pleasure will cloud their judgment to the point where they "can't stop," giving them permission to pursue sexual experiences without seeking consent. The message becomes our bodies are in charge, instead of our hearts or heads.

Lindsey Says

It is common in sex education for people to talk about the "slippery slope" of getting turned on. Erotic massage, or manual stimulation will sometimes be categorized as a "risky" activity, not because it is risky in itself, but because of "what it might lead to." In many ways, we talk about "raging hormones" and the idea that in the heat of the moment you won't be able to make good decisions. I believe that setting young people up to expect that they don't have the power to control themselves once they are turned on is dangerous, and also inaccurate! Of course, you may be more likely to decide to do something risky when turned on, but the fact is that you are still deciding. People must believe that they are capable of being thoughtful about these decisions, even in the moment, if that is what we want them to achieve.

When a student says something about how "you might not be able to stop," I reply, "Imagine you were in a situation where you were feeling super turned on. Everything was perfect and you were feeling great. Now imagine someone comes in with a giant cardboard check and offers to pay you $100,000,000 to stop, put your pants on, and go home. Do you think you could stop?" Everyone always laughs and says "yes," definitely they could stop. If people are resisting that idea, a house fire scenario will usually convince them. "OK, so you are actually totally capable of stopping! You do have control of yourself." Then the conversation can continue about what the things in real life are that motivate us to pause, think, and make a decision about what we want to happen next, since there is probably not a person with an oversized check who is going to help you out with this one.

Another important point in this discussion is that pleasure is not an all-or-nothing situation. Deciding to "stop" might actually mean just choosing one activity instead of another. Both might be extremely pleasurable. Not feeling comfortable with oral sex? How about touching with hands, some serious nipple time, tickling your butt with a feather, or a bit of really intentional, sexy kissing? "Stopping" might just mean taking a moment to put on a condom, or pausing briefly to check in about how you are feeling and what you might like to try next. You don't usually have to actually put your pants on and go back home.

Pleasure and the Sexual Response Cycle: Expanding the Way We Think About Sexual Function

One way that body function seems to be the assumed measure of pleasure is through the use of the sexual response cycle as one of the main ways to assess for sexual health, function, and (assumed) satisfaction. In 1966, Masters and Johnson established a widely used model of sexual response with defined stages: excitement, plateau, orgasm, and resolution. This model focused on physical, measurable changes in the body (and mainly based on sexual response involving penises and erections). While groundbreaking and helpful in many ways, this model does not include any explicit mention of pleasure. The assumption seems to be that if a person's body is functioning according to this cycle, pleasure will be present. However, as we discussed earlier, that is not always the case.

Helen Singer Kaplan had the revolutionary idea that desire is a part of the sexual response cycle (Kaplan, 1979). Desire and pleasure are two different experiences, but are also intertwined. Desire plays a crucial connecting role between physical arousal and sexual pleasure: If the signs of physical arousal are not desired responses, there is often no pleasure in them. When desire is present, pleasure is often experienced as well. However, pleasure is not specifically included in Kaplan's sexual response model, either.

Sexual response models continue to shift and change (Bancroft & Janssen, 2000; Barlow, 1986; Basson, 2001; Janssen & Bancroft, 2007; Loulan, 1984; Stoleru & Mouras, 2007). Loulan included the concept of pleasure and made distinctions between emotional and physical elements of arousal in her sexual response cycle (1984). Basson made the case for emotional or relational factors as the reason for initiating sex (2000), and established the concept of responsive desire: Desire may not be present before people start to be sexual, but arrives at some point after sexual activity is started (Basson, 2002b). She and her colleagues also pointed out that women's subjective experience of arousal is not always connected to physical signs of arousal in the genitals (Basson, 2002a; Basson et al., 2004; Laan & Everaerd, 1998). While men report a higher connection between physical arousal and the subjective experience of being aroused than women do (Chivers, Seto, Lalumiere, Laan, & Grimbos, 2010), men also report experiencing a wide range of physical (genital and non-genital), mental, and emotional signs that indicate sexual arousal (Janssen, McBride, Yarber, Hill, & Butler, 2008). Basically, there is a lot more to arousal for men than just erections.

However, the seemingly obvious component of pleasure is still not frequently addressed directly in sexual response models. Perhaps this reflects an emphasis on the medical model of physical signs and symptoms, or perhaps it is due to the perceived "slipperiness" of pleasure: Because the experience of pleasure is seen as impossible to pin down, focus is given to the observable and measurable physical responses instead. Sexual response models can be useful tools for describing what people might experience from their bodies during sexual arousal, while understanding that everyone's body function is different. When I use a sexual response cycle with a client or student, I make sure to ask where in the cycle they tend to experience pleasure and where they might not. It is wonderful when various forms of pleasure (physical, mental, emotional, relational) are present throughout the entire sexual response cycle. If they are not, I would want to know if the person is OK with pleasure being absent during part or all of the cycle. It may be that they know their pleasure happens at a different point in the sexual arousal cycle and they are happy with that. It may be that they are not happy with it or that this represents an unwelcome change in their body function. If so, there may be ways to adjust with permanent changes, or reverse non-permanent changes in order to have a more pleasurable experience.

Sexual health professionals need to be assessing for pleasure along with asking about physical function. While physical function can be an important piece of the puzzle, it is not always the most important concern of many people seeking professional assistance. A body can function "normally" but that isn't a guarantee that the person who inhabits that body is experiencing pleasure. Or a body can function differently and the person inside can be having a fabulous time. The people I work with usually care about how their genitals work, and understanding how physical arousal tends to function in the body can be helpful information for them. But it usually isn't their primary concern. Instead, they want to know, "How can I have more pleasure with myself and others? How can I be happy about sex and enjoy myself more? How can I make my sexual experiences more like what I would like them to be?"

Banishing the Pleasure Police

Too often US culture skews our definition of pleasure in what ends up being a game of "Have you achieved the correct and most amazing form of sexual pleasure possible to humanity? Not sure? Then you aren't doing it right." Clients who do not currently have orgasms discount the good feelings they do have because they are reaching for an experience that society touts as the ultimate goal of sex. Students who do have orgasms discount them as being too small, too quick, or not the kind of orgasm they were hoping to have. People have all kinds of rules about the "best ways" to get pleasure. Some people think solo pleasure is less valid than partnered pleasure. Some people say orgasms aren't "real" if a person uses a vibrator or sex toy to get them. People with vulvas are told all sorts of things about where the best orgasms come from: the clitoris, the vagina, the g-spot, the cervix, and don't forget to try for uterine contractions! People with penises are told their pleasure depends on their ability to get hard, stay hard, and penetrate for as long as possible. People who don't fit into the boxes that society constructs around gender, orientation, age, or ability are often assumed not to have pleasure at all. Have you ever heard someone rudely question, "How do they even do it?" Well, if "they" have a body, mind, and emotions, they likely "do it" in whatever way makes them feel good.

At some point in our lives, most of us (and most of the people we work with) have probably fallen into the trap of policing our pleasure and attempting to train it to behave in the ways we have been told are the "best." Without education about pleasure, clients and students are working off of cultural myths and stolen porn moves, which may be hot in stories and fantasies but don't always hold up in real-life situations. Sexual health professionals have a unique opportunity to help clients and students stop policing themselves. Working with pleasure means providing pertinent information on pleasure anatomy (which is often different than reproductive anatomy) and function. This starts them on the path to explore and define pleasure on their own terms and to define their own pleasure however they choose.

As professionals, we need to be careful not to become the pleasure police ourselves; we need to avoid the idea that there are certain superior ways to find pleasure and we know exactly what they are. Pleasure is different for every person, even different for the same person from day to day, and professionals need to be clear that there is no flow chart that will guarantee a great experience. There are no specific steps that will work every time. Researchers in the field warn against pleasure education establishing a "pleasure imperative" (Allen, 2012, Allen & Carmody, 2012): that professionals would indicate there are set, established ways to create pleasure or that teaching about pleasure will make people feel that pleasure is the only or best goal of sexual expression, rather than one of many possible goals. However, working through the lens of pleasure makes room for a wide variety of perspectives, encouraging people to examine their experiences of pleasure, exploring whether these experiences have been empowering or disempowering, and facilitating goal setting for the role each person wants pleasure to play in their life. It also includes being frank about the somewhat indefinable nature of pleasure while supplying information about bodies, arousal, sexual response, communication, and relationships—not in a prescriptive way, but rather to give people the building blocks of knowledge they need to become the architects of their own experiences.

Being Aware of Our Biases as Professionals

> The majority of research, theories, and practices in sexual and relationship therapy tend to have a heterocentric, white, western bias. Consequently, we may have a limited view of human sexual behavior that contributes to unrealistic expectations of sexual activity and satisfaction, which is likely to be detrimental to minority [sic] populations.
>
> (Boul, Hallam-Jones, & Wylie, 2008, p. 15)

When helping others figure out pleasure's role in their lives, professionals must be mindful of our own biases. Our perceptions of sexual pleasure and health are defined by the dominant narratives in our cultures. In addition, our own personal experiences, backgrounds, intersecting identities, and beliefs will shape our expectations about pleasure.

As clients and students explore their own belief systems around pleasure they can create meanings that are relevant to their own lived experiences rather than to a dominant discourse that may not include their experiences or beliefs. As sexual health professionals, we must strive to be aware of our backgrounds and biases so we can better help clients to find their own definition of sexual pleasure (rather than inadvertently putting ours upon them). One way to navigate the interplay between our viewpoint and those of the people we work with is to encourage them to develop their own definitions of pleasure. Chapter 6 will cover this important issue.

Pleasure Is a Professional Issue

When people hear the term "sexual health" they may think about condoms, barrier methods, and how to avoid getting STIs. They don't always think about increasing arousal, orgasms, masturbation, or pleasurable partner sex. However, pleasure has a number of positive effects on physical health, mental health, and relationship satisfaction. Pleasure can also be an important way to take back control of one's body and heal from sexual pain or trauma.

Pleasure Is a Health Issue

Pleasure improves physical health. Sexual pleasure and orgasm improve the immune system and reduce stress (Charnetski & Brennan, 2001). Sexual pleasure and orgasm provide relief from pain (Hambach, Evers, Summ, Husstedt, & Frese, 2013; Komisaruk & Whipple, 2000) and frequent ejaculation may be associated with lower risk of prostate cancer (Giles et al., 2003; Kotb, Beltagy, Ismail, & Hashad, 2015; Leitzmann, Platz, Stampfer, Willett, & Giovannucci, 2004). Sexual activity and/or orgasm during menstruation may help protect against endometriosis (Meaddough, Olive, Gallup, Perlin, & Kliman, 2002). These benefits contradict popular cultural perception that sexual pleasure is bad for your health in a variety of ways, such as assuming it will lead to STI transmission, unwanted pregnancies, and or behaviors that "put people at risk." While it is true that there are risks associated with sex, these risks can be managed and sometimes avoided entirely. Much of the sex people have is not actually risky.

Pleasure has a positive effect on mental and emotional health, too. The DSM-V includes "loss of interest or pleasure" as one of the two necessary criteria for Major Depressive Disorder (American Psychiatric Association, 2013). While the DSM does not specify sexual pleasure in this criterion, reduced levels of sexual interest and arousal are common in people experiencing depression (Kennedy, Dickens, Eisfeld, & Bagby, 1999). In fact, women's lack of sexual desire reveals underlying depression in up to 26% of cases and major depression is associated with decreased sexual interest in more than 40% of men (van Lankveld & Grotjohann, 2000), providing yet another reason to include sexual pleasure questions in intakes or assessments. People experiencing depression can benefit from regular exercise, and the endorphins people get from pleasure and orgasm are very similar to those released during exercise. It doesn't seem like much of a stretch that regular sexual pleasure may also benefit people experiencing depression.

Pleasure improves our relationships with others. If we don't know how to create pleasure in our own bodies, it is much less likely that a partner will be able to figure out how to create pleasure in our bodies. Understanding our own pleasure systems can help us communicate and share them with others. Pleasurable experiences often matter more to couples than sexual frequency. A recent study found that a "satisfying sex life" and a "warm interpersonal climate" contributed to relationship satisfaction while frequency of sex mattered less (Schoenfeld, Loving, Pope, Huston, & Štulhofer, 2016). Northrup, Schwartz, and Witte (2012) found that of people reporting they were happy in their relationships, 73% described their sex lives as "making love—a deep physical and emotional connection." Only 2% of people who were happy in their relationships described their sex lives as "just getting it over with." Obviously, this does not mean good sex is the only determinant of happiness in a relationship, but it certainly seems like there is a strong connection between the two.

When we professionals work with pleasure, we are helping students and clients create better physical health, more positive body experiences, and often, more satisfaction in their relationships. Working with pleasure issues results in better health outcomes related to unwanted pregnancy and STI transmission as well. For more information, see Chapter 2.

The Experience of Pleasure Affects the Experience of Self

> As our clients accept their right to pleasure, not only does it enrich their sex lives and deepen their bond with their partner, it also enhances their sense of personal well-being.
>
> (Resnick, 2002, p. 6)

When people create sexual pleasure, either by themselves or with partners, they get to feel the powerful capabilities of their fabulous bodies. People deepen their self-knowledge, self-love, and their relationship with their bodies through the pleasure they create. As I see the people I work with become more confident in creating pleasure for themselves, I see the way they carry themselves change. They seem to stand a little bit taller, walk into a room in a more confident way. Not necessarily with swagger, but perhaps more at home in their bodies. Learning how to create pleasure with partner(s) can be a mix of excitement, vulnerability, daring, asking for what you want, stating what you can give, and sharing a part of yourself—what an amazing experience. Sexual pleasure is powerful, whether solo or partnered.

Pleasure can happen easily or it can be an experience people work for. People who struggle to create pleasure, in their own body or with partner(s), often feel that something is wrong with them or with their relationship. Struggles creating pleasure can affect self-esteem, sexual self-concept, general happiness, and relationship difficulties. Sometimes students or clients have unrealistic expectations due to a lack of information about how bodies actually work. When they receive information on pleasure anatomy and function as well as how to better identify their experiences of pleasure, they sometimes find they were experiencing more pleasure than they even realized. At very least they can see how pleasure is not a mysterious experience that other people have and they do not, but rather there are skills and information available to help them create more pleasure for themselves. Not only that, but there are professionals available to help them: educators, therapists, doctors, physical therapists, and more.

Pleasure as a Way Out of Trauma and Pain

When people have experienced trauma they sometimes find their body has become a place of at best neutrality, and at worst fear or pain. Clients or students who live with injuries or chronic pain often struggle to identify their bodies as safe or pleasurable spaces. Learning to create or find pleasure in their bodies can help to counteract states of pain, depression, or sadness. By working with pleasure, professionals can offer clients and students new ways of relating to themselves and being in their bodies. Harnessing the power that they have to create pleasurable experiences for themselves is a powerful intervention against feelings of loss of control. For students and clients whose life situations are dangerous, chronically stressful, or unpredictable, understanding how to find pleasure in their bodies can give them an opportunity for small but powerful moments of liberation from difficult circumstances.

The Right to Sexual Pleasure

The global community has been taking positive steps toward advocating for sexual pleasure. In fact, pleasure is included in many sexual health organizations' writings as not just an important factor in sexual health, but a human sexual right. A World Health Organization (WHO)–convened international consultation included pleasure in its definition of sexual health: "Sexual health requires a positive and respectful approach to sexuality and sexual relationships, as well as the possibility of having pleasurable and safe sexual experiences, free of coercion, discrimination and violence" (WHO, 2006).

The Sexuality Information and Education Council of the United States (SIECUS; n.d.) lists sexual pleasure as a human right in its statement of sexual rights. The Declaration of Sexual Rights from the World Association for Sexology (WAS): "Reaffirms that sexuality is a central aspect to being human throughout life, encompasses sex, gender identities and roles, sexual orientation, eroticism, pleasure, intimacy, and reproduction" (WAS, 2014). WAS goes on to define the possibility of pleasure as a sexual right: "Everyone has the right to the highest attainable level of health and wellbeing in relation to sexuality, including the possibility of pleasurable, satisfying, and safe sexual experiences" (WAS, 2014).

Pleasure concerns affect the people we work with. By working professionally with pleasure we have the power to positively affect their lives in a variety of ways. When we do not address pleasure issues, we are putting our patients, clients, and students at a significant disadvantage. Sexual health professionals need to be on the forefront of the movement to claim pleasure as an important and valid professional topic. This book aims to help that happen.

References

Allen, L. (2012). Pleasure's perils? Critically reflecting on pleasure's inclusion in sexuality education. *Sexualities*, *15*(3/4), 455–471.

Allen, L., & Carmody, M. (2012). "Pleasure has no passport": Re-visiting the potential of pleasure in sexuality education. *Sex Education*, *12*(4), 455–468.

American Psychiatric Association. (2013). *Diagnostic and statistical manual of mental disorders* (5th ed.). Arlington, VA: American Psychiatric Publishing.

Bancroft, J., & Janssen, E. (2000). The dual control model of male sexual response: A theoretical approach to centrally mediated erectile dysfunction. *Neuroscience and Biobehavioral Review*, *24*, 571–579.

Barlow, D. H. (1986). Causes of sexual dysfunction: The role of anxiety and cognitive interference. *Journal of Consulting and Clinical Psychology*, *54*, 140–148.

Basson, R. (2002a). A model of women's sexual arousal. *Journal of Sex and Marital Therapy*, *28*(1), 1–10. doi: 10.1080/009262302317250963

Basson, R. (2002b). Women's sexual desire—Disordered or misunderstood? *Journal of Sex and Marital Therapy*, *28*(s), 17–28.

Basson, R. (2001). Human sex-response cycles. *Journal of Sex & Marital Therapy*, 27(1), 33–43.

Basson, R. (2000). The female sexual response: A different model. *Journal of Sex & Marital Therapy*, 26(1), 51–65.

Basson, R., Leiblum, S., Brotto, L., Derogatis, L., Fourcroy, J., Fugl-Meyer, K., . . . Schultz, W. W. (2004). Revised definitions of women's sexual dysfunction. *Journal of Sexual Medicine*, 1, 40–48. doi: 10.1111/j.1743-6109.2004.10107.x

Basson, R., & Schultz, W. W. (2007). Sexual sequelae of general medical disorders. *The Lancet*, 369(9559), 409–424.

Boul, L., Hallam-Jones, R., & Wylie, K. R. (2008). Sexual pleasure and motivation. *Journal of Sex & Marital Therapy*, 35(1), 25–39.

Charnetski, C. J., & Brennan, F. X. (2001). *Feeling good is good for you: How pleasure can boost your immune system and lengthen your life*. New York: St Martin's Press.

Chivers, M. L., Seto, M. C., Lalumiere, M. L., Laan, E., & Grimbos, T. (2010). Agreement of self reported and genital measures of sexual arousal in men and women: A meta analysis. *Archives of Sexual Behavior*, 39, 5–56.

Giles, G. G., Severi, G., English, D. R., McCredie, M. R. E., Borland, R., Boyle, P., & Hopper, J. L. (2003). Sexual factors and prostate cancer. *BJU International*, 92, 211–216. doi: 10.1046/j.1464-410X.2003.04319.x

Glickman, C. (n.d.). *Sex positivity*. Retrieved from http://charlieglickman.com/sex-positivity/

Hambach, A., Evers, S., Summ, O., Husstedt, I. W., & Frese, A. (2013). The impact of sexual activity on idiopathic headaches: An observational study. *Cephalalgia*, 33(6), 384–389. doi: 10.1177/0333102413476374.x

Janssen, E., & Bancroft, J. (2007). The dual-control model: The role of sexual inhibition & excitation in sexual arousal and behavior. In E. Janssen (Ed.), *The psychophysiology of sex* (pp. 197–222). Bloomington, IN: Indiana University Press.

Janssen, E., McBride, K. R., Yarber, W., Hill, B. J., & Butler, S. M. (2008). Factors that influence sexual arousal in men: A focus group study. *Archives of Sexual Behavior*, 37(2), 252–265.

Kaplan, H. S. (1979). *Disorders of sexual desire*. New York: Brunner/Mazel.

Kennedy, S. H., Dickens, S. C., Eisfeld, B. S., & Bagby, R. M. (1999). Sexual dysfunction before antidepressant therapy in major depression. *Journal of Affective Disorder*, 56, 2001–2008.

Komisaruk, B. R., & Whipple, B. (2000). How does vaginal stimulation produce pleasure, pain, and analgesia? In R. B. Fillingim (Ed.), *Sex, gender, and pain: Progress in pain research and management* (Vol. 17, pp. 109–134). Seattle, WA: IASP Press.

Kotb, A. F., Beltagy, A., Ismail, A. M., & Hashad, M. M. (2015). Sexual activity and the risk of prostate cancer: Review article. *Archivio Italiano Di Urologia, Andrologia: Organo Ufficiale [Di] Società Italiana Di Ecografia Urologica E Nefrologica/Associazione Ricerche In Urologia*, 87(3), 214–215. doi:10.4081/aiua.2015.3.214.x

Laan, E., & Everaerd, W. (1998). Physiological measures of vaginal vasocongestion. *International Journal of Impotence Research*, 10, S107–S110.

van Lankveld, J. J. D. M., & Grotjohann, Y. (2000). Psychiatric comorbidity in heterosexual couples with sexual dysfunction assessed with the composite international diagnostic interview. *Archives of Sexual Behavior*, 29, 479–498.

Leitzmann, M. F., Platz, E. A., Stampfer, M. J., Willett, W. C., & Giovannucci, E. (2004). Ejaculation frequency and subsequent risk of prostate cancer. *JAMA*, 291(13), 1578–1586. doi:10.1001/jama.291.13.1578.x

Loulan, J. (1984). *Lesbian sex*. San Francisco: Spinsters Ink.

Masters, W. H., Johnson, V. E., & Reproductive Biology Research Foundation (U.S.). (1966). *Human sexual response [by] William H. Masters, research director [and] Virginia E. Johnson, research associate, the Reproductive Biology Research Foundation, St. Louis, Missouri*. Boston: Little, Brown.

Meaddough, E. L., Olive, D. L., Gallup, P., Perlin, M., & Kliman, H. J. (2002). Sexual activity, orgasm and tampon use are associated with a decreased risk for endometriosis. *Gynecol Obstet Invest*, 53, 163–169.

Northrup, C., Schwartz, P., & Witte, J. (2012). *The normal bar: The surprising secrets of happy couples and what they reveal about creating a new normal in your relationship*. New York: Harmony Books.

Resnick, S. (2002). Sexual pleasure: The next frontier. *SIECUS Report, 30*(4), 6–11.

Schoenfeld, E. A., Loving, T. J., Pope, M. T., Huston, T. L., & Štulhofer, A. (2016). Does sex really matter? Examining the connections between spouses' nonsexual behaviors, sexual frequency, sexual satisfaction, and marital satisfaction. *Archives of Sexual Behavior*, 1–13.

Sexuality Information and Education Council of the United States (SIECUS) (n.d.). *Position statements*. Retrieved from http://www.siecus.org/index.cfm?fuseaction=page.viewPage&pageId=494&parentID=472

Stoleru, S., & Mouras, H. (2007). Brain functional imaging studies of sexual desire and arousal in human males. In E. Janssen (Ed.), *The psychophysiology of sex* (pp. 3–34). Bloomington, IN: Indiana University Press.

World Association of Sexology (WAS). (2014). *Declaration of sexual rights*. Retrieved from http://www.worldsexology.org/wp-content/uploads/2013/08/declaration_of_sexual_rights_sep03_2014.pdf

World Health Organization (WHO). (2006). *Defining sexual health*. Retrieved from http://www.who.int/reproductivehealth/topics/sexual_health/sh_definitions/en/

Chapter 2

Dangerous Pleasure

How the United States' Fears Shape the Work of Sex Educators and Therapists

Fish live in the water they swim in, and for sexual health professionals in the United States, it seems we are often swimming in a culture of fear, confusion, and silence. Our country's shame and mistrust around sex, and especially pleasure, shapes our work in a variety of ways. It also affects our professional selves, creating a fear of not being perceived as legitimate that many other professionals do not have to deal with. Because of this, sexual health professionals may feel compelled to justify the validity of their work, and one proven way to do so is to turn to fear: fear of more people contracting STIs or having unwanted pregnancies; fear of porn and erotic materials, "sex addiction," and out-of-control sexual behaviors. Focusing on scary or possibly harmful aspects of sex may seem to prove legitimacy, but it also changes the tone of our work to one that is often perceived by students and clients as shaming or frightening.

This tense cultural atmosphere sometimes creates a "stick to the facts" kind of attitude for working with sexuality. Even though pleasure is a factual topic, it often gets left out because it is perceived as riskier than other topics. If sexual health professionals include pleasure, we increase the risk that our work—which is already frequently under question—will be further discredited. It seems safer to take the position of "protecting" the people we work with from the aspects of sexuality that could "harm" them than to promote the ways they could add more fun and enjoyment to their sex lives.

However, as we will see in this chapter, including pleasure information actually keeps people safer, not to mention happier and more in charge of their own decision making. Incorporating pleasure information increases positive health outcomes, aids in harm reduction, and strengthens people's abilities to make empowered sexual choices. Information on pleasure can be appropriately included with information about birth control, barrier methods, consent, safer sex, and abstinence. In fact, pleasure belongs with all these topics.

The Long-Term Connection Between Sex Education and Sexual Health

I frequently meet with grown people who do not have basic understandings of their own anatomy, sexual function, or skills for communicating about sex with partners. I regularly see couples who have never had pleasurable sex, despite trying for years, people who thought they would "figure it out" at some point, but that hasn't happened. Many blame themselves or their relationships, but I believe it is the direct result of typical sex education in the United States (or lack thereof). It's not their fault they don't know this fundamental information. No one taught them as young people. In addition, they are unlikely to seek out information once they are adults, since adults are "supposed to know what they are doing" already.

Our society tends to be fearful and suspicious of teenage sex, and thusly we are also sometimes fearful and suspicious of sex education for youth. However, when we skip the sex ed for young people, how are they supposed to figure out how to have pleasurable sex when they become adults? Fear of young people being sexual is not an appropriate reason to withhold important information from them. Regardless of whether society at large "approves" of the sex people are having, knowledge about one's own body and how it works is a human right. Limiting sexual health information also does not prevent teens from being sexual. We as a country are failing our young people and our adults alike.

Lindsey Says

When talking with people about my work, people often assume that working with young people must be so difficult (or entertaining), because they "don't know anything" about sex yet. It can be true that school aged people don't know much, but in reality I find that most adults don't know much more. I frequently notice that most of the questions asked by 30, 50, and 70 year olds are the exact questions asked by 13 and 17 year olds. Adults have typically had a lot more sex, but still believe the same myths and stereotypes. In fact, in some ways, it seems that the adults are working against a bigger challenge, because there is a greater assumption that they "should" know everything, and therefore they take a greater risk in admitting they don't by asking a question.

Adults will often speak up in class to exclaim with frustration that they never got to talk about this stuff while they were growing up. Adults frequently want to shake my hand after a discussion to express their appreciation for the first open and respectful dialogue they have had about sexuality in their life. I have had discussions with people who have birthed babies that honestly thought that the baby came out of their anus. How do we have a system that allows for this silence around sexuality to continue? Somehow, many of the professionals that we are interacting with at various points along our different journeys (teachers, doctors, therapists, and more) are failing to utilize opportunities for discussion, growth, and learning.

Once people (of any age) see that it is safe to be vulnerable (i.e. nobody in class will laugh at them), the questions start flying. It is so great to be able to help answer these questions, but at the same time pretty tragic that they never felt safe asking anyone else before they were 60 years old. It isn't really that surprising, given the nature of the sex ed that most adults today received as children, and the secrecy that surrounds skills for sexual satisfaction. We tend to act like you should never have to discuss it, but then also be really good at it, and that good sex has more to do with how you look than what you do or say. That is a pretty dangerous set of assumptions. When we take on pleasure positive sex ed with young people (who are naturally so eager to learn), we have a tremendous opportunity to do so much more to set them up for lifelong success.

Sex Education in the United States Today

Let's take a look at the sex education the young people of today (the adults of tomorrow) are currently receiving. First of all, what kind of education do their parents want them to receive?

Parents Support Comprehensive Sex Education

Regardless of political leanings or religious affiliation, the majority of adults in the United States favor medically accurate, age-appropriate education that includes information about both contraception and abstinence. In a cross-sectional survey of people aged 18–83 living in the United States, Bleakley, Hennessy, and Fishbein (2006) found that, regardless of political leanings, approximately 82% of respondents supported comprehensive sex ed (defined as teaching students about both abstinence and methods for preventing pregnancy and STIs), while 68% of respondents supported teaching how to properly use condoms. In contrast, abstinence-only education programs (defined as promoting abstinence until marriage and not including methods for preventing pregnancy or STIs) received the lowest level of support (36%) and the highest level of opposition (about 50%) (Bleakley et al., 2006).

While the narrative of sex education in schools is often painted as a conflict between political parties, self-identified conservative, liberal, and moderate respondents all supported comprehensive sex education. The extent of support varied significantly, but even among self-described conservatives, 70% supported comprehensive sex ed, and almost 40% opposed abstinence-only sex education. Another popular narrative is that people who are religious are against sex education in schools. However, among religious respondents (i.e., those who attend services more than once a week), comprehensive sex ed was supported by 60% (Bleakley et al., 2006).

These kinds of results are not just seen in one study. Overwhelmingly and consistently, the majority of parents in the United States support comprehensive sex education for a wide variety of ages, some as young as elementary school (Barr, Moore, Johnson, Forrest, & Jordan, 2014; Eisenberg, Bernat, Bearinger, & Resnick, 2008; Herrman, Solano, Stotz, & McDuffie, 2013; Tortolero et al., 2011). Comprehensive sex education is also supported by the American Medical Association and the American Psychological Association (AMA, 2009, APA, 2005).

Despite these findings, abstinence-only education is still frequently what our schools provide. In 2015, Congress passed a two-year extension of the Title V Sec. 510 program, which funds the implementation of ineffective and stigmatizing abstinence-only programs that the majority of Americans do not wish their children to be taught. There seems to be a sharp disparity between the sexual education parents want their children to receive and what our politicians think they should fund.

Sex Education Standards Vary by State

There are no national requirements for sex education in the United States, and individual state's requirements of sex education vary widely. Only 23 states require sexual education at all. Of those, only 13 states require that sex education be medically accurate. Take a moment to let that sink in: The majority of states do not require sex education to be based on factual medical information. Only 18 states require that sex ed include information on contraception. However, 37 states require including information on abstinence, and of these 25 require that abstinence should be stressed, while 19 states require including instruction on the importance of engaging in sexual activity only within marriage. Only eight states require that a sex ed program must provide instruction that is appropriate for a student's cultural background and not be biased against any race, sex, or ethnicity (Guttmacher Institute, 2016). All this variation can make a confusing minefield for educators and does not serve students well. In fact, even when there are guidelines for the topics that sex ed should cover, that doesn't mean that schools actually meet them. The Centers for Disease Control (CDC) recently found that the percentage of schools providing sex education that meets their criteria is generally low and varies widely by state (Demissie et al., 2015).

Instead of basing educational requirements on data about what produces the best health outcomes, some mandates seem to be based on creating fear. For example, 13 states require the inclusion of information on the negative outcomes of teen sex and pregnancy. Four states require *only* negative information on sexual orientation be provided (Guttmacher Institute, 2016). This requirement itself is confusing. Everyone has an orientation: Are educators supposed to supply negative information about everyone? Clearly this is thinly veiled anti-LGBTQ language.

These numbers can feel overwhelming and depressing. However, it is not all bad news. Nine states require information on sexual orientation to be inclusive, while 27 states require teaching skills for healthy sexuality including avoiding coerced sex, making healthy decisions, and family communication (Guttmacher Institute, 2016). Medically accurate, inclusive, culturally appropriate, comprehensive sex education for young people does exist. There are many amazing educators who do great work with young people on a daily basis, but more work needs to be done to make sure all of our youth get the sex education they need and deserve.

Where Does Pleasure Education Fit In?

No state currently mandates teaching pleasure, or even the positive effects of sex within the context of a loving relationship. The very suggestion of teaching pleasure to young people seems frivolous and dangerous to many people. If young people know sex is pleasurable, they will want to have it, right? But if we flip that thought, the converse is more frightening. If young people are never told sex should be pleasurable, they have no reason to expect pleasurable sex. In this case it makes all the sense in the world that the reasons they choose to have sex will be about social status or making someone else happy. Certainly, it gives them no instruction on what to do if sexual activity is painful or just doesn't feel right. It gives partners no reason to stop and check in if they do not witness the other person receiving pleasure. It distorts the whole concept of what sex is and can be, while normalizing all the things we hope sex will not be—scary, dangerous, and likely to feel like a mistake. Teaching about pleasure in a developmentally appropriate way is teaching skills for healthy sexuality and letting young people know that pain, discomfort, or dislike should not have to be part of their sexual experience.

Lindsey Says

I often teach classes for parents on how to talk about sex with their children. An activity I typically start out with is to have the parents privately brainstorm a list of things they want to teach their children about sexuality, and then share with the group. The predominant messages are always, in every single group of parents I have ever taught (quite literally thousands of parents), that they want their children to love their bodies, be proud of themselves, to feel that sex is natural and normal and should be pleasurable and fun, that sex is a beautiful thing, that they need to respect the consent of others and always have the right to say no, and that they can talk to their parents when they have questions. The #1 message I hear time and time again is: "I hope my children grow up without the shame that I have grown up with around sexuality. I have been battling that my whole life."

While some people have concerns about providing sexual health information to young people, the reality is when we do not provide education, we leave them without information they need to keep themselves safe, healthy, and happy. As former Surgeon General Dr. Joycelyn Elders stated, "If you don't educate young people and then they end up pregnant or with HIV . . . If we don't provide health education for our young people it really is akin to child abuse" (Clark, 2009).

Results of Sex Education in the United States

So, what kind of health outcomes do we see from typical fear-based United States sex education? Bad ones.

Rates of Teen Pregnancy

The rate of births to teenagers in the United States has hit yet a historic low, down 61% from 1991 (Hamilton, Martin, Osterman, Curtin, & Mathews, 2015), but even with these big reductions we continue to have one of the highest rates among developed countries (Centers for Disease Control and Prevention, 2012; Sedgh, Finer, Bankole, Eilers, & Singh, 2015). US teens are two and a half times as likely to give birth as compared to teens in Canada, around four times as likely as teens in Germany or Norway, and almost 10 times as likely as teens in Switzerland (Kearney & Levine, 2012). While some of these are planned, wanted pregnancies, by far most are not. In half of the estimated 400,000 annual teen pregnancies in the United States, no method of birth control was used; and of these, nearly one third of these teens (31.4%) believed they could not get pregnant at the time (Centers for Disease Control and Prevention, 2012).

Differences across states are quite dramatic as well, indicating that the land of the free seems to be freer for some than for others. A teenage girl in Mississippi is four times more likely to give birth than a teenage girl in New Hampshire—and 15 times more likely to give birth compared to a teenage girl in Switzerland (Kearney & Levine, 2012). Lower socioeconomic status, lower income, and lower education levels are associated with teen childbearing (Penman-Aguilar, Carter, Snead, & Kourtis, 2013). There are clear disparities in US teen pregnancies when we look at race and ethnicity. While the rate of teen pregnancy has decreased in all racial groups named and specified by the CDC, "non-hispanic black" and "Hispanic" teens are still twice as likely to give birth as "non-hispanic white" teens (Hamilton et al., 2015, Table A.). These findings raise serious concerns about how class, race, and socioeconomic status are affecting access to education, contraception, and health care options. The states with the strongest abstinence-only practices consistently have the highest rates of teen pregnancy (Stanger-Hall & Hall, 2011).

STI Transmission Rates

While STIs are common and contracting them should not be a shameful experience, the way that STIs disproportionately affect young people and people of color in the United States is shameful. Despite being a relatively small portion of the sexually active population, young people between the ages of 15 and 24 accounted for the highest rates of chlamydia and gonorrhea in 2014 and almost two thirds of all reported cases. Additionally, young people in this age group acquire half of the estimated 20 million new STDs diagnosed each year (Centers for Disease Control and Prevention, 2015). African Americans and Latinos account for a disproportionate share of new HIV infections relative to their size in the US population (Henry J. Kaiser Family Foundation, 2014). If current rates of HIV diagnoses persist, one in two black men who have sex with men (MSMs) and one in four Latino MSMs will be diagnosed with HIV in their lifetime (Centers for Disease Control and Prevention, 2016). Remember the earlier stat that only eight states require sex ed that is appropriate for a student's cultural background and not biased against any race, sex, or ethnicity? While there are some successful programs that specifically reach out to communities of color, it seems clear that culturally appropriate and anti-bias education efforts deserve priority in more than eight states.

When only 20 states mandate including information about condoms in sexual education (Guttmacher Institute, 2016), and no states mandate information about safer sex tools such as dental dams, the female condom (FC2), or gloves, it is clear the United States could do a better job of protecting and educating its youth.

Lindsey Says

Though our national STI outcomes are staggering, most sex ed does not focus on skills proven to prevent the spread of STIs, nor on developing healthy attitudes regarding safer sex practices, but rather on fear- and shame-based messages about how supposedly terrible it is to have an STI. Students are left feeling like they would never want to be "tarnished for life" like one of "those" people, while we know that half of them will actually contract an STI by the age of 25 (Cates, Herndon, Schulz, & Darroch, 2004). The social stigma that we learn as teenagers makes it difficult to discuss STI status with partners in adulthood. In fact, the worst part of contracting an STI for many people is simply the stigma.

In doing STI lessons with people of all ages, my primary goal is not to run through all the symptoms and show frightening pictures of what could happen if they have sex with the "wrong person," but rather to de-stigmatize STIs overall. I want to normalize the concept of testing, teach skills for discussing safer sex and status with a partner, and make sure everyone knows some tricks for making condoms feel good and be super easy to introduce. For example, I recommend taping a condom to the back of your headboard, so you can whip it out like a sex magician in the moment, without pause. Ultimately, I want to leave people with the feeling that they have the ability to protect themselves reasonably well from STIs, and also that it is pretty normal to get one and it doesn't mean anything bad about you as a person.

Sex is a normal thing for humans to do. We are quite literally built for it. Sex is also an easy way to spread germs. Just because someone gets an STI doesn't mean they are any less cool, sexy, or sweet than they were before. We don't judge people for getting a cold by sharing a sip from someone's water bottle, because we recognize that is pretty normal and can happen to any of us. STIs are fairly similar; they just happen to be spread by body parts we don't feel as comfortable discussing at the dinner table. You don't have to be a "bad" person, or even make a "bad" decision to contract an STI. Wonderful, normal, sexy, good, trustworthy, lovely people get STIs, too. The shame cloud from high school health class doesn't do anything to keep us safe. It is more like a roadblock to building the comfort and confidence required to talk openly about STIs with a partner and a huge barrier to feeling worthy of sexual pleasure and loving affection.

Taking a pleasure-positive approach to an STI talk includes normalizing sexual desire, discussing a wide variety of sexual behaviors, teaching useful skills to manage risk, and assuming that those affected by an STI are still able to be sexual.

Results Beyond the Numbers: Case Studies in Pleasure

There are many effects from our lack of education about sex and pleasure that are not depicted in pregnancy or STI rates. I see them daily in my work as a therapist. I talk with so many adults who are fearful of their bodies and feel that pleasure will never be within their grasp. Rather than seeing pleasure as something that everyone can achieve to varying degrees, or a set of skills you can learn, practice, and build upon, my clients often feel that pleasure is something that either happens or doesn't. Even worse, if it doesn't happen they often blame themselves or decide that something must be wrong with their relationship.

Navi and Michael are a middle-aged married couple who came in to see me after 15 years of struggling through non-pleasurable sex that was often painful for Navi. Despite loving many aspects of their relationship, they were considering splitting up because the stress of bad sex for so many years had become overwhelming. Michael felt rejected by Navi's lack of desire for him. Navi felt sure something was wrong with her because she wasn't enjoying sex. She felt that this was some kind of inner deficiency on her part and had little hope she could do anything about it.

In their first session I started out with three important pieces of information: people with vulvas often need 20 minutes or more of direct, pleasurable stimulation before they become aroused enough to possibly orgasm, 70% report they need direct clitoral stimulation to orgasm (Hite, 1976), and sexual lubrication can work wonders in helping to avoid sexual pain and increase pleasure. These three simple pieces of information often help my clients quickly increase their ability to create pleasure in their bodies.

Michael and Navi came to the next session with wide smiles and a newfound hope that their sexual relationship could be pleasurable and connecting, rather than painful, fraught, and isolating. They still had issues to work through, but a positive experience of creating pleasure together gave them the emotional boost they needed to keep on trying. Happily, Navi had let go of some of the shame and blame she was carrying, instead saying, "Why didn't anyone tell me about this stuff earlier?"

Patty was in her 60s when she came to talk to me about "her problem." She had never been able to have orgasms or pleasurable sexual experiences with her husband. As a young, newly married woman in her 20s, Patty had been diagnosed with cancer and had surgery to remove her uterus. After the surgery her doctor had been silent about sexual issues and Patty had been afraid to ask. When I asked her if she knew which organs had been removed in the surgery—Did she still have ovaries or her cervix?—she wasn't sure. She said that no one had ever had that conversation with her in the 40 years since the procedure. Patty told me her husband was loving and kind, but had stopped attempting to initiate sex many years ago. When I asked her if she would like to bring her husband in for a couple's session, Patty quickly dismissed this idea stating that this was "her problem" and she needed to figure it out.

Are you noticing a theme here? I work with too many women who come in feeling that somehow they are the problem. Often they blame themselves for difficulty creating pleasure without realizing they are missing crucial information about how to do so, and the fact that no one gave them that information is not their fault. Pleasure education is providing information about how bodies commonly work during arousal so that people can create more pleasure in their own bodies and better understand what to expect from themselves and their partners. But it is not just women who have unrealistic expectations of their bodies.

Will is in his early 20s and currently enjoying having sex with other male identified people. At least, this is what he tells me at first. When we talk a bit more it becomes clear that while he likes seeking out sexual adventures, he could definitely be enjoying them more. Will feels a lot of pressure to perform during sex and impress his sexual partners. He tells me he is concerned he isn't able to "last long enough" and he keeps losing his erection. When I ask how long a typical erection lasts for him he replies "only 15 to 20 minutes" and tells me he feels like he needs to be able to last at least an hour. Of course, this is not how most human bodies work, but Will has gotten the idea (probably from fantasy material like porn and erotica sprinkled with a bit of regular old self-doubt) that his body should absolutely be able to keep an erection and maintain penetration for at least an hour. When I tell him that 15 to 20 minutes is actually a pretty long amount of time to keep an erection, he is surprised. We talk about how erections frequently come and go during sexual activity and that is a totally normal way the body works—not necessarily a sign that he is losing interest in the sexual encounter.

Then I ask him, "Are you sure your partners even want penetration for an hour? That would feel like a really long time for lots of people and might be more painful than fun. Have you ever asked a partner what the most pleasurable part of being sexual is for them?" Will laughs at me, and I laugh too. "I know, that probably sounds like a dorky thing to ask, but why not? Everyone is different. How are you supposed to know what they like if you don't ask? Maybe fucking isn't even their favorite part but they are doing it because they think *you* want to." We talk about how vulnerable this conversation could feel but how it could also be worked into sexy talk beforehand. Will brings up his concern that people don't tend to have these conversations with casual partners and I say, "Well, that's too bad. Especially if you might only have one time to get it right, it would help to know what they like. It seems like you would have more chance of a repeat date if they know you are super into helping them feel good."

Without pleasure education it is easy for students and clients to assume sex is about how long penetration lasts, how hard a penis gets, how many orgasms are had. While many people find those things pleasurable, everyone will answer the question, "What is the most pleasurable part of being sexual?" differently. No one knows until they ask. When we aren't encouraging people to ask pleasure questions, we miss an opportunity to teach about pleasure as the basis of connection and consent.

Can Reshaping How We Teach About Sex Really Make a Difference?

To answer this question, let's look at how other industrialized nations handle sex education and how it affects their health outcomes, as well as cultural perceptions of sex.

Lindsey Says

Cultural norms about coming of age sexually vary greatly across the globe. Impressive health outcomes are widespread in nations with more progressive attitudes towards the normalcy of sex and the reality of pleasure in sex, and it is not surprising. We see many western European nations with successful social marketing campaigns that normalize condoms using pleasure and humor. Magazines for youth sometimes include sexually explicit information and imagery, normalizing teen interest in sexuality. Nudity is more casual and there is generally more comfort with bodies.

In France and Germany, political and religious interest groups have little influence on public health policy. Instead, these policies are based on research. Youth have convenient access to free or low-cost contraception. Sex education in schools is usually integrated across school subjects and at all grade levels. Educators provide accurate and complete information in response to students' questions and families have open, honest, consistent discussions with teens about sexuality. (Advocates for Youth, n.d.). What are the results? The teen birth rate in Germany and France are roughly one third of the US rate (Ventura, Hamilton, & Mathews, 2014). Switzerland has exceptionally low teen pregnancy, birth, and abortion rates (8, 2, and 5 per 1,000 15–19-year-olds, respectively). It also has long-established sex education programs, free family planning services, widely available low-cost emergency contraception, open and direct family communication around sexual debut, and the expectation that sexually active teens will use contraceptives (Sedgh et al., 2015).

Lindsey Says

In the United States, teen interest in sex is often viewed as a sin, a moral failure, a disgrace to the family. If one has sex "too early," they must "suffer the consequences" of unplanned pregnancy, sullied reputation, and the implied shame of getting tested for disease. If we contrast our US norms with the Netherlands, we see that many Dutch parents view teenage sexual interest as a normal and healthy part of growing up. They expect that adolescents would find romantic partners and that those relationships would likely include sexual experimentation. Dutch parents see their role as a more of a guide through this process, teaching valuable relationship skills and having frequent family conversations about sexual initiation (Schalet, 2011).

These belief systems could hardly be more different. So, what are the results? US teen girls ages 15–19 were more than six times more likely to give birth than their Dutch counterparts (Sedgh et al., 2015). Dutch teens are more than twice as likely to use hormonal contraception as US teens, and also twice as likely to use both hormonal methods and condoms at the same time. STI rates are dramatically higher in the United States, and US teens are more likely to report that their first sexual experience was unwanted, that they did not enjoy it, or that they did not feel like it was within their control (Schalet, 2011).

While many people in the United States feel uncomfortable with teen sexuality, few would argue they want a young person to have an unpleasant, painful, or out-of-control first sexual experience. Yet, we can plainly see that our health outcomes are lower across the board than nations who take a sex-positive, open approach, and acknowledge that sex is normative and pleasurable. What is the price our young people pay for our discomfort in talking about pleasure?

Simple changes in the way we teach about sex, pleasure, and relationships can make big differences in health outcomes and (bottom line) in people's lives. While systemic policy changes are needed, every sexual health professional can make a difference with their students and clients.

Reshaping Pleasure Education for Adults

While comprehensive sex and pleasure education is a huge piece of helping today's youth make empowered choices for their sexual futures, it will not help adults who have already gone through the school system. Working with pleasure issues with adults can heal some of the wounds and fill the gaps left by inadequate sex ed.

We tend to think the phrase "developmentally appropriate" applies exclusively to the ways we talk with children and young people. However, adults and elders need developmentally appropriate pleasure education too. As people age, bodies, life situations, and pleasure change. Adults need pleasure information that fits their life situation. Some examples might include various stages of pregnancy and post-partum; during illness or physical injury; dating after divorce or death of a spouse, during menopause, after menopause, as erections change, and within nursing homes or assisted living situations. While improving sex education in schools is vital, developmentally appropriate pleasure education needs to be accessible long after high school graduation—in community centers, health care settings, sex toy stores, couple's retreats, online, and more.

Pleasure Actually Keeps Us Safer and Healthier

We have been raised to fear the *yes* within ourselves, our deepest cravings. But, once recognized, those which do not enhance our future lose

their power and can be altered. The fear of our desires keeps them suspect and indiscriminately powerful, for to suppress any truth is to give it
strength beyond endurance.

(Lorde, 2007)

Can pleasure education keep us safer and provide better health outcomes? Sexual health scholars have long advocated for the inclusion of pleasure in sexual
education and discourse (Fine, 1988; Fine & McClelland, 2006; Hirst, 2013;
Philpott, Knerr, & Boydell, 2006; Tolman, 2002). However, relatively few educational programs put pleasure at the forefront, making research on its efficacy
difficult to find. However, it makes sense that sex-positive emotions support
harm-reduction practices. When people have information about how to make
sex pleasurable they are more likely to talk about what is working or what
might work better. If an individual feels positively about the sex they are having,
it becomes possible to go to the store for condoms, and to the clinic for birth
control and testing, without fear or embarrassment. These factors make for better
health outcomes as well as greater happiness and satisfaction with sexual relationships and experiences.

Teaching pleasure-positive skills (communication, pleasurable condom use, etc.)
does not make people start having sex any younger, or have more partners. In fact,
the opposite is true. Comprehensive sex ed programs that encourage both abstinence and condom/contraceptive use have been shown to have a positive impact
on delaying sex, reducing the frequency of sex or number of partners, and increasing condom or contraceptive use. In contrast, programs that encourage abstinence
without encouraging condom or contraceptive use currently have little evidence
that they delay the onset of sex or otherwise affect sexual behavior (Kirby, 2007;
Kirby & Laris, 2009).

Pleasure Matters in Condom Use

Studies show that when people believe condom use will be pleasurable they tend
to use condoms more, while people who think condoms reduce pleasure or interfere with arousal tend to use condoms less (Crosby, Charnigo, & Shrier, 2014;
Graham, Crosby, Milhausen, Sanders, & Yarber, 2011; Newby, Brown, French, &
Wallace, 2013). In a recent study, researchers found that pleasure-related attitudes
had stronger associations with lack of condom use than all sociodemographic or
sexual history factors that were examined. In fact, they found that the greater the
perceived chance of pleasure reduction, the greater the odds of condom nonuse
(Higgins & Wang, 2015).

Lindsey Says

*As sexuality professionals, it is perfectly appropriate for us to help people see how good condoms
can be, as this will make them more acceptable in real-life sexy scenarios. I introduce the topic
like this, "I want to show everyone a few tricks for making condoms feel really good, because that
is obviously important, right?" As I go through all the steps, I emphasize that before putting the*

condom on the penis, you can leave an inch or two of extra space at the tip, and then put a good sized squirt of silicone lube in there before pinching the tip and rolling it down. Then I demonstrate how instead of being tight and dry at the tip of the penis, reducing sensation, this method gives you a lot of material that is really slippery that is going to move around and increase the feelings the penis is getting. I think the lube information is pretty important, but even more important is the simple acknowledgement that their pleasure is valid and important, and not at all incompatible with sexual safety.

Sexual Health Professionals and Fear

It is not just our students and clients who experience fear in connection to pleasure and sexuality. Professionals who work with pleasure issues experience fear as well: fear of not having the right training; fear of repercussions to their programs or themselves; and fear that their professionalism, personality, or identity will be judged. Let's examine these fears—as well as why it is important to challenge them, both in ourselves and in our society.

Fear of Lack of Training

One reason many sexual health professionals don't include pleasure in their work is they didn't get any pleasure education themselves. Other than those who have sought out specialized training, most professionals are not trained to address pleasure, and may not have even received comprehensive sexuality education themselves.

There are currently no set standards regarding sexuality education for medical students, and information on sexual function and dysfunction is generally scant or absent in many medical schools (Shindel & Parish, 2013). There are also no standardized requirements for therapists regarding education in sexuality or pleasure. I frequently get referrals from couples therapists sending me clients because they don't feel competent working with sexual issues. These are not complex or specialized issues, mind you: These are couples who just want to talk about their sexual relationship and are told that their relationship therapist "doesn't work with that." While fear of addressing pleasure issues without training is understandable, silence around pleasure is also harmful to our clients and students.

Fear of Repercussions

Many sexual health professionals hold a very real fear for their jobs or their organization's funding. It was not so long ago that Dr. Joycelyn Elders was forced to resign as surgeon general simply for saying that masturbation is a part of human sexuality and that teaching about it might be a possible way to limit the spread of HIV (Jehl, 1994). What might have happened to Dr. Elders if she had dared to add, "And it feels great!"?

These kind of issues are not just in the past. Recently, deceptively edited videos attempted to imply Planned Parenthood was illegally selling fetal tissue. As a result, 12 states conducted investigations of Planned Parenthood. Congress attempted to defund the organization, which is the largest provider of sex education in the United States (Planned Parenthood, 2014). While Planned Parenthood was cleared of the fetal tissue accusations (Kurtzleben, 2016) and, in fact, the makers of the video were indicted for using false IDs (Ludden, 2016), this kind of situation creates negative perceptions that are not easily reversed. It also creates real concern for sexual health professionals that something like this might happen to them or their organization if they say or do the wrong thing—or perhaps even if they say or do nothing wrong. The fear of words taken out of context, misinterpreted, maliciously edited, or falsified is a real one for sexual health professionals.

Lindsey Says

Sex educators may be very good at helping students feel relaxed and open enough to ask tough questions. There is often a moment of fear, though, when the question turns to pleasure.

"Why would someone want to have oral sex?"

"Does butt sex feel good?"

"What does masturbation feel like?"

"Why do some girls pee during sex?"

The sex educator immediately scans the room to evaluate the looks on the other adults' faces, wondering if they are going to be criticized or end up on the evening news for giving an honest answer, no matter how age-appropriate and important it may be. Sadly, it has happened before—and it will happen again—that a perfectly accurate response to a question about sex has landed someone in trouble. But what happens when we don't answer the question?

Shutting the student down or telling them that their question is inappropriate sends a clear message that they have gone too far, and that student may never ask another sex question again. The myths then carry on and on, and we've lost the opportunity to build understanding of basic sexual functions and a healthy range of expectations for how sex and bodies work. These elements are instrumental in developing self-esteem, self efficacy, and appreciation of difference, and are cornerstones of enjoying pleasurable, consenting sexual experiences in the future. Every question can be answered appropriately. Be confident in the knowledge that the answers to pleasure questions can all essentially tie in to respecting partners and supporting safer sex practices.

Fear of repercussions often leads to over-medicalization of issues and a focus on pathology rather than happiness. Therapists feel justified asking about the "bad" in their client's sex lives: Has anyone had an affair? Any problems with compulsive sexual behavior? Quantifiable questions also seem safe and reasonable: How often do you have sex? How long does it last? How many sexual partners have you had? While all of these are important questions, it is just as important (and in some cases, perhaps more important) to ask pleasure questions of clients.

Box 2.1   Pleasure Questions

Are you happy with the ways you are sexual with yourself?
Are you happy with the ways you are sexual in your relationship(s)?
Is sexual activity pleasurable for you?
Are you having orgasms?
Do you want to have orgasms?
Do you know how to create pleasure in your own body?
Do you know how to create pleasure with your partner(s)?

While these are the results clients tend to be most concerned about—enjoying sex, feeling good in their body, connecting pleasurably with their partner(s)—these questions are often regarded as less professional and more intrusive. However, my experience is when I ask about pleasure, my clients trust me more, open up, tell me about their hopes and goals. Many of them have said, "Thank you so much for asking! We saw a therapist about our relationship for two years, and they were great. Our communication is so much better. But we never talked about sex." Or, "I know it's silly because you are a sex therapist, but I was afraid of bringing this up."

Fear of bringing up the subject is not unique to my clients. In fact, 68% of clients cite fear of embarrassing a provider as the reason for not bringing up sexuality issues when visiting medical professionals (Marwick, 1999). As much as professionals fear bringing up the subject of pleasure because we might offend the people we work with, the people we work with are just as afraid to bring it up to us. It is the professional's job to be the one to break the silence. If someone does get upset, you can say, "I'm so sorry if I offended you. This is a big concern for many of the people I work with. Studies show about 70% of people are afraid to ask their provider sexuality questions, so I make it a practice to ask all the people I work with. I'm happy to change the subject, but please know I am always here if you have any questions or concerns in the future."

Fear of Scrutiny of the Professional Self

Sexual health professionals may feel extra pressure to present a rigidly "professional" appearance to combat any misconceptions or devaluations of their work. I had this experience while taking a photo for my website. Myself and a few other friends who needed professional photos had hired a photographer and we were chatting as we waited for our turn in front of the camera. When I looked over the possible outfits I had brought with me, I saw clothing I found to be professional and flattering, matching who I am and what I bring to my practice. I had also brought items I found professional and frumpy, but I felt might give me more "credibility." As I was weighing my options, one of my friends said to me, "My friend asked if sex therapists have sex with their clients. Do you?" The sick feeling of fear hit my stomach and I reflexively grabbed the frumpiest blouse I had brought. I hated that photo every time I looked at it afterward. I don't present this story to be disrespectful to sexual surrogates or sex workers. Instead, I would like to reflect fears I frequently hear echoed from sex therapist colleagues: "I don't wear makeup to work. I don't want people to get the wrong idea," "Is this blouse too low cut? It seemed OK when I put it on this morning, but maybe I should put a scarf over it?" "What books are appropriate to display in my office? Maybe I'd be better off keeping some of the more sexual titles at home." All of these concerns boil down to, "Am I presenting myself non-sexually enough to be respected as someone who is qualified to talk about sex?"

One professional I know told me:

> I can speak on the part of being a person of color and working in the field of sexuality. There is a certain look society has when they envision a "professional" sex therapist. There is a stigma when working with folks within my own community as a female working in the field of sexuality. I have my tongue pierced and folks automatically correlate that to "kinky sex" or "no wonder you're into sex therapy." In addition to needing to appear like a professional and dressing like one, I feel I am constantly having to prove myself.
>
> (P. M. Moua, Personal Communication, October 1, 2015)

The sad truth is that our professional "look" and selves will be scrutinized. Our subject matter may be deemed less respectable if we appear less traditional, less conservatively dressed, or if we dare to show any signs of being a sexual human being. Of course, the reason for this is at least partially related to sex negativity. This presents a difficult situation where bowing to the expectations of what "professionals" look like may mean that we are contributing to sex negativism and in some cases even oppression (when we assume that "professionals" should be white, straight looking, presenting binary gender, etc.).

One thing all sexual health professionals can do to combat this is challenge our own views of what "professional" means to us. Do we value what people say and do as a professional or do we value what they wear while they say it? Who do we pay attention to and who do we dismiss? Do we listen only to people with doctorates while ignoring others who have many years of experience in the field? Do we avoid people who do hands-on sexual work (sexual surrogates, hands-on sex educators) while privately thinking to ourselves that some of our clients could possibly benefit from this work? Do we strive to separate ourselves from sex workers and porn performers while encouraging our clients to watch their educational videos? While we continue to fight against stigma in our larger world, how can we better support each other within our professional communities? Choosing not to give in to fear of including pleasure is one big way to change our field. If we stand up proud, professional, and confident when working with pleasure, the world will take notice.

Shifting the Conversation

As sexual health professionals, we have an opportunity to shift US culture by standing up for the power (and professional value) of pleasure. Outlining the positive effects that pleasure education has on health outcomes can back up the validity of this choice. Don't let fear determine what you teach or talk about. Choose your topics, interventions, and curricula based on the needs you see in the people you work with. When professionals are intimidated by the issue of pleasure, they communicate that message of fear to the people they teach. When working with

pleasure issues, be confident. Back up your confidence with facts about the positive
benefits of pleasure. Make your reasoning evident by explaining these benefits to
students and clients. Don't hesitate to point out the consequences of *not* talking
about pleasure (see Chapter 3 and 4 for further discussion) and point out links
between teaching pleasure and teaching consent (Chapter 4). Don't let fear keep
you from working with the important topic of pleasure.

References

Advocates for Youth. (n.d.). *Adolescent sexual health in Europe and the United States,* the *case for a
rights. respect. responsibility.® approach.* Retrieved February 12, 2016, from http://www.advo
catesforyouth.org/storage/advfy/documents/adolescent_sexual_health_in_europe_and_the_
united_states.pdf
American Medical Association. (2009). *An updated review of sex education programs in the United
States.* Retrieved February 12, 2016, from http://www.gprhe.org/IMG/pdf/AMA_Updated_
Review_on_Sex_Education_Programs_2009.pdf
American Psychological Association. (2005). *Resolution in favor of empirically supported sex education
and HIV prevention programs for adolescents.* Retrieved February 12, 2016, from http://www.apa.
org/about/policy/sex-education.pdf
Barr, E. M., Moore, M. J., Johnson, T., Forrest, J., & Jordan, M. (2014). New evidence: Data doc-
umenting parental support for earlier sexuality education. *Journal of School Health, 84,* 10–17.
Bleakley, A., Hennessy, M., & Fishbein, M. (2006). Public opinion on sex education in US schools.
Archives of Pediatric & Adolescent Medicine, 160(11), 1151–1156.
Cates, J. R., Herndon, N. L., Schulz, S. L., & Darroch, J. E. (2004). *Our voices, our lives, our futures:
Youth and sexually transmitted diseases.* Chapel Hill, NC: University of North Carolina at Chapel
Hill School of Journalism and Mass Communication.
Centers for Disease Control and Prevention. (2012). *Prepregnancy contraceptive use among teens
with unintended pregnancies resulting in live births—Pregnancy Risk Assessment Monitoring System
(PRAMS), 2004–2008.* Retrieved February 12, 2016, from http://www.cdc.gov/mmwr/pre
view/mmwrhtml/mm6102a1.htm
Centers for Disease Control and Prevention. (2015). *CDC fact sheet; reported STDs in the United
States, 2014 national data for chlamydia, gonorrhea, and syphilis.* Retrieved February 12, 2016, from
http://www.cdc.gov/nchhstp/newsroom/docs/factsheets/std-trends-508.pdf
Centers for Disease Control and Prevention. (2016). *CDC newsroom release; lifetime risk of HIV
diagnosis.* Retrieved April 29, 2016, from http://www.cdc.gov/nchhstp/newsroom/2016/
croi-press-release-risk.html
Clark, A. S. (2009, February 6). Ex-surgeon general: Lack of sex ed "akin to child abuse." *The Jer-
sey Journal.* Retrieved from http://www.nj.com/hudson/index.ssf/2009/02/exsurgeon_gen
eral_lack_of_sex.html
Crosby, R. A., Charnigo, R., & Shrier, L. A. (2014). Prospective associations between perceived
barriers to condom use and "perfect use". *American Journal of Preventive Medicine, 47*(1), 70–72.
Demissie, Z., Brener, N. D., McManus, T., Shanklin, S. L., Hawkins, J., & Kann, L. (2015). *Characteristics of health programs among secondary schools.* U.S. Department of Health and Human Services,
Centers for Disease Control and Prevention. Retrieved February 2, 2016, from http://www.
cdc.gov/healthyyouth/data/profiles/pdf/2014/2014_profiles_report.pdf
Eisenberg, M. E., Bernat, D. H., Bearinger, L. H., & Resnick, M. D. (2008). Support for compre-
hensive sexuality education: Perspectives from parents of school-age youth. *Journal of Adolescent
Health, 42,* 352–359.
Fine, M. (1988). Sexuality, schooling and adolescent females: The missing discourse of desire. *Har-
vard Educational Review, 58*(1), 29–53.
Fine, M., & McClelland, S. (2006). Sexuality education and desire: Still missing after all these years.
Harvard Educational Review, 76(3), 297–338.

Graham, C. A., Crosby, R. A., Milhausen, R. R., Sanders, S. A., & Yarber, W. L. (2011). Incomplete use of condoms: The importance of sexual arousal. *AIDS and Behavior*, *15*(7), 1328–1331. doi: 10.1007/s10461-009-9638-7.x

Guttmacher Institute. (2016). *Sex and HIV education.* Retrieved February 18, 2016, from http://www.guttmacher.org/statecenter/spibs/spib_SE.pdf

Hamilton, B. E., Martin, J. A., Osterman, M. J. K., Curtin, S. C., & Mathews, T. J. (2015). Births: Final data for 2014. *National Vital Statistics Reports*, *64*(12). Retrieved February 12, 2016, from http://www.cdc.gov/nchs/data/nvsr/nvsr64/nvsr64_12.pdf

Henry J. Kaiser Family Foundation. (2014). *The HIV/AIDS epidemic in the United States.* Retrieved February 12, 2016, from https://kaiserfamilyfoundation.files.wordpress.com/2014/04/3029-15-the-hivaids-epidemic-in-the-united-states1.pdf

Herrman, J. W., Solano, P., Stotz, L., & McDuffie, M. J. (2013). Comprehensive sexuality education: A historical and comparative analysis of public opinion. *American Journal of Sexuality Education*, *8*, 140–159.

Higgins, J., & Wang, Y. (2015). The role of young adults' pleasure attitudes in shaping condom use. *American Journal of Public Health*, *105*(7), 1329–1332.

Hirst, J. (2013). It's got to be about enjoying yourself': Young people, sexual pleasure, and sex and relationships Education. *Sex Education*, *13*(4), 423–436.

Hite, S. (1976). *The Hite report: A nationwide study on female sexuality.* New York: Macmillan.

Jehl, D. (1994, December 10). Surgeon general forced to resign by white house. *The New York Times*. Retrieved from http://www.nytimes.com/1994/12/10/us/surgeon-general-forced-to-resign-by-white-house.html

Kearney, M. S., & Levine, P. B. (2012). Why is the teen birth rate in the United States so high and why does it matter? *Journal of Economic Perspectives*, *26*(2), 141–166.

Kirby, D. (2007). Abstinence, sex, and STD/HIV education programs for teens: Their impact on sexual behavior, pregnancy, and sexually transmitted disease. *Annual Review of Sex Research*, *18*, 143–177.

Kirby, D., & Laris, B. A. (2009). Effective curriculum based sex and STD/HIV education programs for adolescents. *Child Development Perspectives*, *3*(1), 21–29.

Kurtzleben, D. (2016, January 28). Planned parenthood investigators find no fetal tissue sales. *National Public Radio.* Retrieved April 29, 2016, from http://www.npr.org/2016/01/28/464594826/in-wake-of-videos-planned-parenthood-investigations-find-no-fetal-tissue-sales

Lorde, A. (2007). *Sister outsider: Essays and speeches.* Berkeley, CA: Crossing Press.

Ludden, J. (2016, January 26). Anti-abortion activists indicted on felony charges in planned parenthood case. *National Public Radio.* Retrieved April 29, 2016, from http://www.npr.org/2016/01/26/464469813/anti-abortion-activists-indicted-on-felony-charges-in-planned-parenthood-case

Marwick, C. (1999). Survey says patients expect little physician help on sex. *JAMA*, *281*, 2173–2174.

Newby, K. V., Brown, K. E., French, D. P., & Wallace, L. M. (2013). Which outcome expectancies are important in determining young adults' intentions to use condoms with casual sexual partners? A cross-sectional study. *BMC Public Health*, *13*(1), 1.

Penman-Aguilar, A., Carter, M., Snead, M. C., & Kourtis, A. P. (2013). Socioeconomic disadvantage as a social determinant of teen childbearing in the U.S. *Public Health Reports*, *128*(Supplement 1), 5–22.

Philpott, A., Knerr, W., & Boydell, V. (2006). Pleasure and prevention: When good sex is safer sex. *Reproductive Health Matters*, *14*(28), 23–31.

Planned Parenthood. (2014, January). *By the numbers.* Retrieved April 29, 2016, from https://www.plannedparenthood.org/files/9313/9611/7194/Planned_Parenthood_By_The_Numbers.pdf

Schalet, A. T. (2011). *Not under my roof: parents, teens, and the culture of sex.* Chicago: University of Chicago Press.

Sedgh, G., Finer, L. B., Bankole, A., Eilers, M. A., & Singh, S. (2015). Adolescent pregnancy, birth, and abortion rates across countries: Levels and recent trends. *Journal of Adolescent Health*, *56*(2), 223–230.

Shindel, A. W., & Parish, S. J. (2013). Sexuality education in North American medical schools: Current status and future directions. *Journal of Sexual Medicine*, *10*(1), 3–17.

Stanger-Hall, K. F., & Hall, D. W. (2011). Abstinence-only education and teen pregnancy rates: Why we need comprehensive sex education in the U.S. *PLoS ONE*, *6*(10), e24658. Retrieved from http://doi.org/10.1371/journal.pone.0024658

Tolman, D. L. (2002). *Dilemmas of desire: Teenage girls talk about sexuality*. Cambridge, MA: Harvard University Press.

Tortolero, S. R., Johnson, K., Peskin, M., Cuccaro, P. M., Markham, C., Hernandez, B. F., . . . Dennis, H. L. (2011). Dispelling the myth: What parents really think about sex education in schools. *Journal of Applied Research on Children*, *2*(2), 5.

Ventura, S. J., Hamilton, B. E., & Matthews, T. J. (2014). National and state patterns of teen births in the United States, 1940–2013. *National Vital Statistics Reports: From the Centers for Disease Control and Prevention, National Center for Health Statistics, National Vital Statistics System*, *63*(4), 1–34.

Chapter 3

Pleasure for All People

How the Professional Focus on Reproductive Health Puts Everyone at a Disadvantage

Sexual health is an umbrella that includes a wide variety of topics: anatomy and physiology, communication, consent, STI and pregnancy, pleasure, values, and more. However, most sexual education programs focus almost exclusively on two topics: reproductive health and STI prevention. Most reproductive health and STI lessons address sexual behaviors only between someone with a penis and someone with a vulva. In addition, it is common for little to no information about arousal and pleasure for women to be provided since this is not necessary for reproduction. The result is that the people who are most able to infer health and pleasure information from sex education are cisgender men who are exclusively interested in being sexual with cisgender women.

Who is disadvantaged by this approach? Everyone, but most dramatically people with vulvas, people who identify as LGBTQ, and people whose bodies function differently than "standard" sexual response. Sadly, the curriculum that sex educators are most often allowed to teach in schools perpetuates a sexist, heteronormative view of sexuality.

Reproductive health education and STI prevention information is very important, but if it is applicable to certain people only, others are left without education. Changes and additions need to be made to comprehensive sex ed in order for it to be beneficial for everyone, and pleasure is a missing piece that could help include more people in the puzzle. Whether working in schools or with adults who are long past high school health class, incorporating pleasure will help to include more people and give them the information most relevant to their lives.

Reproductive Anatomy Versus Pleasure Anatomy

Our sexuality is with us from birth to death, although it manifests differently at different developmental stages, of course. Reproduction is an important part of some people's lives. Pleasure is hopefully present throughout our whole lives and intertwined with all our sexual experiences, reproductive or not. When pleasure is excluded from the conversation, the majority of people's sexual experiences are excluded as well.

Reproductive health gives information on reproductive anatomy, which is often very different from pleasure anatomy. Reproductive anatomy lessons for people with penises at least involve a major pleasure organ: the penis. Reproductive

FRONT VIEW of VULVOVAGINAL ANATOMY

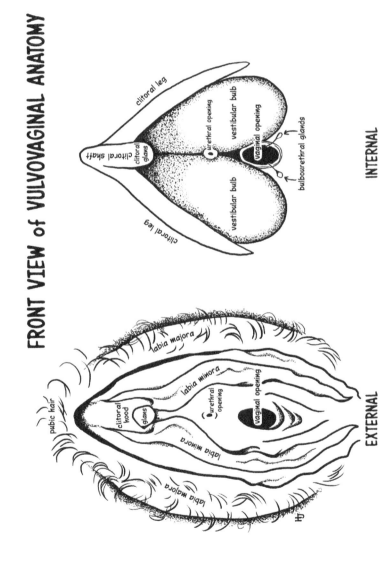

INTERNAL

EXTERNAL

Figure 3.1 A Diagram of Vulvovaginal Anatomy That Puts Focus on Pleasure Anatomy—The Internal Structure of the Clitoris

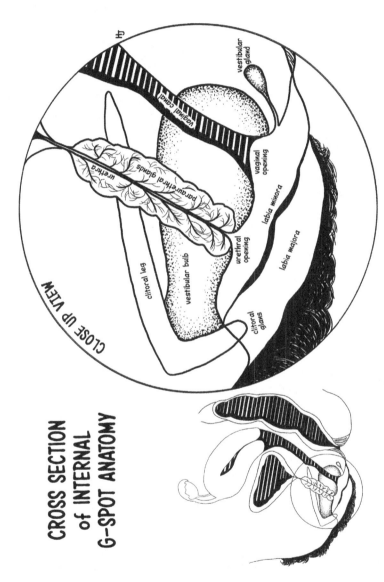

CROSS SECTION of INTERNAL G-SPOT ANATOMY

CLOSE UP VIEW

clitoral leg
urethra
paraurethral glands
vestibular bulb
vaginal canal
clitoral glans
urethral opening
vestibular gland
vaginal opening
labia minora
labia majora

Figure 3.2 By Emphasizing the G-Spot Rather Than Concentrating on the Vagina, Uterus, and Fallopian Tubes, Pleasure Anatomy Is Given Focus

© Hannah Jorden, published with permission of Hannah Jorden.

anatomy lessons for people with vulvas may not even use the word "vulva." The focus is on menstrual cycles, ovaries, uteri, and vaginas. The body part most people with vulvas report getting the most pleasure from—the clitoris—unfortunately does not need to be mentioned when explaining reproduction.

In contrast to the familiar cross-section often used in reproductive anatomy (vagina, uterus, and ovaries), Figures 3.1 and 3.2 emphasize pleasure anatomy (the clitoris and g-spot). Providing a view of the body that might be similar to what a person would see if they looked at their vulva (or a partner's), Figure 3.1 attempts to normalize—rather than medicalize—the vulva. When I use these with clients and students, I make sure to say that this is just one way a body might look and that genitals differ in appearance, just like their owners do.

Lindsey Says

I was once doing a parent and staff night in preparation for a sex ed unit beginning at a senior high school. This was a chance to preview the lessons and materials that the students would be using and ask questions. The anatomy diagrams were very straightforward, clear, and accurate drawings. The school's director was fine with the diagram of the penis, but very uncomfortable with the diagram of the vulva.

"Do we have to include the clitoris?" She asked, concerned. "Our students are just so innocent."

That it never occurred to her to censor information about the penis, but that information about the clitoris would spoil the "innocence" of the students, is very telling. Can you imagine if we actually removed the clitoris from the picture, and then all the people who go home to look at their vulvas in the mirror after the anatomy lesson are shocked and scared to find they have an extra body part?

The pleasure of the penis is routinely included in sex education, as early as in puberty lessons, but clitoral and vaginal pleasure are mysteriously missing. Pick up nearly any puberty book—not only will you find that it is all about "becoming a guy" or "becoming a girl," with nothing speaking to trans or nonbinary young people; you will likely see the "boy" version includes info about masturbation, erections, orgasm, and ejaculation. The "girl" version will basically address periods, and say nothing of positive sexual feelings, attraction, or function. Oh, and there are usually some beauty tips thrown in, too.

Table 3.1 shows the differences between the body parts necessary to cover in reproductive education and those that are involved in pleasure education. Notice how many important body parts involved in pleasure are left out when the focus is strictly on reproductive education.

Since the penis is a largely external organ, it lends itself to more familiarity and easy exploration than a vulva, which often requires a mirror and some determination to examine visually. There are many other biological and cultural factors that may make pleasure information about the penis more "self evident" than pleasure from the vulva. Pleasure information being left out of or banned from sex ed curriculum means that no information is provided to help young people (and the adults they become) navigate this issue.

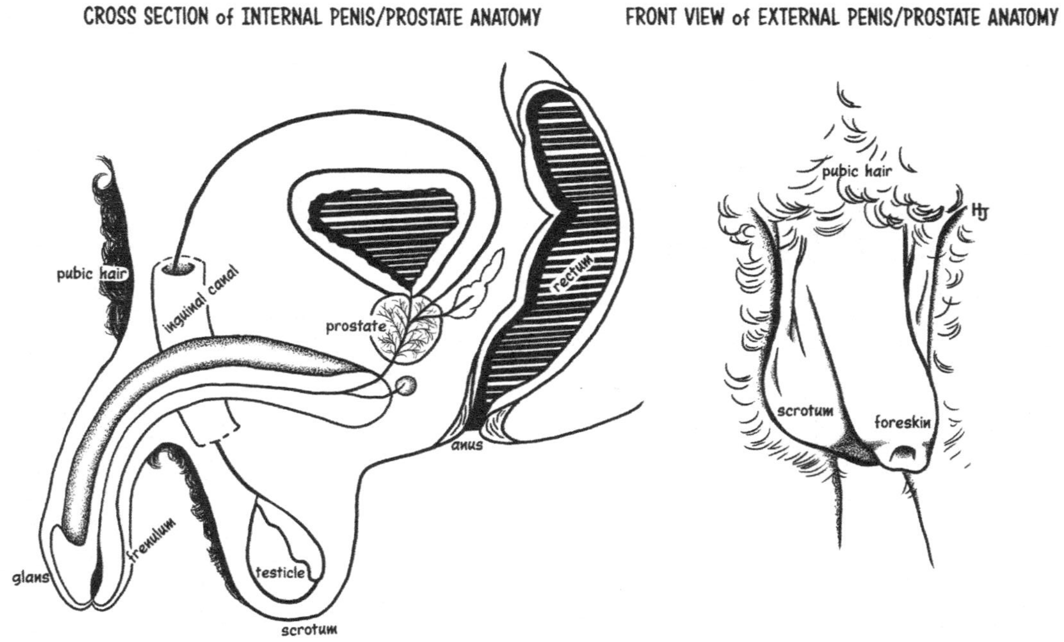

CROSS SECTION of INTERNAL PENIS/PROSTATE ANATOMY   FRONT VIEW of EXTERNAL PENIS/PROSTATE ANATOMY

Figure 3.3 Internal and External Penis/Prostate Anatomy

Table 3.1 Body Parts Taught in Reproductive Anatomy and Body Parts Involved in Pleasure Anatomy

Body Parts Taught in Reproductive Anatomy	*Body Parts Involved in Pleasure Anatomy*
Penis	Penis
Testes	Frenulum
Prostate (possibly included,	Scrotum
but usually not information about prostate	Prostate
pleasure)	Anus/rectum
Vagina	Nipples
Cervix	Clitoris
Uterus	Vulva
Ovaries	Vagina
Fallopian Tubes	G-spot
	Anus/rectum

Notice the emphasis on pleasure education in Figure 3.3. Including a front view of the penis rather than just the internal cross-section puts emphasis on the skin and nerve endings. Providing a view that would be similar to a person looking at their own (or a partner's) body makes the diagram more applicable in daily life and hopefully less medical or intimidating. Including internal pleasure organs such as the prostate also puts the emphasis on pleasure. Again, when using this with clients and students I would emphasize that this is one way a body might look, and while this drawing shows an uncircumcised penis, many people have circumcised penises as well.

Types of People Who Are Disadvantaged When Pleasure Education Is Excluded

Many different types of people are disadvantaged when pleasure education is left out. Here are some examples of the people impacted and the negative effects they suffer as a result of the exclusion of pleasure information.

People With Vulvas

One of the most frequent things I do when starting therapy with clients who have a vulva (or whose partner does) is give out basic health and pleasure information about vulvas. I generally don't have to do this for people with penises. People with vulvas gain virtually no understanding of how arousal and pleasure function in their body from reproductive health information. While the process of erections and ejaculation are included in basic reproductive health education, people with vulvas frequently hear nothing about desire, arousal, increased blood flow to the genitals, changes in breathing, lubrication, clitoral stimulation, g-spot stimulation, ejaculation, or orgasm. Excluding pleasure information leaves out a vast part of the picture for more than 50% of the population.

Reproductive health education leaves women with very little information that could be helpful if they are not experiencing pleasure in their bodies. Even worse, excluding pleasure information and focusing on reproduction reinforces seriously harmful stereotypes such as women do not experience pleasure at all or people with vulvas should get pleasure exclusively from penetration with a penis. When pleasure education is left out, it reinforces the notion that women's sexuality is for reproduction only and subject to the needs of others. When sex education is taught without ever mentioning pleasure for people with vulvas, the message often received is that sex isn't something a person with a vulva is expected to enjoy, but rather tolerate.

People Who Identify as LGBTQ

Current sex ed in schools is not serving LGBTQ youth well. Remember that only 12 states require discussion of sexual orientation in sex education, and, of those, three require the teaching of negative information (Guttmacher Institute, 2016). In several studies, LGBTQ youth report inadequate sexual health information through their schools' sex education programs, and they felt that their needs were left out of the curriculum (Garcia, 2009; Kubicek, Beyer, Weiss, Iverson, & Kipke, 2010; Kubicek et al., 2008; Pingel, Thomas, Harmell, & Bauermeister, 2013).

Most abstinence-based sex education promotes heteronormativity through active silence around anything other than heterosexuality (Fisher, 2009). By focusing on reproductive health education only, sexual behaviors that are nonreproductive are often completely ignored. This leaves people who want to have sexual experiences that do not involve penis-in-vagina sex with almost no information on how to do so pleasurably and safely. That is a lot of people and a lot of information left out. Important interventions like normalization of queer pleasure and modeling boundaries in a variety of non-hetero situations are nonexistent, which can easily leave many people wondering what might be wrong with them that no one ever mentions their desires, fantasies, or identities.

It is a terrible blow to the self-esteem to be rendered invisible. This kind of devaluing of identities is likely to damage empowered decision making and the ability to protect oneself. Kubicek et al. (2010) studied how and where young men who identify as gay, bisexual, or MSM found sexual health information. They found that they received very little information in school sex ed that was applicable to their sexual lives, and instead turned mainly to the Internet, friends, and sexual partners for information:

> While resourceful in learning about sex, many young men still had significant gaps in their sexual knowledge at the time of their sexual debut. This led many to engage in high-risk sexual activities and often to be ill equipped to advocate for their own sexual preferences or health.
>
> (Kubicek et al., 2010, p. 258)

Kubicek et al. (2010) collected many stories of first sexual experiences from their study participants, and the lack of applicable sexual education shows in the accounts they gathered: "More experienced partners often determined the nature of the sexual experience because they 'seemed pretty educated.' These partners typically controlled the sexual encounter, and respondents reported 'doing what he told me'" (p. 254). While we can't assume these were negative sexual experiences (and the study doesn't elaborate on how the respondents felt), it seems clear that lack of pleasure education resulted in less sexual agency, and the need to follow the lead of their partner. This dependence can certainly be seen as a potential vulnerability.

Pain was another frequently reported outcome in these first sexual experiences: "Reporting painful sexual debuts was not unusual among the qualitative respondents. Young men reported that they did not know how to prepare themselves or their body for anal intercourse, particularly those who 'bottomed' or engaged in receptive anal intercourse" (Kubicek et al., 2010, pp. 255–256).

> Experiences such as these led some young men to believe that anal sex was supposed to be painful. Given that most young men did not have people in their lives with whom they felt they could talk, they reported that they just "assumed it was supposed to feel that way." This realization made some question their sexuality further, believing that they would never be able to engage in a pleasurable or healthy sexual relationship.
>
> (Kubicek et al., 2010, p. 256)

Unfortunately, many of the people I have worked with have similar stories. Accurate and appropriate information about pleasure would have gone a long way towards keeping these men safer and enabling them make more empowered choices. Including LGBTQ topics and identities in sex education can combat stigmatizing silence and in fact improve the general safety of school for LGBTQ students (Snapp, McGuire, Sinclair, Gabrion, & Russell, 2015). Providing information on ways to increase both pleasure and safety helps clients and students make informed decisions. Student and clients may choose safer options if they know how to make them pleasurable, and if they do choose riskier options it is because it is the right choice for them, not because they don't know there are other possibilities.

Lindsey Says

Witnessing that no teen sex ed curriculum was created with LGBTQ youth specifically in mind, I decided to make that happen in my own setting, at Family Tree Clinic in St. Paul, where I am the Director of Health Education. We developed a peer education group for teens, to run during the summer at our clinic. The students named the group KISS (Keeping It Safe and Sexy). We began in 2010 and since its inception, the program has been a huge success. Each year we have grown by leaps and bounds. A real strength of the program is that we have the freedom to constantly evolve and adjust based on the expressed interests of the participants. LGBTQ experiences are centered throughout, and we have made a real diversion from how typical programs define and discuss anatomy and sexual practices. We are more frank, specific, and open-ended with our discussion of the multitude of ways that people give and receive pleasure. The truth is that programs for heterosexual cisgender people would benefit from this model too. Each year, the enthusiasm grows and the biggest piece of feedback we hear from the students is that they wish we had more sessions and the sessions were longer. We are already meeting for 16 three-hour sessions during summer vacation, but they never want it to end.

KISS members develop a passion for sexual health that they carry with them into their relationships, families, and communities, because this is sex ed that speaks to their real needs, desires, and experiences. One unanticipated outcome that was especially exciting was the effect on communication between KISS members and their parents. We measured significant increases in frequency and quality of family conversations about sex, and many KISS members decided to come out to their parents about their sexual orientation or gender identity after building this foundation of respectful conversation in the family and increasing self-esteem and confidence by participating in a program in which they could see themselves reflected.

People Who Are Questioning or Confused

When reproductive sex is presented as the only option, people may not understand that there are many other ways to be sexual. Without being presented with other options, people who may be questioning their orientation, or just feeling confused about their sexuality in general, may not receive information that would help them better understand their own desires and selves. Normalization of questioning, ambivalence, and fluidity of sexual identity and/or experiences goes a long way toward helping people feel better as they learn more about themselves. Information about solo pleasure (masturbation and fantasy) can be tremendously helpful for people who are figuring themselves out. It is also a relatively risk-free way to explore sexuality that is left out of many sex education curricula, for fear that it would be seen as inappropriate or encouraging sexual behavior.

People Who Are Intersex

"'Intersex' is a general term used for a variety of conditions in which a person is born with a reproductive or sexual anatomy that doesn't seem to fit the typical definitions of female or male" (Intersex Society of North America, 2016). For those people whose reproductive anatomy may be different than what is taught in standard reproductive health classes, pleasure education may offer more helpful information about their bodies and experiences. Learning about a wider variety of body parts and body functions, nerve endings, and how pleasure works in the body is more inclusive and more likely to be helpful.

People of Various Gender Expressions

While people who identify as transgender, nonbinary, genderqueer, gender variant, gender creative, or otherwise not cisgender may enjoy reproductive sex, they are likely to enjoy other forms of sexual expression as well (like the vast majority of people do). Currently no state mandates teaching about gender identity as part of sexual education and (as we will cover in Chapter 4), sex education is often based off of gender stereotypes that are harmful to people of all gender expressions. Pleasure education that emphasizes negotiation of sexual experiences, communication about likes/dislikes, and does not assume preferred sexual behaviors based on gender or body parts may serve these folks (and their partners) better.

Heterosexual, Cisgender Men

Speaking of stereotypes, focusing only on reproductive sex reinforces a narrow definition of heterosexual male sexuality. Heterosexual men who enjoy anal play, prostate pleasure, oral sex, and non-penetrative sexual expressions with partners are not receiving any information on their preferred sexual expressions through reproductive health education. When people do not see their interests represented in the information provided, they are likely to assume their desires are outside the norm—something secretive or shameful. This also gives partners the impression that the men they want to be sexual with will only enjoy penis-in-vagina sex.

Heterosexual, cisgender men who prefer penis-in-vagina sex are also disadvantaged by a lack of pleasure education. A strict focus on only reproductive information sets expectations that pleasure is not a valued or important part of their or their partner's sexual experience (not to mention leaves them with a lack of skills for creating pleasure in themselves and others). This gap in information can easily lead the inaccurate and dangerous stereotypes covered in Chapter 4, such as "Women never enjoy sex so you have to convince them to let you do it," "Pain/discomfort is totally normal during penetration," or "Being a good lover depends on the size of your penis and how long your erection lasts."

Straight Couples

When penis-in-vagina sex is the most talked about (and most taught about) sexual behavior, many male/female couples feel that this is the sexual activity they should like best. I have had many of these couples come to therapy with the initial complaint that they are having a "big problem" in their sex life. When I ask them what is going on, they report many great things about their sex life: They are happy with their connection and chemistry, they feel they have sex about as frequently as they would like, they are able to have pleasure and orgasms, and they feel comfortable talking about sex. In general, they seem to be doing really well.

When I ask them why they are coming to therapy they say: "We don't like penetrative sex that much. It's fine but we don't enjoy it as much as oral or hand sex. Yes, we can orgasm from it, but we orgasm at different times and she needs clitoral stimulation. Something must be wrong if we are not having penetrative sex, with simultaneous orgasms from penetration only, all the time." When I tell them that lots of couples prefer forms of sex other than penetration, that clitoral stimulation is necessary for most women to orgasm, and that none of this means there is something wrong with their relationship, they are often surprised and relieved.

People With Physical Disabilities or Differences

When reproductive education is given the focus, people whose bodies function differently may think that sexual expression and pleasure are not available for them. Many people with disabilities find their bodies do not function according to the standards on which many of the DSM-V sexual diagnoses are based on, but this does not mean that they are incapable of pleasure and sexual satisfaction: "Current diagnostic schemes may serve to label the sexual response of a disabled person as dysfunctional when, in reality, it may be highly functional for the individual" (DiGiulio, 2003, p. 54). Tepper (2000) illustrates how people with spinal cord injuries (SCI) were left at a disadvantage from a lack of pleasure education and an over-focus on genital intercourse:

> The absence of quality sexuality education combined with learning about sex primarily from having genital intercourse, led to sexuality embodied in the genitals and cognitively focused on perfect performance with the goal of orgasm. This genitally focused and performance oriented conception of sexuality presented developmental challenges to optimizing sexual potential after injury for all participants.
>
> (p. 288)

In contrast, pleasure education is able to address the issue of how to cultivate pleasure in each person's individual body. This is not just about physical arousal and orgasms. As we mentioned in Chapter 1, pleasure can be physical, emotional, mental, relational, or any combination of these. No matter how a person's body functions, there is always the possibility of pleasure.

> Participants who relearned how to experience pleasure and even orgasm after SCI believed early on that there was more possible and that their sexuality was their responsibility. They learned more about their spinal cord injured bodies, introduced fantasy; embraced the disability and rejected sexist and ableist ideals, and were fortunate enough to experience sex with a significant sexual partner. The deliberate inclusion of pleasure in this research brought to light the most compelling issues around sexuality and disability for the participants.
>
> (Tepper, 2000, p. 289)

People with SCI are only one example. People with long-term physical illnesses, injuries, disabilities, and whose bodies do not follow normative physical arousal patterns could all benefit greatly from a focus on pleasure.

People With Developmental or Cognitive Disabilities

It is often assumed that people with developmental or cognitive disabilities are not going to have children and thus are not in need of sexual education. Whether or not this is true varies from person to person, but a common effect is that those with cognitive disabilities are typically seen as either completely desexualized (living in a permanently innocent childlike state), or their sexual behaviors are perceived as being "out of control" or criminal (Gomez, 2012).

Fifty-six percent of students with mild intellectual disabilities and 84% of students with moderate to profound intellectual disabilities do not receive sexual education in school (Barnard-Brak, Schmidt, Chesnut, Wei, & Richman, 2014). This study's authors encouraged readers to consider the ramifications of not providing sex ed to students with intellectual disability (ID), pointing out that people who have ID are three times more likely to be sexually assaulted than people who have not been diagnosed with ID. Without sex education these students are less likely to have skills to protect themselves or let caregivers know what is happening if they do experience abuse.

Of course, many people with cognitive and developmental disabilities will grow up to experience sexual feelings and desires just like most other people do. When they are taught nothing about appropriate context, boundaries, and expressions of sexuality (whether alone or with a partner) these individuals are set up for personal frustration and left at risk of violating some otherwise commonly understood boundary that they were never made aware of. Though a person may be classified as a "vulnerable adult," it is still normal for them to have a need for sexual pleasure, and there are appropriate ways for supporting professionals to make space for this in each individual's life. For some, these pleasures might not even be specifically genital, but may be romantic and intimate in nature. The ability to seek satisfying relationships and experience bodily pleasure is a human right.

People Experiencing Fertility Issues

If sex is mainly about reproduction, what does that say to couples who have fertility issues? Struggling to conceive is a tremendous stress on couples to begin with. When they do not have good information about how to cultivate more pleasure in their sexual connection, they are left without important relationship tools in an already stressful time.

People as They Age

Our bodies go through many changes as we age and our pleasurable parts are not immune to the changes. In fact, sometimes they are the exact places where changes are happening. Later-life body changes are not generally covered in high school health class, so most people receive no formal education regarding these issues. People going through menopause, noticing changes in erections, or noticing general changes in sexual function need their professionals to bring up the subject of pleasure with them. I have had many clients who suffer through dryness, chafing, or pain during penetration who didn't know there were options available to them (lubrication, consulting their doctor about medical options). Many relationships suffer because one or both people's bodies are changing with age and they just assume, "Well, I guess sex is over for me/us." Just because people are older or their bodies change does not mean they want to be finished with sexual pleasure. When professionals assume someone doesn't need pleasure information because they are over a certain age, they are overlooking an important opportunity, and the people they work with lose out.

Everyone

The majority of sex acts in your life will not be reproductive. I say that confidently even though I probably don't know the details of your sex life. The average person will have 2.5 instances of sex that lead to reproduction. However, the number of sexual experiences (with self and/or others) in an average lifetime is likely to be much higher than 2.5. A fun game I like to play in some of my classes is "name a sexual behavior that is not reproductive." As the class yells out their answers, the list becomes incredibly long and varied. People suggest partnered and solo activities, genital and nongenital activities, and words that make some people in the class ask, "What does that mean?" It becomes clear very quickly that sexuality and reproduction are two separate (though sometimes intersecting) topics, and there are a wide variety of sexual behaviors that are not reproductive.

Comprehensive reproductive health education is essential. Education regarding STI transmission (especially inclusive of non-heteronormative sexual behaviors) is crucial. But pleasure education is in every way as valid and important as both of these. Leaving out pleasure education means we leave people needlessly ignorant in ways that negatively affect their self-esteem, self-confidence, and sexual relationships.

The Myth of the Beautiful People

Sex sells. Pleasure sells. The idea that a product is pleasurable or sexy can make big money for companies. The image we are often "sold" of pleasure is that it is easily available . . . as long as you are young, traditionally beautiful, and have a fit/thin/busty/muscular body. I call this the Myth of the Beautiful People: Somewhere out there is a group of people who are easily fitting all of society's ideals, who have all the partners they could want to have, and pleasure flows effortlessly throughout their sculpted, youthful bodies.

The danger of the Myth of the Beautiful People is that people buy into it and try to live up to it, or assume that pleasure is not available to them if they fall outside of these narrow and difficult-to-meet standards. So they try to change their appearance in order to find pleasure, when pleasure does not depend on any type of appearance. They choose not to pursue sexual pleasure because they assume they cannot have it, when pleasure is within everyone's reach. Or, maybe they meet society's criteria for youth and beauty but feel ashamed because despite appearing to "have it all" pleasure is not happening "naturally," when really, there is no "natural" when it comes to pleasure.

Without pleasure education, it is easy for people to assume The Myth of the Beautiful People is accurate. After all, that is the way it looks in movies and in porn, two of the most prevalent sources where people absorb pleasure information when it is not included in sex education. We see pleasure connected to certain bodily features rather than a knowledge of the way bodies work. We see pleasure connected to finding the "perfect" partner rather than communicating and practicing with a (wonderfully, awkwardly) human partner.

Because most people do not have many confidants they share the details of their sex lives with (especially if those details are not happy and glamorous), they don't get the chance to hear that the amount of pleasure one experiences is not connected to age, looks, race or ethnicity, abilities, gender, body type, or any other one factor. However, I do get to talk with many people about their sex lives. The broader picture I see is this: The people who have the most pleasure in their lives work for it. They prioritize pleasure by working on communication, better understanding their own and their partner's bodies, and seeking help or information when they need it.

No Pleasure for You!

It is not just the general population that falls into believing the Myth of the Beautiful People: Sexual health professionals can do this as well when they assume they don't need to bring up the topic of pleasure with certain people. Sometimes professionals do not intend to ignore the topic of pleasure with certain demographics but do so without realizing it. Stereotypes and pleasure negativity run deep and fuel assumptions about clients and students for all of us. Seniors, people of all different body sizes, people with disabilities, people living with mental illness, people with cognitive disabilities, and people with long-term physical illnesses often have pleasure concerns or questions. They are also frequently overlooked by professionals who may assume these clients or students are not interested, are "busy dealing with other issues," or not in need of pleasure education. Sometimes professionals feel awkward bringing up the topic of pleasure because they feel it might seem rude or it feels inappropriate because of differences in age, gender, or culture.

Pleasure information is even more important for these populations precisely because it is often overlooked or not discussed. When other people (especially professional people) assume pleasure is not a priority for you, you are likely to believe them, even if that does not match your own priorities. In addition, people who are marginalized receive many messages that imply that finding sexual pleasure and sexual partners is likely to be more difficult for them (Tepper, 2000).

Assumed or experienced scarcity of partners, and difficulty finding pleasure information that is applicable or inclusive, is the exact kind of set-up that leads people to say "yes" to sexual experiences or partners they would really rather say "no" to. When people believe sexual pleasure will be difficult to find or are unsure how to get it without a partner, they are more likely to put themselves into dangerous or risky situations. What a difference it can make to know that pleasure is something you can cultivate in your own body, something you can find good information about and support around. These are the attitudes that can shift thinking from a scarcity model of "take what you can get" to one of goal setting and "what do I want?" This is one of the many ways pleasure education contributes to health, safety, and self-esteem.

Clients or students who may not be able to have partners due to concerns about ability to consent are likely still in need of pleasure education. Everyone needs to know how sexual pleasure may function in their bodies, how they may be able to find solo pleasure, and what appropriate boundaries might look like. Every person needs to have professionals in their lives whom they can bring pleasure questions to, because these are body functioning questions, questions of self, and questions of sexual health. When sexual pleasure in the body changes (difficulty getting or maintaining erections, difficulty with lubrication, changes in arousal, or pain) it may indicate the presence of other medical conditions that are important to diagnose. Professional attention to masturbation is not frivolous or perverted. Solo pleasure is an important part of wellness and changes in masturbation functioning can be the canary in the coal mine, alerting a professional that medical attention may be needed.

Access to information about sexual pleasure is particularly important for people who may be coping with issues such as physical or mental illness, pain, depression, or anxiety. As we covered in Chapter 1, pleasure is good for people in a variety of mental and physical ways. Pleasure is a way to comfort and soothe ourselves, and it can be a way to positively connect with others. Sexual pleasure and body pleasure can help people through hard times in life. All (beautiful, human) people, not just "The Beautiful People," need access to accurate pleasure information.

Building Pleasure Skills

If pleasure education is potentially for everyone, this means that professionals are likely to work with lots of different people, with differing needs, and from diverse communities. Sometimes professionals think specific training is needed to work with people in specialized populations, or populations that the professional is not a part of. Training is a wonderful thing to pursue, when it is available. However, training in these areas is often difficult to find. It is (unfortunately) unlikely that each professional will be able to find trainings on sexual pleasure specific to every specialized, marginalized, or educationally neglected community.

If there is another professional in your area who specializes in working with people in a specific community, referral can be a responsible option. However, clients and students sometimes feel that referral is another way that their needs are put off or considered "too complicated" for them to get prompt support. My own experience is that often the need outnumbers the specialists available, and very few specialists of any sort are trained in working with pleasure issues. Here are a few ideas for addressing pleasure issues sensitively with a wide variety of people:

- Don't make assumptions about someone's sexual function or capacity for pleasure because they use a wheelchair or a cane or because of a diagnosis they may have. Just as we can't assume whether any random person is able to get erections, whether they have pain or pleasure during sex, or whether they enjoy certain types of stimulation, we also can't make assumptions just because we can see a person uses adaptive equipment or because we have some (unrelated) health information about them.
- Ask questions rather than making assumptions.
- Ask about how their specific circumstances affect pleasure with themselves and others. For example, "Do you feel depression and anxiety have affected your ability to have sexual pleasure?" or "How do you feel cancer is affecting your relationship with your body? How about your sexual relationships?"
- Don't assume whether sexual pleasure is or is not a priority for your client or student. The only way to really know is to ask.
- Don't assume an individual or couple's difficulty is directly related to an illness, disability, age, orientation, or any other aspect of their identity or life. Instead, ask questions to help you understand their perception of the problem (if they think this is a problem) and how it may intersect with many aspects of their life.
- Even if you are not able to access a local training on how to better serve the clients and students you are working with, there are resources available. Traveling to trainings is great when possible and Internet trainings are a great option if you can't travel.
- Reach out to other professionals who work with these issues and ask them what trainings, books, or other resources they recommend.

- Ask your student or client if they feel they are getting what they need from you or if they think they might benefit from searching out a specialist. While it is always the professional's job to make sure they are able to give competent care, the people we work with often have a good sense of whether they are getting what they need from our services. Their perception matters.
- Do your own research. Read books, watch movies that are recommended, and try to gain perspective on your client or students' experience or community. Specifically look for resources created from within the community your student or client belongs to rather than outside voices commenting on the community. But of course . . .
- Don't assume you know something about your client or student because you know something about a demographic they belong to.
- Ask questions based on norms and expectations to gain information or normalize what may be happening for your student or client. Phrasing your question so that it is not an assumption is important. For example, "Have you noticed any changes in your body's lubrication in the past few years? Some people notice a difference postmenopause," or "Many people who have an ostomy bag want to discuss how to talk about it to people they are dating. Is that something you are interested in discussing, or not really?"
- Rather than using a best guess or something you think you heard once, don't be afraid to answer a question with, "I don't know." Then make sure you follow up with, "Let's try to find information about that."

Talking about sex therapy for disabled individuals or couples, DiGiulio says, "In essence, the core tenets of empathy, sensitivity, caring, listening, and understanding are the same regardless of the clientele" (2003, p. 64). No matter the kind of sexual health professional or the kind of clientele, these principles offer a solid basis to start from.

Pleasure as Empowerment

> In touch with the erotic, I become less willing to accept powerlessness, or those other supplied states of being which are not native to me, such as resignation, despair, self-effacement, depression, and self denial.
>
> (Lorde, 2007)

When people are struggling—because they are trying to understand more about themselves, because they don't know anyone else like them, because their body is "different," because the world tells them they are lesser—knowledge is power. When people are not given information about key parts of their bodies, the ways their body functions, and the wide variety of sexual expressions, they are more likely to struggle. When no one ever normalizes a desire for pleasure, or encourages people to explore their own bodies, people often feel that pleasure is not for them or assume pleasure is scary and bad. Working with pleasure issues and providing pleasure education can lead to empowerment for all kinds of people—really, for all of us. Sexual health professionals need to present information that is applicable and useable to a wide variety of people. Teaching and talking about sexuality through the lens of pleasure is an important way to open the discussion and include more people.

References

Barnard-Brak, L., Schmidt, M., Chesnut, S., Wei, T., & Richman, D. (2014). Predictors of access to sex education for children with intellectual disabilities in public schools. *Mental Retardation, 52*(2), 85–97.

DiGiulio, G. (2003, Spring). Sexuality and people living with physical or developmental disabilities: A review of key issues. *The Canadian Journal of Human Sexuality, 12*(1), 53.

Fisher, C. M. (2009). Queer youth experiences with abstinence-only-until-marriage sexuality education: "I can't get married so where does that leave me?" *Journal of LGBT Youth, 6*, 61–79.

Garcia, L. (2009). "Now why do you want to know about that?" Heteronormativity, sexism, and racism in the sexual (mis)education of Latina youth. *Gender & Society, 23*(4), 520–541.

Gomez, M. T. (2012). The S words: Sexuality, sensuality, sexual expression and people with intellectual disability. *Sexuality and Disability, 30*(2), 237–245.

Guttmacher Institute. (2016). *Sex and HIV education*. Retrieved February 18, 2016, from http://www.guttmacher.org/statecenter/spibs/spib_SE.pdf

Intersex Society of North America. (2016). Retrieved January 24, 2016, from http://www.isna.org/faq/what_is_intersex

Kubicek, K., Beyer, W. J., Weiss, G., Iverson, E., & Kipke, M. D. (2010). In the dark: Young men's stories of sexual initiation in the absence of relevant sexual health information. *Health Education & Behavior, 37*(2), 243–263.

Kubicek, K., Carpineto, J., McDavitt, B., Weiss, G., Iverson, E. F., Au, C. W., . . . Kipke, M. D. (2008). Integrating professional and folk models of HIV risk: YMSM's perceptions of high-risk sex. *AIDS Education and Prevention: Official Publication of the International Society for AIDS Education, 20*(3), 220.

Lorde, A. (2007). *Sister outsider: Essays and speeches*. Berkeley, CA: Crossing Press.

Pingel, E. S., Thomas, L., Harmell, C., & Bauermeister, J. (2013). Creating comprehensive, youth centered, culturally appropriate sex education: What do young gay, bisexual and questioning men want? *Sexuality Research & Social Policy: Journal of NSRC: SR & SP, 10*(4). Retrieved from http://doi.org/10.1007/s13178-013-0134-5

Snapp, S. D., McGuire, J. K., Sinclair, K. O., Gabrion, K., & Russell, S. T. (2015). LGBTQ-inclusive curricula: Why supportive curricula matter. *Sex Education, 15*(6), 580–596.

Tepper, M. S. (2000). Sexuality and disability: The missing discourse of pleasure. *Sexuality and Disability, 18*(4), 283290. doi: 10.1023/A:1005698311392.x

Chapter 4

Pleasure and Consent
How Teaching Pleasure Combats Rape Culture

Pleasure education is a vital component of teaching consent. When we instruct people to continually check in with partners in order to collaborate on increasing pleasure, we combat the idea that sex with someone who is of diminished capacity, drunk, passed out, silent, or unresponsive is something that "just happens sometimes." Pleasure education encourages people to own their desires rather than acquiescing to other people's desires. When sexual health professionals portray pleasure as one of the most important parts of sex, we set the standard for people to expect pleasurable experiences and encourage them to speak up when they have non-pleasurable or bad experiences.

Desire can be ambivalent, which makes consent more complex than "Yes means yes and no means no." Sometimes a "yes please" can turn into a "wait a second." Sometimes your partner is feeling a solid "maybe." Pleasure education offers important information on how to navigate these situations. When we teach that pleasure is not intuitive to anyone, we take performance pressure off and people who were previously too embarrassed can now check in about their partner's experience during sex.

Pleasure-Positive Culture Can Combat Rape Culture

There is a lot of discussion and disagreement about what the term "rape culture" entails.

Lindsey Says

Rape culture is not as simple as a culture in which rape happens, because that will unfortunately happen anywhere, but rather a culture in which the societal trend is that rape and assault are seen as typical, excusable, to be expected, even romanticized, where the aggressors are seen as the ones being taken advantage of, where the victims are blamed or assumed to have wanted it. Here is the most clear and succinct definition of rape culture I have seen so far: "A rape culture is a complex of beliefs that encourages male sexual aggression and supports violence against women. It is a society where violence is seen as sexy and sexuality as violent" (Buchwald, Fletcher, & Roth, 2005).

While rape culture creates a power dynamic that greatly disadvantages women, it negatively affects everyone, cisgender men included. The assumptions prevalent in rape culture create a system in which cisgender men are taught not to recognize sexual assaults that may have happened to them (because they are told men cannot be assaulted because all men love sex and want all the sexual contact that happens to them all the time). Trans and nonbinary people are also greatly endangered by rape culture. If you don't "play by the rules" of gender, rape culture would say that you "deserve what you get." This is unfortunately evident in the appallingly high rates of sexual assault on trans and nonbinary people.

While rape culture is an expansive subject, in this chapter when we refer to "rape culture" we are referring to the overt or unspoken belief that:

- Sexual pleasure makes people incapable of controlling or less responsible for their sexual behaviors.
- Sexual violence can be justified because of something someone did (what they wore, who they went out with, actively seeking sexual pleasure, etc.).
- Sexual pleasure is only for certain people and is not possible, important, or permissible for others.
- Sexual pleasure is an appropriate reason to override someone's "no" or push the limits another person's consent.
- It is justifiable to be violent toward or devalue another person based on their sexual choices, gender, or orientation.

Sex Education Without Pleasure: An Inaccurate and Dangerous Picture

Sex education without pleasure paints an inaccurate and sometimes dangerous picture. Vital contextual information and partner skills are frequently left out when pleasure is excluded from sexual health. For example, let's look at the sexual behavior that is most often covered by reproductive health education: penis-in-vagina penetration, as described without pleasure information. In many lessons, not much more information than "the penis goes into the vagina" is conveyed, possibly with some messages about preventing pregnancy or STI transmission. The "this part goes here" approach does not give any information about how firmly or gently to put "this" part "here." It does not cover how much time it might take to be aroused enough to enjoy "this part" going "here." It makes no mention of partners discussing wants and needs, what pleasure might look like, what pain might look like, or how to stop and have a conversation with your partner if you aren't sure "this part going here" is going well for them. It does not suggest options for how to make any "part" feel good, or supplies like lubrication that many bodies need in order for "this part" to attempt to go anywhere. Nor does it suggest that it is OK if people prefer to do other sexual things besides "putting this part here." All of this important information is what pleasure education conveys.

Teaching about pleasure includes teaching that it is separate from physical arousal. Many people experience physical arousal (erections, lubrication, orgasm, and other physical reactions) during unwanted and nonconsensual sexual activities. When people are not taught that physical arousal does not necessarily mean a person "wants it," we set people up to misunderstand their bodies and the bodies of their partners. We also leave victim/survivors in a place of confusion, knowing they did not feel right about this sexual experience and perplexed by their body's response. We set them up for self-doubt.

Conversely, when people aren't told to expect pleasure in their partner's reactions, they sometimes don't. Not because they are predators, but because they are terrified, embarrassed, don't even know what to look for, and no one ever encouraged them to ask. Take George and Jill, for example. Married for 27 years, they have raised three kind and caring children together. In my office they frequently laugh together and it is clear they love each other. However, when we talk about sex Jill looks at the floor and her eyes fill up with tears. George becomes stone faced. Sex for Jill has never been pleasurable and in the past few years it has become painful. George worries that Jill doesn't love him anymore, and maybe has never loved him in a sexual way. After a few solo sessions with Jill, she and I have a chance to talk over her grief, frustration, and anger about the years of "putting up" with sex. Over time, Jill begins to understand what might help her enjoy sex more as we talk about lube, vibrators, and take the focus off penetration for now.

Then a funny thing happens: Jill and George come in for a couple's session and tell me they were sexual together and it was great. They both felt pleasure and enjoyed themselves. But now, in session, they are angry at each other. George gets mad that it took all these years before Jill told him what felt good to her. He says, "I would have done whatever she asked! It could have been like this long ago!" Jill is angry at George for turning their first pleasurable experience together since they were dating into a fight. She yells at George, "Well, why didn't you ask me then? You had to see I wasn't enjoying it. Did you care how I was feeling? If you wanted to make it better why didn't you ask me how?" There is silence in the room for a moment and then I (very gently) ask George, "What do you think about that? Did you ever ask Jill how you could make sex feel better for her?" George looks at me wide-eyed with this realization and says, "No, I didn't. I should have. I'm embarrassed. How did I never think to ask that?"

George is a kind man who loves his wife. He would have loved to make sex more pleasurable for her from the start. However, George and Jill were both raised with absolute silence around female sexual pleasure, which affected both of them deeply and in ways neither of them realized. I have worked with so many Jills and Georges. I do not tend to see this issue in queer couples, who often seem to be more skillful at negotiating what they want, maybe because there are fewer assumptions made about what behaviors sex "should" consist of. Heterosexual gender stereotypes about what sex is and who will get pleasure from it are keeping the Jills of the world thinking bad sex is normal and the Georges from asking how to make it better.

Gender Stereotypes Teach Misinformation About Pleasure

Gender stereotypes are harmful to everyone. They cast cisgender women as desire-less victims, cisgender men as lust-controlled perpetrators, and leave out everyone else. Let's take a moment to explore the implied conclusions behind messaging commonly found in a variety of sex education materials as well as messages that clients and students tell Lindsey and me they received through their families, religions, and cultures.

Cisgender Girls/Women

You are exclusively heterosexual and you will need to protect yourself from boys/men who always want sex and might pressure you. Guys only want "one thing"—and if they want sex from you, it means they don't respect you. You don't really have sexual desire, but at some point you'll probably be pressured to have sex to keep a relationship. Boys/men always want sex from you but if you have actually been sexual with partner(s) they won't want you because that makes you dirty.

Lindsey Says

If you do something sexual, it means you don't have any self-respect. Some programs even go so far as to say that your purity essentially belongs to your dad and represents your family, until another man marries you and thus takes ownership.

Implied message: Don't expect sex to be pleasurable for you and don't expect to want it. If you do want it, there might be something wrong with you. Interest in sexual pleasure will negatively affect your desirability as a partner as it might make you "easy" or "slutty." Your job is to fend off predatory men until you find one that you want to marry. Then sex should be pleasurable, so you should be able to easily and completely switch your mindset at that point.

Cisgender Boys/Men

You are exclusively heterosexual. Your hormones are completely crazy and you think about sex all the time. You want to talk girls out of using condoms, because you are irresponsible, selfish, and only care about feeling good. The only way to be honorable is to abstain from sex because you won't be able to control yourself otherwise. Once you start having sex with an approved partner your job is to know everything she wants without ever having to ask. If you have to ask, your manhood and desirability as a partner will be questioned.

Lindsey Says

Much sex ed messaging doesn't speak to guys at all, just posits them as the aggressor and then all the focus is on warding them off. In each story or example, the guy is pressuring the girl to have sex, not use a condom, doesn't respect her, etc. I have hardly ever seen anything that is about how guys should act in any of these situations. It is all about girls defending themselves, except when there is a dangerous "slut" girl who wants to give him an STI, of course.

Implied message: Desire is a dangerous force that will make men hurt people. We don't expect that you will be able to control yourself when experiencing pleasure, so you must abstain completely. If you push women's boundaries or do something nonconsensual, you aren't as responsible for your actions because you probably can't control them. You will want sex all the time—and if you don't, something is probably wrong with you. You are never victimized by unwanted sexual contact, but it will be easy for you to become a victimizer. It is pretty normal for you to pressure someone to be sexual with you because of your high level of desire and low level of control. Experiencing sexual pleasure will make you keep pushing for more until someone finally makes you stop.

LGBTQ Identified People, Questioning People, and People Who Do Not Fit Into Binary Gender Expression

Most often, these identities are not mentioned and information is presented in a way that assumes heterosexuality.

Implied message: You don't exist or possibly are too dangerous to talk about. Figure it out yourselves and don't bother to expect positive role models or health and safety information that applies to you.

The Dangers of Teaching Gender Stereotypes

The examples just given may seem exaggerated. However, they are very present, both in popular culture and in many sexual education programs. These stereotypes may seem outdated; however, young people today still believe them to be true. Recent research findings show that among college students, men are still conceptualized as sexual initiators and women as sexual gatekeepers, and that men's sexual pleasure is primary whereas women's experience of pleasure is secondary (Jozkowski & Peterson, 2013).

Internalized gender stereotypes impact clients' and students' perceptions of pleasure and consent, and not in a good way. Here are some examples.

Gender Stereotype: Cisgender men are sexual initiators and should know what they are doing sexually. If they are good lovers, they don't need to ask their partner for feedback.

Lindsey Says

Outcome: *In working with a group of highly sexually active young men, a common theme was that the guys were not sexually satisfying their partners. The type of sex they were pursuing was of the no-names-exchanged variety. One might assume that the young men were uncaring, selfishly out to get off and go home. Further discussion revealed a much different truth: They didn't know the first thing about how to please a partner. Rather than try, fail, and look foolish, damaging their reputation of sexual prowess, they opted to act like they didn't care, often treating partners callously. These young men were missing out on the opportunity to form loving bonds, which they did indeed desire, because they didn't know what to do sexually and were afraid to admit it. We can imagine that this was, at least sometimes, confusing and problematic to their sex partners as well.*

Gender Stereotype: Cisgender men want sex all the time and can enjoy any sex that comes their way. Men easily become sexual predators and are never sexual victims/survivors.

Outcome: Most of the men I have worked with do not talk openly about their own experiences of sexual abuse or assault. Many have experiences they do not characterize as assault or abuse, even when they would meet the technical definition. However, if you ask them whether they have had experiences where they felt unsettled, uneasy, or unhappy during or after a sexual experience they often share stories of being touched by a babysitter, pursued by an older person, having a partner pressure for sex when they had already said no, or being told by partners, "If you don't want to do this, why do you have an erection?" Many times they tell me about feeling confused that they didn't enjoy the experience, saying, "I know any of my guy friends would have loved to have that happen to them." They don't give themselves permission to view these experiences of unwanted contact as assault.

Lindsey Says

I hear these stories nonstop when talking with boys about sexual violence.

When men do acknowledge an experience of sexual abuse, they often expect that it won't have any affect on their lives and are confused when it does. I regularly hear statements to the effect of: "I don't know why I can't just shake this off. It happened, so what. I should just get over it." Sometimes with men who have children, I say, "If this experience happened to your son, how would you feel? Would you think it was fun and OK? Would you want your son to be able to talk to someone about it? To take time to process it so they can feel better?" Often this lets them think about their experience with new perspective and give themselves permission to heal in whatever way feels right to them.

Gender Stereotype: Cisgender women don't want sex, but they do want relationships. Having sex is a requirement of long-term relationships, so they put up with it.

Outcome: "It's actually hurt for a long time. A few years now. But I didn't say anything because I'm embarrassed that I can't get turned on and I don't want him to feel bad." "He thinks I'm orgasming but I'm not. I have been faking so long I don't feel like I could tell him the truth. He would be so hurt." I have heard these kinds of statements many times. So many women assume that their pleasure is not important, that they can't expect sexual pleasure, or that something is wrong with them because they are not experiencing it. In addition, some male partners assume that women don't get much pleasure from sex and don't register their partner's disinterest or discomfort in the way we would want them to (for example, stopping sexual activity to check in and talk to their partner). On the flip side, women who do want and enjoy being sexual sometimes express feeling bad about their capacity to feel pleasure and desire.

Gender Stereotype: Cisgender women aren't supposed to want sex, so sometimes they say or indicate "no" when they really mean "yes."

Outcome: This myth is incredibly harmful. It puts women in a double bind where they are allowed no agency. If women say "yes" and mean it, they are acting inappropriately. If they say "no" and mean it, their "no" may be questioned or disregarded. Saying "no" when they mean "yes" sets up a disturbing power dynamic with their partner(s). It reinforces the idea that their choices should be about social acceptability rather than what they actually want and denies their partner(s) genuine feedback or consent.

Research indicates that women and men assess and express consent in different ways, and these differences seem to relate directly to gender stereotypes frequently found in sex education. For example, women were more likely than men to indicate consent through "Passive Behaviors" and "No Response Signals" (Jozkowski, Sanders, Peterson, Dennis, & Reece, 2014), complying with the stereotype that women yield to sex for the sake of their male partners. Men are more likely to look for nonverbal signals to indicate consent than women, possibly leading to easier confusion about whether consent has been given (Jozkowski, Peterson, Sanders, Dennis, & Reece, 2014).

This stereotype has horrible effects on men as well, implying they cannot take their female partners at their word and that "some resistance" is a normal expectation in sexual experiences. This can easily convince men that pushing past their partner's "no" is an expected sexual behavior. In fact, Jozkowski, Sanders, et al. (2014), found that men who endorsed this type of gender stereotype (defined as "token resistance and rape myth acceptance") were more likely to report engaging in behaviors that are on the verge of pressure to consent to sex (taking a partner somewhere private, shutting a door, or continuing to move forward with sexual behaviors or actions unless a partner stopped them).

Gender Stereotype: We know what men and women are like and how they have sex with each other. If you fall outside of the gender binary or are not straight, who knows what you do?!

Outcome: The lack of positive LGBTQ and nonbinary identities and experiences presented in sex education has serious negative effects. When I worked in outpatient chemical dependency treatment for LGBTQ-identified people, I frequently heard statements like, "I didn't know how to be a gay man/lesbian/queer person. After a few drinks at the bar it all seemed easier to manage"; "I wanted to be sexual but I didn't know how. When that [very much] older person hit on me, I figured they would be able to show me. I wasn't attracted to them and didn't really like them, but I didn't know if I would get another chance." This is certainly not to imply that all LGBTQ people turn to substances to navigate sex and identity issues. However, when education does not offer information about the kinds of sex that people are interested in and provides no positive examples of relationships, we put LGBTQ people at risk of taking what they can get, rather than looking for what they want and believing they deserve it. As covered in Chapter 3, LGBTQ-identified people are disproportionately disadvantaged by lack of pleasure education.

Pleasure Education Increases Empowered Communication

When gender stereotypes are taught in the United States, they are based on the premise that we can make generalizations about all men's and all women's sexuality. However, hearing about how sexuality is taught in other countries reveals that our assumptions about gender are not shared with the rest of the world. In addition to keeping us stuck in a binary gender system that leaves many people out, American stereotypical assumptions about gender are not keeping us safer, healthier, or happier.

Dutch researchers found more similarities than differences between boys' and girls' experiences of sexuality (Schalet, 2011). However, these researchers also noticed sex stereotyping that assumed boys were supposed to be more active and girls more passive in sexual interactions. So educators in the Netherlands began teaching negotiation and interaction skills to all young people, including the expression of sexual wishes and boundaries. How did this turn out for the Dutch adolescents? A 2005 national survey found high levels of these skills in young people of all genders, including "letting the other person know exactly what feels good" and not doing things one does not want (Schalet, 2011). What a great example of how pleasure education is vital to teaching consent; pleasure education teaches how to tell your partner what feels good to you and how to say "no thanks" to the experiences you don't want.

While the United States continues to consider the subject of pleasure too lascivious, frivolous, or dangerous, the Netherlands teaches pleasure in a way that helps young people feel more in control of their choices. Did teaching pleasure send the Dutch population into a frenzy of sexual violations? In fact, it may have done the exact opposite. The rate of reported rapes in the United States is three times higher than that in the Netherlands (NationMaster, 2016a).

Perceptions of first sexual experiences are also very different for young people in these two countries. Dutch youth described their first sexual experiences (broadly defined to include many different activities rather than focusing on intercourse) as well timed and fun. They also felt more in control of their first sexual experiences than their US peers (Schalet, 2011). While some people may feel uncomfortable with the idea of young people beginning sexual relationships, Dutch education is succeeding in teaching young people that they are in control of their sexual choices rather than leading them to believe that pleasure "takes over" to the point where you cannot be held accountable for your decisions. Dutch teens' experiences of well-timed and fun first sexual experiences set them up to expect the same from sexual experiences later in life. Youth feeling empowered to let partners know what feels good and what they do not want helps keep them safer from abuse and sets the norm that sexual relationships will progress according to people's mutual enjoyment and preferences, rather than by a set sexual script.

Pleasure and Sexual Assault Prevention

One of the reasons pleasure has been cast as dangerous is because of the frightening realities of sexual assault and abuse. These horrible actions are often cast as the result of people who are so overtaken by their own desire for pleasure that they violate others to get it. This narrative encourages us to think about pleasure as dangerous and corrupting.

Getting accurate numbers about rates of sexual abuse and assault is difficult for many reasons: Sexual violence is underreported, respondents' perceptions of whether an unwanted sexual experience qualifies as "abuse/assault" differ, and wording questions to obtain the most accurate data is a complex and contested process. However, it is true that the United States has a problem with sexual violence. Out of 57 countries where data on rate of reported rapes was available, the United

States ranks ninth (NationMaster, 2016b). In a nationally representative survey of adults, about one in five women reported being raped at some time in their lives (Breiding, 2014; Centers for Disease Control, 2012). More than 43% of women and 23% of men experienced other forms of sexual violence during their life-times (Breiding, 2014). Evidence suggests that rates of men who have experienced nonconsensual sexual contact are likely much higher than society tends to assume (Stemple & Meyer, 2014) estimating that one in six or one in seven men experi-ence an abusive sexual encounter before age 18 (Briere & Elliott, 2003; Dube et al., 2005). Rates of sexual assault are higher for LGBTQ-identified people than for people who identify as heterosexual (Centers for Disease Control, 2010). Horrify-ingly, 64% of transgender people report experiencing sexual assault (Grant, Mottet, Tanis, Harrison, Herman, & Keisling, 2011).

Of course, there will always be predators in the world, and it is important to acknowledge the role that power plays in sexual violence. However, the messages common in the ways sex is currently talked and taught about support the idea that sexual assault behaviors are normal. As sexual health professionals, we are in a criti-cal position to either dismantle rape culture or perpetuate it by the way we address these messages.

Why am I so confident that changing sex education can help fight sexual vio-lence? Because teaching about pleasure is teaching about consent. Given that the majority of sexual assault survivors know their perpetrator (Breiding, 2014), the task becomes less about protection from masked strangers hiding in the bushes, and more about addressing the cultural issues at play that perpetuate rape and inadver-tently condone assault behavior.

Connections Between Pleasure and Danger

Looking at the disheartening statistics about sexual violence in the United States, it could be easy to be scared into excluding pleasure and focusing on danger. However, when danger is covered and pleasure is left out, we are missing the chance to deepen the discussion and include real-world scenarios that people are likely to encounter in life. In fact, a study that assembled a focus group of sexual exploitation victim/survi-vors found that universally, respondents felt that sex education (with an emphasis on relationships) is one of the best ways to prevent exploitation and abuse (Hennepin County No Wrong Door Initiative, 2015). The most comprehensive and honest way to teach about sexuality likely means acknowledging that pleasure and danger exist together and influence each other. As Cameron-Lewis and Allen point out,

> It is impossible to separate out all sexual experiences as either positive or nega-tive. Sexual intimacy is not experienced in such simplistic dualistic terms. Even when sexual experiences are seen as existing along a continuum, with positive at one end and negative at the other, this does not take account of the way in which in reality positive and negative experiences may occur simultaneously.
>
> (2013, p. 126)

Pleasure and danger go together in the lives of many of our clients and students. One of my clients, a woman in her 70s struggling with desire issues, told me the following story when I asked her whether she had positive memories of pleasure in her body: "Well, there was one time when I was young. My sister and I went down to the river and, rather impulsively, we decided to take all of our clothes off and swim naked. I remember really enjoying that day. The cool water felt so good on my body. Then my mother came down to look for us and when she saw that we were naked, she beat us. That's the last time I tried anything like that." Pleasure has been dangerous in many clients' and students' lives. Ignoring this connection means ignoring their reality.

Pleasure and Danger for Youth

This is not just an issue for past generations: Pleasure can be dangerous for young people as well. Deborah L. Tolman, who interviewed many female high school students for her book *Dilemmas of Desire*, noticed her subjects perceived danger in describing their experiences of desire and pleasure: "Several girls mentioned in interviews that they would not want their teachers knowing what they were telling me about themselves because they feared they might be thought less of by these adult women in their lives" (2002, p. 31). Tolman also noted the girls she interviewed were often reticent to talk about desire in front of other girls, concerned that their statements about their sexual experiences would be used against them (2002). It is vital that sexual health professionals pay attention to these dynamics. If clients and students fear judgment from us or from others, they are less likely to talk honestly or ask the questions they need to ask.

Pleasure and Danger for Cisgender Men

We tend to think of pleasure being dangerous for women, but the truth is that people of any gender can experience dangerous sexual situations. I noticed while working with cisgender men using hook-up apps to meet other guys that they would arrange dates at someone's apartment whom they had never met before. When I asked if they took precautions to make these situations safer, it seemed that no one had ever talked to them about dating safety. It was assumed that as cis-men they would not be in danger or should be able to take care of themselves. I conveyed a lot of safety techniques I had been taught at a young age, because as a cisgender woman it was assumed I would likely need them (carry your keys between your fingers if you need protection, tell a friend where you are going and if you don't call by the end of the date they should call the police). Being raised as men, they were not taught these (to me) basic safety skills.

However, there was another assumption that many of these men brought up to me: Because they were into casual sex, they were less deserving of safety. This is one of the ways that vilifying pleasure contributes to rape culture—assuming that if you seek out pleasure, you deserve what you get if something goes wrong. It would have been easy for me to encourage these clients to stop hooking up because it was "too dangerous," but I would have devalued their preferences and pleasure goals in the process. Instead, we had in-depth conversations about hooking up: What was enjoyable about it, what was not so fun, how important was it to them, how concerned were they about safety issues, how to make hook-ups safer, what kind of balance did they want between possibility of pleasure and risk of danger, and how to get through feelings of shame or unworthiness to realize they absolutely deserved both safety and pleasure.

Pleasure and Danger for Nonbinary People

People who are gender variant, trans, nonbinary, gender fluid, intersex, or otherwise differ from societal assumptions of binary gender are often at higher risk when it comes to seeking pleasure. The possibility of violence from partners when they disclose information about their gender or body is unfortunately a very real concern. I have worked with many people who fear that if they are true to who they are, they will never find a partner who finds them desirable and enjoys all the parts of them. Sometimes their body has physical reactions during arousal that they don't enjoy or that don't fit with their gender, making the experience of pleasure a contradictory and sometimes unpleasant experience. It is difficult not to internalize negativity and discrimination when it is reflected all around you in society. Many trans and gender-creative clients I have worked with have said something like, "I probably don't deserve pleasure and if something bad happens to me while I'm trying to find pleasure it is probably my fault."

It is important for sexual health professionals to understand that gender-variant people often find themselves navigating danger daily. Professionals must be able to hold both realities— pleasure and danger—and hear their clients' and students' perceptions of how both are present in their lives. Pleasure is an incredibly important topic to bring up with gender-variant students and clients, to reaffirm that they do deserve pleasure, solo and in relationships.

Pleasure and Danger for People of Color

Racism can make pleasure dangerous. Springer writes:

> The culture that's embedded in these subtle and not-so-subtle passing judgments tries to take away my right to say yes to sex by making me feel like if I do, I'm giving in to centuries of stereotypes of the sexually lascivious black woman.
> (2008, p. 77)

Springer also points out: "Puritanical views on sexuality are not confined by race. In the case of the black community, however, our silence is further enforced by traumatic intersections of race, sexuality, and often violence" (2008, p. 83). Sexual health professionals cannot afford to be unaware of the ways that intersections of race and/or culture affect client and student perceptions of pleasure. In addition, the race/culture of students and clients will interact with the race/culture of the professional who is working with them. It is the professional's job to be aware of how these elements may impact their students' or clients' sense of safety or danger in engaging with sexual health professionals about pleasure issues.

Seeking to Understand Pleasure and Danger Within Our Intersectional Identities

The relationship between pleasure and danger will be different for each student and client, and so professionals need to purposefully seek to acknowledge each person's experiences of pleasure and danger. This includes exploring the influences their gender, orientation, race, culture, ability, religion, peer group, relationship status, family of origin or of choice, and countless other factors have had on their ideas about pleasure. Our multiple identities never exist in isolation from each other. The intersectionality of identities we each experience means that we are affected in a myriad of ways unique to each of us, and that these are evolving throughout life. Pleasure has been and continues to be dangerous for many people, but it can also be a path to healing. However, when sexual health professionals blithely proclaim pleasure as perpetually wonderful, without nuance and without inquiring about or acknowledging the negative experiences of their clients and students, this valuable information can come off as insensitive and inapplicable to their lives.

Teaching Pleasure and Danger Together to Increase Efficacy

> For college students, both women and men, specific factors related to comfort/safety and agreement/wantedness were the most important predictors of quality of sexual intercourse. Consent is often thought about as a necessity to prevent sexual assault; however, these findings suggest that aspects of internal consent may also be important in regard to improving the quality of an individual's sexual activity. These findings bridge the fields of sexual assault prevention and sexual enhancement with consent as a link.
>
> (Jozkowski, 2013, p. 270)

What might teaching pleasure and danger together look like? The Sexual Assault Resistance Education (SARE) program is one example. At three Canadian universities, SARE offered first-year female students a four-phase sexual assault prevention class that included risk assessment and self-defense, as well as sexuality and relationship education. This education included "a wide range of possible sexual activities beyond intercourse and health and safer-sex practices, and a context to explore their sexual attitudes, values, and desires and to develop strategies for sexual communication" (Senn et al., 2015). Educating beyond intercourse (shifting the focus from reproduction to sexual pleasure) as well as exploring sexual desires and communication strategies are forms of pleasure education. This was in contrast to the control group, who were only given brochures on sexual assault (teaching about danger but not pleasure). This program demonstrated significant positive results. Women who participated in SARE were at significantly lower risk of completed rape, attempted rape, attempted coercion, and nonconsensual sexual contact than those in the control group. In contrast to previous health initiatives, the efficacy of the program was sustained throughout the one-year follow-up period. (Senn et al., 2015).

The SARE program is an excellent example of how to incorporate pleasure education into sexual assault prevention programs, and the results are very encouraging. One critique of this program might be that it focuses on potential victims rather than on possible perpetrators, which could be seen as putting responsibility on victims rather than changing perpetrator behavior. To address this issue and provide better education for all, it would be great to see this kind of program available to not just first-year female students, but all students.

Lindsey Says

When talking with young people about consent, one fun activity is to brainstorm a long list of all the ways people can check in with their partner during sexual encounters, both leading up to and throughout the whole experience. Someone will often bring up the idea of signing a contract or taking a video beforehand to document that consent was given, which provides a great opportunity to point out that this isn't going to cut it, because consent can be withdrawn at any time and for any reason. Instead, we need both subtle and explicit ways to understand how it is going for everyone involved as we go along. Inviting students to find their own words they could say that won't interrupt the moment or make them look anything less than suave is super helpful, because hearing these phrases and seeing them written on the board helps people to be able to recall them later when they need to put them into action. Young people are notoriously bad at reading body language and vocal tone (thanks to the not-quite-done-developing prefrontal cortex) so being very clear is important. Also, emphasize that it is always good to check in multiple times, in a variety of ways, to make sure you've got it right. A short sampling of possible answers:

Nonverbal feedback:

Making "yum" noises
Nodding your head "yes"
Raising your eyebrows and pausing, while holding your hand on the button of your pants, waiting for a response to a silent question

Verbal feedback:

Using your sexy voice to whisper:
Can I unbutton your shirt?
Do you like this?
Is this good?
You ready for me?
I want you to tell me what you want.
Like that?
Do you want more?
How about this?
Are you sure? I don't want to rush you. Let's take our time, baby.
Harder or softer?
You could also discuss signs that the person is possibly not that into it and it might be time to stop and check in.

Nonverbal feedback:

They push your hand away.
They aren't touching you back.
They are looking away from you.
They are not making any noises at all.
They seem distant.

Verbal feedback:

Um, I guess so.
Maybe.
I don't know.
Well . . .
Hold on . . .
If they suggest something else to do

Another part of getting consent is understanding the difference between an unsure, hesitant, "Um, well, I guess so . . . " and a resounding, excited "HELL YEAH!" I have found that the idea of "yes means yes" is really useful to articulate with young people. Not only does the person need to communicate "yes" in some fashion, but they need to actually mean it for consent to be real. This means that you didn't have to talk them into it, convince them, or use any sort of trickery or coercion to get "yes" out of them. When people practice clear consent, they can trust that they won't be under pressure to do anything they aren't comfortable with. This is a key for great sex, as everyone can relax and feel confident that they are each enjoying what is going on.

Pleasure-Positive Culture Supports Active Consent

> If a young woman is unable to view herself as a legitimate sexual subject, how is she able to articulate her consent or lack of consent in a sexually intimate situation? How is she able to articulate her boundaries and her desires if she is not permitted to think about them? How can schools expect young people to know their sexual selves and assert their needs if their sexual agency is denied by sexuality education? Furthermore, why would a young person be able to consider the needs and desires of a sexual partner if they are not able to consider their own?
>
> (Cameron-Lewis & Allen, 2013, p. 124)

This statement is not just true of young people or women/girls. I have worked with countless adults, elders, and people of all genders who struggle to make sexual choices, express desires or dislikes, and have mutually fulfilling sexual relationships with loved partners because they lack sexual agency. We as a society fear to teach these skills to young people because we think they are too young, and we also provide almost no sex education for adults. The assumption is that adults will "pick it up along the way" or that skills will be gathered through trial and error in relationships. Sometimes that happens and many times it does not. Frequently people endure traumatic experiences as they try to piece it all together with little to no guidance. Pleasure skills are a vital component of forming a sense of sexual autonomy and sexual personhood that fights rape culture. Pleasure education teaches sexual autonomy and personhood by saying: "What gives *you* pleasure? How can you communicate that to partners? Then your next responsibility is to find out what gives your partner(s) pleasure."

Four Guidelines of Pleasure and Consent: Aware, Actively Participating, Collaborative Decisions, and Feedback

"Previous research suggests that when consent is expressed in more explicit terms (i.e., verbal cues), individuals are more likely to experience a higher quality sexual encounter" (Jozkowski, 2013). This quote illustrates the connection between consent education and pleasure education. Sexual health professionals teaching pleasure will also be teaching important elements of consent: being aware, actively participating, making collaborative decisions in their sexual choices, and giving/seeking constant feedback. Following are some of the ways that these four guidelines unify the topics of pleasure and consent. I hope these examples clarify how teaching these two concepts together can strengthen our students' and clients' understanding of both.

All Sexual Partners Will Be Aware

- *All sexual partners will have enough awareness of their situation to be able to consent.*
- *All sexual partners will be aware of accurate health information that could inform the sexual choices they make.* This means that as sexual health professionals we are providing education that is medically accurate, comprehensive, and applicable to the kinds of sex the learner might want to have (penis-in-vagina information isn't going to cover everybody). Students and clients will be taught what body responses might be expected and which may indicate that something is not going well. They will also be aware that body responses alone cannot fully indicate consent.
- *All sexual partners will be aware that pleasure is an expected outcome for all sexual participants.* They will be aware that partners frequently make decisions to start, stop, pause, or adjust during sexual experiences in order to increase pleasure or respond to discomfort. They will know while pleasure may not happen in every situation, pain or dislike is an alternative that no one needs to accept.

All Sexual Partners Will Be Actively Participating

- *All sexual partners will be actively participating during all of the sexual experience.* This is likely to include positive noises, changes in breathing, body movements, and physical evidence of pleasure accompanied and verified by verbal evidence of pleasure and consent. Participants will understand that any one of these actions alone can be misunderstood and so will seek multiple expressions of pleasure and consent throughout the experience.
- *All sexual partners will actively participate in safer sex and contraceptive decisions.* One partner should not be able to override choices about another partner's body. All partners will consider it part of their responsibility to contribute to discussion of these important issues, and to share financial burden when appropriate.

All Sexual Partners Will Make Collaborative Decisions

- *All sexual partners will make collaborative decisions regarding what experiences they want to have together.* Since there are many ways to be sexual and all people have different preferences, partners cannot assume what sexual activities might take place. Established sexual partners are unlikely to want to have sex the exact same way every time, so collaborative decision making is not only necessary for each sexual experience, but it can also add to excitement.

• Partners need to talk about what they want before, during, and after any sexual experience. In order to have pleasure, communication is vital, adjustments are to be expected, and checking-in is needed.

All Sexual Partners Will Be Giving and Seeking Constant Feedback

• *All sexual partners will be giving and seeking constant feedback in a variety of ways.* These may include asking questions, listening for positive noises, or observing body responses. However, the best way to increase pleasure and create/maintain a connection with a partner is to check in with them in a combination of all of these ways.

• If a partner freezes up, stops answering, or sounds unsure in their answers, it is important to stop and check in more thoroughly with them to understand what is happening.

Pleasure Before, During, and After

All sexual partners should have pleasure before being sexual with a partner (enjoying sexual discussion and negotiation), during (checking in, making adjustments), and after (asking how the experience was for your partner, sharing a satisfying ending whether that means cuddling or high fiving).

Shifting to a Pleasure-Positive Culture

> The onus for improving women's sexual health outcomes should not solely be the responsibility of individual women. The need for culture-level intervention is especially salient given the sexual double standards apparent in Western culture.
>
> (Satinsky & Jozkowski, 2015, p. 422)

While each student or client can increase pleasure in their own lives, significant change won't occur without a culture-wide shift in the way we view sexual pleasure. Yes, I'm suggesting sexual health professionals can start a revolution. Pleasure education needs to be designed for people of all genders and orientations, and must actively seek to dismantle gender stereotypes. Pleasure education helps people feel happier, more confident, and more empowered. In addition to these being wonderful things to feel, it is much more difficult to victimize happy, confident, empowered people.

References

Breiding, M. J. (2014). Prevalence and characteristics of sexual violence, stalking, and intimate partner violence victimization—National Intimate Partner and Sexual Violence Survey, United States, 2011. *Morbidity and Mortality Weekly Report. Surveillance Summaries (Washington, DC: 2002), 63*(8), 1.

Briere, J., & Elliott, D. M. (2003). Prevalence and psychological sequelae of self-reported childhood physical and sexual abuse in a general population sample of men and women. *Child Abuse & Neglect, 27*(10), 1205–1222.

Buchwald, E., Fletcher, P. R., & Roth, M. (Eds.). (2005). *Transforming a rape culture*. Minneapolis, MN: Milkweed Editions.

Cameron-Lewis, V., & Allen, L. (2013). Teaching pleasure and danger in sexuality education. *Sex Education, 13*(2), 121–132.

Centers for Disease Control, Division of Violence Prevention. (2010). *NISVS: An overview of 2010 findings of victimization by sexual orientation*. Retrieved February 20, 2016, from http://www.cdc.gov/violenceprevention/pdf/cdc_nisvs_victimization_final-a.pdf

Centers for Disease Control, Division of Violence Prevention. (2012). Sexual violence: Facts at a glance. Retrieved February 20, 2016, from http://www.cdc.gov/ViolencePrevention/pdf/SV-DataSheet-a.pdf

Dube, S. R., Anda, R. F., Whitfield, C. L., Brown, D. W., Felitti, V. J., Dong, M., & Giles, W. H. (2005). Long-term consequences of childhood sexual abuse by gender of victim. *American Journal of Preventive Medicine, 28*(5), 430–438.

Grant, J. M., Mottet, L., Tanis, J. E., Harrison, J., Herman, J., & Keisling, M. (2011). *Injustice at every turn: A report of the national transgender discrimination survey*. Washington, DC: National Center for Transgender Equality.

Hennepin County No Wrong Door Initiative. (2015). *Voices of safe harbor: Survivor & youth input for Minnesota's model protocol on sexual exploitation and sex trafficking of youth*. Retrieved February 26, 2016, from http://www.hennepin.us/~/media/hennepinus/your-government/projects-initiatives/documents/no-wrong%20-door-voices.pdf?la=en

Jozkowski, K. N. (2013). The influence of consent on college students' perceptions of the quality of sexual intercourse at last event. *International Journal of Sexual Health, 25*(4), 260–272.

Jozkowski, K. N., & Peterson, Z. D. (2013). College students and sexual consent: Unique insights. *Journal of Sex Research, 50*(6), 517–523.

Jozkowski, K. N., Peterson, Z. D., Sanders, S. A., Dennis, B., & Reece, M. (2014). Gender differences in heterosexual college students' conceptualizations and indicators of sexual consent: Implications for contemporary sexual assault prevention education. *The Journal of Sex Research, 51*(8), 904–916.

Jozkowski, K. N., Sanders, S., Peterson, Z. D., Dennis, B., & Reece, M. (2014). Consenting to sexual activity: The development and psychometric assessment of dual measures of consent. *Archives of Sexual Behavior, 43*(3), 437–450.

NationMaster. (2016a). *Crime: Netherlands and United States compared*. Retrieved February 25, 2016, from http://www.nationmaster.com/country-info/compare/Netherlands/United-States/Crime

NationMaster. (2016b). *United States crime stats*. Retrieved February 25, 2016, from http://www.nationmaster.com/country-info/profiles/United-States/Crime

Satinsky, S., & Jozkowski, K. N. (2015). Female sexual subjectivity and verbal consent to receiving oral sex. *Journal of Sex & Marital Therapy, 41*(4), 413–426.

Schalet, A. T. (2011). *Not under my roof: Parents, teens, and the culture of sex*. Chicago: University of Chicago Press.

Senn, C. Y., Eliasziw, M., Barata, P. C., Thurston, W. E., Newby-Clark, I. R., Radtke, H. L., & Hobden, K. L. (2015). Efficacy of a sexual assault resistance program for university women. *New England Journal of Medicine, 372*(24), 2326–2335.

Springer, K. (2008). Queering Black female heterosexuality. In J. Friedman & J. Valenti (Eds.), *Yes means yes!: Visions of female sexual power and a world without rape* (pp. 77–88). Berkeley, CA: Seal Press.

Stemple, L., & Meyer, I. H. (2014). The sexual victimization of men in America: New data challenge old assumptions. *American Journal of Public Health, 104*(6), e19–e26.

Tolman, D. (2002). *Dilemmas of desire: Teenage girls talk about sexuality*. Cambridge, MA: Harvard University Press.

Part 2

Skills for Professional Practice

Chapter 5

Talking Professionally About Pleasure

Sexual health professionals sometimes hold themselves back from addressing pleasure issues because they fear being perceived as inappropriate. The skills presented in this chapter will help bridge the gap between knowing that pleasure is an important topic and feeling confident working with this valuable subject. With some forethought and practice, talking about pleasure can become second nature. Instead of being worried about being perceived as unprofessional, you will be putting your clients and students at ease with your knowledge and comfort in addressing pleasure issues.

Appropriate and Factual

When addressing pleasure issues, it can be helpful to consider two questions: "What is factual information about this topic?" and "What is appropriate based on the setting and my role in this situation?" Sometimes I imagine these two questions standing before me like the goalposts on a football field. I imagine "appropriate" written down the left post and "factual" written down the right. Whatever I say has to sail right down the middle, between them both. This is probably the only football fantasy I have ever had in my life. In fact, I had to look up the term "goalposts" as I wrote this to make sure I was using the right term. When in doubt, or in a situation that is making you sweat as you try to find words, just remember the "factual and appropriate" goalposts.

Standards for what is appropriate vary according to the situation. Therapists talking with long-term clients may be more frank or familiar than educators talking to a group of students they have never spoken to before. Medical language may be appropriate in some settings and may alienate clients or students in others. Your professional role in each situation will also guide how you respond. I may feel comfortable offering basic sex education in a therapeutic context but I would not ask someone about their personal trauma history in the context of a public class. As a professional, you must learn to read the people in the room and pick up on subtle feedback cues that communicate how your students and clients are receiving the information. It is always a good idea to check in with them directly if you are not sure.

Some situations may pose more professional difficulty than others. Therapists may be working with young adults who have important pleasure questions but whose parents are concerned about what is being said in therapy. School administrators may have an agenda for sex education that may not be in line with what sex educators know brings the best health outcomes. Answering a question using factual information can offer evidence-based knowledge to the listener and a rationale for the professional should they be asked to justify their statement. Much information about pleasure is based on anatomical and physiological facts, and pleasure info can almost always be related back to teaching about healthy relationships and boundary-setting skills. Backing up your work with research findings is one way to ensure you can justify your message should anyone ask. Furthermore, double-checking your statements through citing research, anatomy, or function is a great practice as it can help educators and therapists identify and address their own biases.

One of the ways I use this in my practice is to cite the statistic that 70% of women need clitoral stimulation to have an orgasm (Hite, 1976). Many of my clients come to therapy believing that penetration should be enough stimulation to lead to orgasm and feeling disappointed that this has not happened for them. Providing this factual information about pleasure functioning helps them realign their expectations of bodies and allows them to let go of any judgments they had been putting on their sexual response or their connection as a couple. This statistic also helps me check my own bias toward clitoral stimulation. If 30% of women report they do not need clitoral stimulation to have an orgasm, it is an important for me to remember not to assume all my clients will need, want, or enjoy clitoral stimulation even if I think it would be a great idea for them to try it.

Lindsey Says

When teaching in a more permissive school I may be able to plainly say, "The clitoris is incredibly sensitive and it really exists just to provide pleasure. Some people think it feels really good to touch it directly, while others prefer touching more towards one side, and some don't like it to be touched at all. More people experience orgasm through touching the clitoris than penetration alone. Lubrication is really important here, as dry rubbing will be irritating to some." Let me tell you that speaking plainly about the clitoris has the entire group hanging on my every word. Of course, I must change my tune a bit in more conservative sex ed programs, but even in restrictive settings, it is possible to include small bits of information about pleasure. It may look more like this: "The clitoris has more densely packed nerve endings than the end of the penis, so it is extremely sensitive!" I might need to stop there, or I may add, "Every person's body parts are going to respond differently, but typically the clitoris is sensitive in a good way." Some of it is left a bit vague, hoping that the students will put two and two together, but I feel like it is my duty to at least point them in the right direction. Saying that the clitoris is typically more sensitive than the penis is really just an anatomy factoid. It is true, and it is not like I am directly telling them to go home and try it out (though I hope they do).

Whenever I feel uncertain about the boundaries in the setting I am in, I check to make sure that what I am saying is factually accurate and is rooted in creating respect for one's self and one's partner, or reinforces skills for healthy relationships (i.e. communication, consent, safety). Nearly always, I feel there is a strong connection to at least one (if not all three) of these criteria, and then I feel confident that I will be able to justify my choice of words if I am called to.

Choosing Language and Phrasing

It is vital that sexual health professionals give thought to how they choose their language and then practice these skills before getting in front of clients or students. When professionals struggle to establish language around pleasure issues, it is more likely that students and clients will be confused or embarrassed. It may seem gentler to have vague conversations about "intimacy." However, one party might be talking about physical sexual contact while the other is referring to emotional connection. Professionals sometimes think euphemistic language gives the client comfort and privacy. However, using clear language and asking questions when conversation becomes unclear establishes your space as a safe place to talk about their sexual concerns. This can be a freeing experience for clients or students who may have never had a place where it was appropriate to talk openly about sex and pleasure.

I've talked with some professionals who are concerned that if they introduce the topic of pleasure, their students or clients will say something inappropriate. The truth is, they might. However, in the vast majority of cases, they won't do so on purpose or maliciously. Unless you are working with a population that has a history of boundary-breaking behavior, the vast majority of people want to act appropriately. But asking a therapist, teacher, or medical professional about sex is a situation Ms. Manners probably didn't cover, and people often struggle to figure out what they "should" or "shouldn't" say in these situations. You as the professional set the tone for these interactions by the way you carry yourself and the comfort you display with your role. Language can be a large indicator of your comfort levels. My own experience has been that the people I work with follow my lead and rarely try to be inappropriate. This also means if I don't lead the conversation to pleasure issues, they often stay silent about this important information.

The Internal "Ick" Factor

Let's be real for a second. As much as sexual health professionals often consider it our job to be unbiased and unflappable, we all have our own internal reactions to words, concepts, and ideas. Pleasure words can bring up strong reactions both for us and the people we work with. Even when we are not judging anything as "wrong," we likely all have words we prefer and some that set off our "ick" factor. This means we have to practice dealing with that internal response so it doesn't come out in a shaming way with clients and students.

Let's take a look at some words that might be used in a conversation about pleasure:

Erotic
Horny
Arousal
Asshole
Cock
Orgasm
Sexy
Succulent
Sweet

Lubricate
Hard
Busted
Pussy
Cream
Ejaculate
Penis
Fuck
Loose
Sensual
Thick
Tits
Anus
Peehole
Ripe
Flaccid
Wet

You probably like some of those words more than others. There are a few on that list that made me wonder, "Do I really need to include *that one*?" But I typed them anyway, knowing that the words I don't like might be some of your favorites. The words we choose reflect our cultural background, personal experiences, personal eroticism, and what we have been taught (or not taught) about sexual language. This is not about some words being "right" and some being "wrong" but rather building an awareness of why you may choose or avoid certain language.

On first thought it may seem most appropriate to always use medical or clinical language when talking about pleasure in a professional context. However, medical language is alienating to many people and not applicable to some. Clinical language can be confusing. How many sex therapists use the word "engorgement" in session without thinking twice? I know I have. But this term could easily be confusing for clients who may be embarrassed to speak up or stop a session to clarify language.

Another option is using whatever language the client uses. Mirroring client language is a way of being approachable, respecting the client's language choices, and demonstrating active listening. There are many advantages to mirroring client's language and this can be a valuable approach. However, it becomes more complex when a client chooses words that are uncomfortable for you, reflect a culture that is not your own, are unclear terms, or go against your values. If you feel awkward saying a word you probably sound awkward saying that word. If you are finding yourself uncomfortable mirroring a client's language, ask yourself why. If you personally dislike the word "horny" but your client uses it all the time, can you push yourself to become more comfortable with it?

Listening for the Meaning Underneath

Clients and students often enter professional spaces unsure of what is OK to say to a professional. They may ask questions clumsily or phrase their concerns awkwardly due to a lack of experience talking about pleasure. Sometimes they may use language that could be considered offensive, perhaps because that is the only language they have or maybe that is the language they feel most comfortable with. Actively listening to their language gives you information about their experience of pleasure. "Cumming" implies a different kind of experience than the more clinical "orgasm." When a student or client uses words some people might consider crude—like "cunt," or "fuckhole"—they may be offering a window into their eroticism or into the norms of a sexual community they identify with. Clients who use words like "down there," "my stuff," or "doing it," may be showing a lack of sex education or possibly nervousness or shame about sexual issues. It is important not to jump to conclusions about client's experiences or values based on their language choices alone. However, this can be a great starting place for conversations with students and clients about how they choose their language.

I was working with a cisgender female client, let's call her Marta, and I noticed she used the word "slutty" a lot. She would call certain clothing slutty, mention how "no one wants to be seen as slutty," and she would label other women's nonsexual behavior as slutty. I listened without comment about the word for the first few sessions. A few sessions later, after I felt Marta trusted me a bit more, she said something or someone was slutty and I said, "Tell me about that word. You use it a lot and I wonder how you feel about it." She said, "Do I? Huh." As she thought about it she realized her friend group frequently used the word. This led to a talk about sometimes feeling like her friends policed each other's sexual behavior. She brought this topic up again the next session and she later told me she continued to think about how she felt about it for a while after that. I was careful in all these conversations never to tell Marta that she shouldn't say "slutty." It wasn't my job to change her language, but it was important for me to better understand what was beneath it.

Just as listening to and reflecting client language is important, it can also be important for the professional to offer language that may be informational or helpful to their client. Medical language is a language of power. People will often get better medical or professional care if they can access this language, but not everyone receives sex education that includes this information. Deliberately linking casual language to medical language is a way to educate while respecting the chosen words of the person you are working with. Dropping simple connecting phrases into conversation such as "your perineum, or like you said, your taint," show the client or student you are listening to them while giving medical language to use if they so choose.

Openly acknowledging that differing situations may necessitate different language can start important conversations about the different worlds your clients may have to navigate. People who face discrimination due to sexual orientation, gender expression, sexual practices, nontraditional relationship structures, culture, or race probably already realize the ways in which language affects how they are treated and they will likely be happy to have a straightforward conversation about the issue. However, as a professional you need to be respectful of their experiences. There is a difference between providing information that can be helpful and "educating" a client to speak the way you would prefer.

Lindsey Says

When working with both youth and adults outside of school settings, there is typically some serious slang flying around. If I am not sure what a term means, I just ask. People are more than happy to explain, and appreciate that I am interested in them. I let them know that there are a lot of different words people like to use, and that is fine. I explain that I am going to mostly use the "medical terms" so that they can get more comfortable with them, in case they find themselves in a situation where they would like to speak like that, like if they are talking with their doctor. Of course, when someone is with their own friends, or they are getting sexy with someone, or if some other term just feels better for them, they should just use whatever words feel the most comfortable in the moment. This makes it seem comfortable for us to proceed with me, the professional, using "technical" terms and it not feeling too artificial or out of touch. It is nice to be able to role model using words like "vulva" and "anus" with ease. Typically, group participants will be saying those words more naturally by the end of class.

One activity I use with teens when talking about language is to have them brainstorm a big list of terms that we commonly use for sexual body parts or sexual acts, talk about where these words come from and how they make us feel, and then give the students markers and invite them to cross anything off the list that they dislike. We agree as a group to try our best to stick to the words that are left standing, so that everyone can feel comfortable and respected in the learning environment. It is a fun exercise in awareness of the origins and the effects of our language, and how our words may impact others.

The Importance of Inclusivity in Language

Due to the ever-changing landscape of identities colliding with societal discrimination and ignorance, certain populations are often left out of professional discussion. People who identify as lesbian, gay, bisexual, transgender, queer, pansexual, intersex, nonbinary, gender variant, gender creative, or genderqueer, as well as people who have a relationship style that differs from monogamy, rarely see their identities or relationships reflected in standard language. Sexual health professionals are in a unique position to create a more inclusive and welcoming environment for all people through language. Often this can mean the difference between our students and clients feeling heard and seen, or feeling ignored, or worse, discriminated against.

Some professionals receive training on inclusive language and others do not. Most of us don't just naturally have these skills. It takes time and practice to seamlessly choose inclusive language without tripping over your words. However, simple adjustments in the words you choose can help to make a wider variety of people feel comfortable and welcomed.

Inclusive Language in Presentation or Group Settings

Some phrases are more inclusive and welcoming than others. Saying "partner" includes more people than husband, wife, girlfriend, or boyfriend. "People with penises" or "people with vulvas" may feel more inclusive to gender-variant people and helps avoid falling into gender stereotypes like, "men experience such and such" or "women tend to prefer the other thing." But of course, this can be complex, too, as sometimes people don't want to be equated with their genitalia. I generally try to use "people with penises" or "people with vulvas" in group settings and for classes. When I am working one-on-one with people I make sure to have a conversation asking what pronouns and terms they would like me to use, and then I make sure to do so.

Using "they" instead of "he" or "she" is a wonderful way of welcoming people no matter what gender they identify with. I frequently use "they" in the singular, and for the most part people don't have any trouble understanding what I am saying. In fact, this usage has become so prevalent that the American Dialect Society voted the gender-neutral singular pronoun "they" as the Word of the Year for 2015 (American Dialect Society, 2016). Saying "person" instead of "man" or "woman" is often an easy adjustment that doesn't make assumptions. "Folks" can be useful and "ya'll" works well unless you sound as hopelessly Midwestern as I do.

When talking to a group, it can be helpful to use a variety of terms to talk about general or hypothetical situations. Saying "If you are going to try this with your (*alternately sub in some of the following: husband/wife/partner/boyfriend/girlfriend*)" throughout your conversation will hopefully include most people in the room at some point. Substituting the phrase "all genders" instead of "both genders" can avoid enforcing the gender binary and create space for people of many genders. Saying "partner or partners" can include people who are not in a monogamous relationship.

It is wise to avoid using words like "all" or "everyone," even for statements that seem universal because there is always an exception to the rule. The minute you say, "Everyone loves an orgasm," you will meet a person who feels unpleasantly out-of-control during orgasm and has felt like the odd one out all of their life because of it. I know because that's what happened when I said it. Saying, "Just about everyone loves an orgasm" would have let them feel included. Changing professional language to include fewer absolutes can help us remember to think about exceptions to the rule. This can be useful in broadening our own assumptions around sex and pleasure.

Phrases such as "all men" or "all women" encourage the listener to think in gender stereotypes. Even in moments where it seems appropriate, such as "all women have a clitoris" or "all men have a penis," we are leaving out people who identify with a gender that is different than the sex of their genitals, as well as people who have experienced clitoral circumcision, had surgery for penile cancer, or intersex people whose genitals did not conform to binary standards at birth. Statements such as "all men want sex" or "all women want relationships" reinforce harmful gender stereotypes, exclude people who likely already feel excluded, and can make people who don't identify with those statements feel like they have something wrong with them.

Starting therapy groups, classes, and workshops by sharing your gender pronoun (he/she/they/zie/hir/something else entirely) and encouraging participants to do the same can create an atmosphere that is welcoming. You may be surprised by how people's pronouns vary from what you may have assumed. Offering stickers or name tags for all group members to write their name and pronoun down can help everyone have respectful conversations with each other in situations where groups may be too big for individual introductions. Professionals might also choose include their own pronouns in their email signature or on their business card to let people know they are aware that pronouns are a way to show respect.

Why Is All This Important?

If you aren't already familiar with these ways of using language, the last few paragraphs probably sounded like a long list of rules. At this point you may be wondering, "This seems exhausting. Do I really need to think about all of this? How am I going to say 'people with penises' and not feel ridiculous? This won't work in the kinds of situations I work in." Here's the thing: There are a lot of people who constantly feel excluded because their identities and experiences are not acknowledged. Making sure all people have access to pleasure education is vital.

I have also questioned the necessity for using this kind of language in every setting, especially when feeling insecure because I am presenting in a new place or to a new group of people. There was one class that I was feeling so nervous about that I was really considering using more traditional, gendered language. I had a lot of information to cover in very little time. I was a new presenter at this facility, so I didn't have the benefit of having already established a good relationship with the clients. I knew that my class had been seen as controversial and that a staff member had to fight to get it approved. I was just plain anxious and coming in with odd-sounding language felt like it might be the step too far. I tried to justify this choice to myself because it was a residential treatment center for mothers who were recovering from substance abuse. I thought to myself, "What would be the harm in just saying 'women' and dropping the 'people with vulvas' this time? They are all mothers in a women's treatment facility. What are the chances that I will alienate someone?" I even had the thought, "Maybe I would be more likely to alienate someone by saying 'people with vulvas.'" Then I started rethinking whether I needed to make sure I wasn't assuming genders of partners during this presentation. I thought, "Well, they are moms. I guess it seems like they are having sex with men." I was talking myself out of my own standards for teaching classes because of my anxieties.

When I got to the class, my fear intensified. A few people appeared to be sleeping (this is somewhat common if people are in withdrawal from substances, but still doesn't boost the ego). Just about everyone else in the room was eyeing me suspiciously. I launched into my standard class intro and then I skipped going around the room to have them introduce themselves because I didn't want to ask their gender pronouns. I immediately felt wrong. I was chickening out and I knew it. I thought to myself, "OK, enough of this. Just use the language you know is important and if they hate it, then we'll talk about it." So I started in with "people with vulvas" and "people with penises."

Sometimes your listeners may need some education around why you are choosing the phrases you choose. This was one of those times. I could tell by everyone's faces that they were trying to figure out what the heck I was talking about. I put on my best calm face and said, "Are you noticing that I am saying 'people with vulvas'? I'll probably also say, 'people with penises' during this workshop too. I do that because I want to be respectful and inclusive of people whose gender identities may be different than their physical sex." One of my students said, "Huh?" As I was opening my mouth to explain, another student said, "Like my cousin." It turns out

I didn't have to explain anything. Instead, I got to watch silently at the front of class while one of my students explained the difference between gender and physical sex to another one of my students. What a wonderful moment.

Feeling more confident, I continued using inclusive language, including making sure my terms did not assume the gender of their partners. One of the participants asked me, "Why do you keep saying 'whether you are being sexual with someone who has a penis or someone who has a vulva?" I replied, "Because I don't know who everyone in this room is being sexual with. I don't want to make assumptions." A participant sitting in the corner quietly said, "I sleep with women sometimes." A few others started to tease her and before I could step in she said, "Whatever, I like it and there's nothing wrong with it." "That's right," I told her, to make sure I offered some support. Before class was over another participant told the group that she also slept with women sometimes and didn't feel comfortable talking to her counselor at the program about it. Others chimed in to reassure her by sharing supportive experiences they had talking with their counselors about sex.

I walked out of that class feeling overwhelmed. I had been so nervous to teach to this new group, but not only had they responded positively to the inclusive language, they had even felt safe enough to share vulnerable information about themselves. How fabulous and brave of them. I started to think about how different class would have been had I not used inclusive language. My students probably would not have felt comfortable sharing these parts of themselves and likely would have felt overlooked in the room—because I would have been overlooking them. I felt so thankful that I had managed to find my own bravery (even if a little late) and promised myself I would never again compromise on inclusive language issues out of fear. I promise I did not make that story up in order to convince you to use inclusive language. I feel grateful to have had that experience so that I can always think back on it when I am feeling nervous about being as inclusive as possible. I hope that reading that story will give you courage to teach in ways that might require some extra explanation, but that you know will have positive impact.

That class could possibly have gone another way, with participants pushing back against the language or tuning out because of it. But truthfully, I have taught many classes and I have never had students push back about inclusive language in a way that significantly derails the class. While I have feared that I might lose work due to using inclusive language, I have never to my knowledge lost opportunities or not been asked back because of trying to include people. Part of that may be luck, or the politics of the area where I live and work—but another part of it is having confidence. Knowing the important reasons why I choose this language helps me calmly and confidently explain it to the people I am working with. Again, the professional sets the tone: The more confident you are in presenting your material, the more likely the people you work with are to feel calm, at ease, and open to learn.

When We Make Mistakes

Every professional will have times when they struggle or become tongue-tied, especially around gendered language. Gender duality is so ingrained in our culture that it can be difficult to find language that does not make assumptions. Succeeding in using inclusive language some of the time is better than giving up on using it all together. Any way professionals can create space for people's varied identities is valuable.

Try not to feel guilty or shameful if you make a mistake. I say that as someone who has made many language mistakes and will surely continue to mess up sometimes. I say that as someone who has accidentally misgendered people and who still thinks regretfully about some of my worst mistakes years later. It can be painful to know we aren't perfect. However, all of us at some point will use the wrong gender pronoun or alienate someone. If you catch yourself, correct yourself. If someone else brings it to your attention, acknowledge the slip, apologize if appropriate, and change your language going forward.

If you are confused about how you have offended someone, it might be a great time to have a respectful conversation about what went wrong and how you can fix it in the future. These situations frequently bring up strong feelings on both sides and it can be harder than it seems to actually listen to the other person instead of getting caught up in your own emotions. If you go to a place of guilt or shame around your mistaken language it is much more likely you will get defensive, angry, or disengage from the conversation. When this happens to me, I try to remind myself that these are often the conversations where someone decides whether or not to trust me as a professional in their life. It is worth it to push myself to stay engaged in these moments.

Inclusivity When Working With Individuals or Partners

Using broad, inclusive terms when talking with a group of people or someone you don't know well can be welcoming. However, once you know how an individual identifies themselves, their body parts, and their important people, it shows the most respect to use their language. Calling a man's same-sex partner "partner" may feel disrespectful if they are married and he uses the term "husband." While acknowledging marital status tends to be important to most people, it holds special importance to many LGBTQ-identified people due to the long history of marriage inequality.

Inclusivity is sometimes about holding many possibilities rather than assuming we understand someone's identity. It is easy to assume someone is straight when we know they have an opposite-sex partner. It is easy to assume someone is monogamous when we know they are married. It is easy to assume that a cisgender woman who identifies as lesbian fantasizes about cisgender women. But there are many exceptions to these cases.

When we speak to clients or students as if we know these things to be true, we lose the chance to explore with them. When we ask them questions that assume answers, we are more likely to get the answer we had assumed. For example, if you say, "You're so young, you haven't been diagnosed with an STI, have you?" it becomes much harder for them to tell you they had gonorrhea last year. Making sure to ask questions even about the things we think we know and to phrase those questions in an open-ended way is an act of inclusion. For example, instead of, "You've never been diagnosed with an STI, right?" try, "What STIs, if any, have you been diagnosed with?" Instead of, "How often do you and your partner have sex?" try, "Are you and your partner currently sexual with each other? If yes, what does being sexual together include for the two of you?"

More examples of open questions include:

- Do you currently have any sexual partners?
- Are you and your partner sexually monogamous or nonmonogamous?
- How do you identify? (This could apply to sexual orientation, gender and more.)
- What pronouns do you use? How would you like me to refer to you?
- So, tell me about who is in your family; either family of origin or chosen family. (This allows them to designate who they feel is family as well as share names or titles for family members that may be less traditional than "mom" or "dad")

Language and Countertransference

Students and clients put themselves in a vulnerable position when they open up to a professional about sex and pleasure issues. In order to best help them feel comfortable opening up, the professional needs to be aware of their own areas of discomfort. If as professionals we continually find ourselves struggling with student or client language choices or accidentally excluding the same group of people over and over again, it is important to look at why this keeps happening. Our experiences and biases (in both the positive and negative sense) are likely factoring into these difficulties. I can't tell you how many times I have said something during a class and felt myself blush, or realized as someone asks a question, "OK, this is apparently a topic I still feel awkward talking about." We can't always know ahead of time what subjects will embarrass us. However, we can address these issues internally when they come up for us and practice our best poker face in the meantime.

Using Personal Experiences as Examples

As with so many issues in education or therapy, it is easy to think of our own experiences as the measure of "normal." When a client, especially one with similar genitals or experiences to us, mentions an orgasm they have had, our brains are likely to use our own experiences as mental reference. When we are asked by a client or student, "What does an orgasm feel like?" it may seem impossible not to use our own experiences to explain these sensations. After all, our only reference point for how pleasure feels physically is how it feels to us.

Using personal experiences in a professional context can be tricky for a few reasons. First, our experience will not reflect everyone's experiences. Second, sharing personal experiences is a choice that will influence the professional relationship. This is a choice that needs to be made skillfully. Sharing personal experiences can humanize the professional, change the power dynamic, normalize the experience of pleasure, and validate the idea that there is no shame in being a sexual person. However, it can also shift the focus to the professional rather than the student or client, leave openings for people to question our professionalism, and alienate those whose experiences are different than our own. When in doubt, it is easy to avoid this issue by turning a personal experience into a more-removed statement. For example, "I used deep breathing to help me orgasm," can easily be presented as, "some people find that deep breathing helps them orgasm."

Making sure the information you give offers multiple possibilities can include more people's experiences. For example, to answer the orgasm question, "Orgasms feel different to everybody. Orgasms can even feel different to the same person on different days. Some people feel their muscles might clench rhythmically, some feel their muscles relax, and some might not notice what their muscles are doing at all. People use many different words to describe their orgasms, like release, intense, explosive, or 'a warm feeling.'" Providing information about what is happening in the body (and using language that states it as likely, rather than unerring fact) as well as providing many different descriptors, makes space for a multitude of experiences. Talking about how orgasms are experienced differently by different people encourages the student or client to get curious about what their own orgasm feels like.

Using phrases such as "some people," "it is not uncommon to," or "many times people find that," offer helpful norms while preserving space for those who do not fit that standard.

Lindsey Says

Because I am a sex educator, I am often asked questions like, "When did you first have sex?" "What type of birth control do you use?" and so on. It usually isn't the case that the person really cares to know about my personal life. Really, they just trust my opinion and want to know what I would do in their situation. I choose not to share my personal experiences, because I typically don't find that to be helpful. Instead, I say, "Well, as your teacher I am not able to tell you that kind of private info, but I can say that most people have had sex by about age 20." or "You know, it doesn't really matter what type of birth control I might use, because you and I have different bodies and would likely prefer different things anyway. Which of these types is most interesting to you? That is what really matters here."

Choosing Words That Make Room for Pleasure

Language around pleasure shapes students and clients' expectations of themselves. Often, language of achievement is used when we discuss pleasure and body functioning. "Can you achieve orgasm?" "Are you able to achieve erection?" This language indicates an "either/or" situation and doesn't leave room for an experience that lands somewhere in between. However, clients often reflect ambiguity around their own pleasure experiences. Sometimes my clients (almost always clients with vulvas) are unsure about whether they have experienced orgasms. They may experience arousal and sensations they enjoy but question whether they are missing a more dramatic sensation they "should" be having. For many people, pleasurable body sensations can be ambiguous and begin subtly, but our current language does not reflect this. Sometimes this causes people to miss, discount, or ignore pleasurable sensations in their body. If clients are expecting to be run over by the freight train of ecstasy they may miss that warm tingly feeling that could be their ticket to ride.

If we ask a client if they "achieved" orgasm and perhaps they are not sure themselves, they are likely to say no. If they did not "achieve" what we are asking about they are likely to feel like they failed in some way. Pressure and anxiety are huge enemies of pleasure. If we look at the example of "achieving an erection," achievement language could be both anxiety producing and too unspecific to yield helpful information. What constitutes the achievement of erection? How firm does the erection have to be? How long, and in what circumstances, does it need to remain that firm? Asking questions more detailed than "Can you achieve it?" is vital in order to gather the kind of information that will be most helpful. Achievement language also does not address the concept of enjoyment. One can achieve orgasm but find it unfulfilling.

One alternative to achievement language is language that focuses on experiences. Experience-based phrasing can open up space for more detailed answers that report not only body function, but also how the person in question feels about their functioning. It seems to me that people are asked what their experiences are like far less often than they are told what they should strive to achieve. The following are examples of questions that focus on experience-based language.

Experience–Based Questions for Individuals

Are you enjoying your current sexual activities with yourself and/or others?

What kinds of sex do you enjoy, if any?

How do you feel about the way your body works when you are being sexual?

Do you know what pleasure feels like in your body?

Where in your body do you feel sexual pleasure?

Would you describe that feeling to be mild, medium, or intense? Are there other words that make more sense to you?

Do you feel like you have orgasms? If so, what do they feel like? Have you had an experience you would describe as an intense feeling of pleasure in your body? If not, have you had a subtle experience of pleasure?

Experience–Based Questions for Partners

How do you know when your partner is experiencing pleasure?

How do you show your partner that you are feeling good?

What makes a sexual experience with your partner satisfying and enjoyable for you?

What do you think your partner would like to get out of a sexual experience with you? (*Then you can ask their partner what they want and see how close the two answers are.*)

Describe one of your most pleasurable moments with your partner. (*Notice that this request does not even specify the pleasure as sexual, thus opening the question up for partners who may have no history of a pleasurable sexual experience together.*)

These questions can teach clients and students to tune in to their own experiences and be present in their bodies rather than evaluating their experience by outside standards. However, sometimes clients are confused by these questions since they reflect a different way of looking at sexual experience. They may be unsure about what is being asked or what is appropriate information to share. Professionals may need to explain why they are using this kind of phrasing. For example, "Hearing about what pleasure feels like in your body is helpful because sometimes people don't think they have orgasms but they still feel a lot of pleasure. If we focus on what you enjoy doing and what feels good to you, we might be able to find new options for you to increase sexual pleasure in your life." Or, "Understanding how pleasure feels to you and how it happens in your body gives us both more information about what is working well, and might help us understand if anything is not working well."

When we shift the language from medicalized terms to language of experience we also shift power back to the client. When outside standards are central (orgasm, erection, ejaculation, accepting penetration, maintaining sensations "to completion") the client is encouraged to successfully complete a scripted experience laid out for them by professional standards. When the client's awareness of their own experience is central, it conveys that they have the power to set their own goals and change their experiences through self-knowledge.

Lindsey Says

Common turns of phrase used in sex education can lay a preconceived judgment onto a concept, and it is typically a negative one. Following are some examples of simple changes we can make to create a more neutral tone and invite people to create their own meaning.

From	To
Consequence	Outcome
Dirty/clean	Has an STI/doesn't have an STI
Embarrassing	Private
Bad choices	Choices
Should	Could
Ruin your life	Change your life
Can't achieve goals	Face different challenges

Example: *What are the consequences of sex? ("Consequences" sounds like a punishment that you deserve.)*

Instead: *What are the possible outcomes of sex? (These can be both positive and negative.)*

Example: *We know that teens sometimes make bad choices and have sex when they are too young, so we want you to know about birth control in case you make the wrong choice. ("Bad/ wrong" are totally subjective.)*

Instead: *People will all make different choices when it comes to sex, which is why we need to know about protection. When a person decides to have sex, they will need this info! (Appreciating that people make decisions for complex reasons that we can't assume to understand.)*

Example: *Teen pregnancy would ruin your life and keep you from achieving goals. (Most people who became pregnant as teens wouldn't say their lives were "ruined.")*

Instead: How would an unexpected pregnancy change your life? What different challenges might you face than what you were expecting? (Teen parents still achieve goals—they don't need to throw in the towel. But yes, there will be challenges!)

Thoughts on "Normal"

Almost all the people I work with at some point ask me, "Am I normal? Are my fantasies/desires/body functions/behaviors normal?" I tend to dislike the word "normal." Normal is a word that, once again, sets up a "yes/no" dichotomy. Your sexual preferences are either normal or they are not. Your body is normal or it is abnormal. The fastest way to shut down a client or student is to make them feel they are abnormal. However, I understand why people ask the question. They want to hear validation that they are OK, that other people experience what they experience. Most of the time I just tell them, "A lot of people feel the way you do," or "I hear that a lot. I think that is really common."

When someone describes something that might be problematic or indicates a physical functioning problem I might talk about "normal" as being on a spectrum with the middle being "most common" and more unique behavior and experiences on the farther left or farther right. I might say, "What you are describing sounds like it is a little closer to the ends of the spectrum. So how do you feel about it? If it isn't causing you concern or problems in life, then it is probably just fine. If you are concerned about it, let's talk more about what has you worried." Of course, there may be some times when people need to be told to consult a medical professional or when part of working with that client or student may be adjusting an undesired behavior that is causing them problems. Even in these situations I find my students and clients want to hear that yes, many other people are working on these same issues.

The topic of "normal" can be a great jumping-off point for discussion. Asking clients and students about their feelings and experiences with the word "normal" and their sexuality can be a great therapeutic discussion. Addressing the concept of "normal" in a class provides the opportunity to discuss how "normal" is never just one thing, but more like a spectrum, and that a more helpful measure might be whether students are happy with the issue or whether it is causing them problems.

Anatomy and Function

All of this talk about experience-based language and not getting too caught up in what is normal should not discount the importance of understanding sexual anatomy and function. Professionals cannot work effectively with pleasure issues without knowledge of how arousal works in the body. Often, people are taught more about the reproductive capabilities of their bodies than the pleasure capabilities. Studying sexual anatomy and function from the viewpoint of pleasure is vital to educators and therapists. The full range of anatomy and function as it relates to pleasure is outside the scope of this book. However, the following are some skills for incorporating and utilizing this information with clients and students.

Clarifying Body Expectations

The patchwork state of sex education in the United States means that we cannot assume that all adults have a basic knowledge of sexual functioning in the body. In addition, the lack of education about pleasure means few adults have a comprehensive understanding of how to identify and increase sexual pleasure in their bodies. Providing basic information on normative body function can help clear up misunderstandings or unrealistic expectations. If someone expects to be able to have penis-in-vagina penetration for a whole hour they may feel there is something wrong with their body when this doesn't happen, when really, their functioning is totally normative if their erection lasts for about 5 minutes during penetration (Waldinger et al., 2006). In fact, they wouldn't qualify for a diagnosis of premature ejaculation unless they ejaculated in less than 1 minute (American Psychiatric Association, 2013) and neither of these measures matter as much as whether they (and any partners) are enjoying the sexual activity they are having.

Lindsey Says

It is so common for a 15-year-old boy to be bragging about how he needs extra-large condoms and how he lasts for more than an hour of penetration. Statistically, we know this would be only rarely true, but once it is boasted in class and everyone else hears it, it enters the belief systems of "normal" and everyone else feels inadequate.

I like using a simple True/False worksheet that covers expectations of sexual body functions and performance. This is an easy format to begin conversations about the range of penis size and the whole myth that "bigger is better," that vaginas don't get stretched out and "used up" by having sex, that "getting wet" doesn't necessarily always happen when you want it to, nor does it necessarily mean one was turned on, and that penetration isn't everyone's favorite activity and it commonly lasts a fairly short time. We can bust myths about hymens being "proof" of virginity, about volume of ejaculations (for people with penises and vulvas), about anal sex being necessarily painful—the list goes on and on. The activity is fun, even though it is just a true and false, because it is packed with conversation about things that apply directly to students' body and performance anxieties. I love seeing them explain these myths to peers when they hear them in the hallway later on, and am so glad that they may feel better about the size, appearance, or function of their own body as they grow.

Sometimes knowledge of anatomy can change the way clients and students think about sexual expression or possibilities for pleasure. Stating that the anus has many nerve endings, just like the clitoris or the head of the penis, may pique some people's imaginations and confirm the experiences of others. The simple statement that some people can experience orgasm just a few minutes after first arousal while some may need 20, 30 minutes, or more from first arousal to orgasm provides information that could be very important to their experience of partner sex. Now that they know the norms, they can figure out how they want to adjust their expectations and behaviors. I like to tell my students and clients: "Think of yourselves as sexual scientists. This might mean examining how pleasure functions in your body, gathering information without immediately judging it, building hypotheses about what might feel good, and testing these hypotheses for results. Just like in science, hypotheses don't always prove true. If that happens, no need to panic. You can use the information you have gained about your body and your partner(s) body to form new questions to put to the test. Have fun experimenting!"

Arousal in the Body

Supplying clients and students with information about how arousal functions in the body can help them find or increase their arousal. For example, the important role that blood flow and engorgement play in arousal is often overlooked and seldom covered in reproductive health. Discussing the ways in which breathing deeply or holding breath can influence arousal can help clients and students take control of their experiences. Information on how arousal functions in the brain and the importance of fantasy can help clients understand how their mind and body are connected.

Validating the Importance of Pleasure Concerns

When couples come into therapy with multiple concerns or stressors, it can be easy to prioritize other issues over pleasure. Complex issues such as rebuilding trust after infidelity, coping with depression or anxiety, or grieving a loss can seem to cancel out pleasure concerns. However, so often all of these issues influence each other: Working on them together can possibly create more positive change than waiting for resolution of all other issues before addressing pleasure. When I see a couple with multiple conflicts and one of the partners says, "*And* we never have sex anymore!" I know that this is not an unimportant concern for them or they wouldn't be bringing it up. Sharing pleasure can be a powerful way for couples to connect and heal, especially when words fail.

Lindsey Says

When young people talk about pleasure, it is usually treated as inappropriate, as if it is totally uncalled for to suggest that sex feels good. They basically expect to get a stern look from the teacher and a laugh from their peers. They are nervous about how this class is going to go and they want to puff their chests out a little. Students who have never met me usually try to ruffle my feathers. They want to see how far they can push before I get uncomfortable, testing the boundaries. Personally, I love the "shock question" and see it as a productive moment in establishing expectations with a group. Someone enters the room and says, "Oh, we have sex ed today? Well, I have a question. Why do girls like to get it in the booty?" They think they are going to make me blush and get an admonishment from the teacher. I say, calmly, earnestly, and with a natural smile, "That is such a good question. A lot of people wonder about that, so I am glad you asked. You know, to some people the butt and the anus are really sexual. To others, they aren't. There are a lot of nerves there, so for someone who likes the idea of anal sex, it could feel really good. People don't need to do it if they don't want to, but it is pretty common and some people are really into it. Anything else you guys are wondering about this?" Boom. They are hooked. They didn't get in trouble. I gave them a real, honest answer. I wasn't embarrassed. I acknowledged that people like sex and it feels good. They now know that they can ask me anything and I am going to tell them. The floodgates open. They stop trying to get a laugh, and instead get down to what they really want to know. I am now a trustworthy and non-judgmental source of sex info—something young people are thirsty for.

Sexual health professionals are in the unique position of being able to reinforce that pleasure is a valuable topic, worthy of attention in the client's life. While information about anatomy, body function, and partner communication are all important topics, sometimes the most valuable thing a professional can say is, simply: "Wow, that is a great topic to bring up. I'm so glad you asked." Hearing such an affirmation immediately helps a person to relax. They went out on a limb by asking a vulnerable question, and now they know that it was OK to do so. You aren't judging them. They don't have to feel worried or defensive. While all the skills in this chapter can be helpful in talking about pleasure in professional ways, being welcoming and affirming of pleasure concerns is one of the most helpful and simplest ways to support the people you work with.

References

American Dialect Society. (2016). *2015 Word of the year is singular "they"*. Retrieved January 15, 2016, from http://www.americandialect.org/2015-word-of-the-year-is-singular-they

American Psychiatric Association. (2013). *Diagnostic and statistical manual of mental disorders* (5th ed.). Washington, DC: Author.

Hite, S. (1976). *The Hite report: A nationwide study on female sexuality*. New York: Macmillan.

Waldinger, M. D., Quinn, P., Dilleen, M., Mundayat, R., Boolell, M., & Schweitzer, D. H. (2006, February). A multi-national population survey of intravaginal ejaculation latency time. *Journal of Sex Research, 43*(1), 492–497.

Chapter 6

What's Their Pleasure? Helping Clients Discover Their Ability to Feel Good

Difficulties creating and focusing on pleasure are very common: 40–50% of women report experiencing at least one "sexual dysfunction" (a broad category that includes difficulties with interest, desire, arousal, orgasm, and pain). The data indicate that the most frequent sexual dysfunctions for women are desire and arousal dysfunctions (McCabe et al., 2016). These high numbers do not consider the many people who would not meet criteria for a sexual dysfunction but still experience difficulty with pleasure, or who are quietly dealing with these issues without seeking professional help.

This is not just a problem for women: People of all genders may find themselves struggling to find and experience pleasure. While there is disagreement in the field of sex therapy about how to best address these issues (especially around the approval of medication to treat Hypoactive Sexual Desire Disorder in women), one thing is clear: People frequently struggle to find desire and cultivate pleasure, and these struggles cause them personal and relational distress. This chapter provides ways to help clients and students discover what they find pleasurable, amp up the pleasure they are already having, and have a better understanding of how they perceive pleasure so that they can create more of it.

Pleasure and Young People

Lindsey Says

It may sound like discussing pleasure with young people could be pretty scandalous. However, when done carefully, pleasure can safely fit into even the most conservative of settings. As we mentioned earlier, developing our personal understanding of pleasure supports safer sexual practices and careful decision-making. In fact, talk of cultivating pleasure can fit right in line with concepts of abstinence education. We know that most teens "practicing abstinence" in the form of virginity pledges end up initiating sex at the same age as other teenagers, have the same number of lifetime partners, and are less likely to use birth control and condoms when having sex (Rosenbaum, 2009). It would seem that remaining committed to abstinence can be a major challenge. Successful abstinence requires a lot of forethought and skill building.

We can help teens to practice thinking outside of the box and be less goal-oriented about sex. Learning to enjoy pleasures that are both physical and emotional, sexual and nonsexual, may make an individual's commitment to abstinence more manageable. Learning to think for oneself about which actions are desired (and when) can strengthen feelings of personal control over decisions.

Here is a list of sample questions that may be helpful in leading this discussion appropriately with teens:

What kinds of things feel really great to your body, that have nothing to do with sex?

Which of those things would be fun to experience alone? With a friend? With a romantic partner?

What kinds of sexual things seem interesting to you?

Which of those things would you feel comfortable doing right now? Alone? With a partner?

Which of those things do you feel like you might like to experience someday in the future, but not yet?

How will you know it is the right time to try some of those things? What would the situation be like? (Even if this is something you are already doing or have done in the past, you can still imagine the "ideal" situation!)

If you are tempted to do them earlier than you feel comfortable with, how might you stick with your decision to wait? Might you decide it is OK to change your mind? If so, would you need some kind of protection, like condoms?

If you are thinking of doing something new with a partner, how can you discuss it with them ahead of time, to see if they are feeling interested and ready too?

Please note that if working in a group, it would generally not be appropriate to ask teens to share answers pertaining to sexual pleasure aloud. I usually would conduct this as a private writing activity. I ask students to spread out so no one can see other papers, and tell them that they may take this paper with them and won't be turning it in, explaining that answers will be kept private not because they are shameful, but just because they are personal. For discussion, ask process questions rather than ones requiring that anyone disclose their answers: i.e., What was it like to write these things down? What might be the benefits of spending time answering these questions for yourself? Do you think most teens plan ahead for things like this?

Another approach would be to have them brainstorm ideas of pleasurable activities on paper, crumple them up and throw them into the middle of the room, and then go and retrieve someone else's paper to share aloud. This allows for idea sharing with the safety of anonymity. To further ensure privacy, a list of sexual activities could be pre-printed on the paper with check boxes. Include a few blank lines where people can get creative, thus communicating that exploration and creativity are welcome: Your sexual pleasures do not need to come from someone else's list. I always allow people to choose to pass if they like. Obviously, this activity will work only if your environment feels like a "safe space."

Cultivating Pleasure Awareness With Adults

It is easy to miss, overlook, or ignore sensations of pleasure in the body. Many people struggle to tune in to their bodies in general, much less sensations they may have been taught are taboo, dangerous, or shameful. In general, most people aren't taught how to be present in their bodies or build awareness of the sensations and emotions they are experiencing. Introducing the concept of pleasure awareness establishes that people need to look for the signs of pleasure in their bodies if they hope to experience it. If clients and students are not fostering an awareness of pleasure in their bodies, they may assume they do not experience it at all or overlook sensations that could lead to greater arousal if cultivated.

Most often, I begin to develop pleasure awareness with an individual before working on increasing pleasure in a sexual partnership. Helping individuals identify their experience of pleasure in their body can lead to greater ability to communicate with partners about what feels good to them. When people are good at tuning in to their own sensations, they are often better at being mindful and aware of their partner's experience. This is no substitute for direct conversation about wants, needs, boundaries, and goals, but it is a helpful ability that often changes the experience of sex for all partners.

Tuning In to the Body

Often I find it helpful to start with basic exercises, like asking clients or students to spend a moment just noticing their breath or paying attention to their heartbeat, in order to become more aware of their body in general. Questions regarding where in the body an emotion or feeling "lives" can be helpful. "What places in your body do you tend to feel pleasure?" "What words would you use to describe pleasure in your body?" "Where in your body does the feeling of 'sexy' (or arousal, hotness, sensuality, whatever words they prefer) live?" Many times the answers have been surprising to both the client and myself. Naming and giving words to feelings of pleasure helps clients and students call these sensations up again the next time they want to feel sexual.

Meditative, exploratory, "close your eyes and tune into your body"–type exercises are great to use in groups or workshop settings. Your participants can quietly observe what happens for them and then write about it privately. Or the group can have a discussion where participants who feel comfortable can share aspects of their experience while others are free to just listen.

Kegel Exercises

Kegel exercises, repeatedly squeezing and releasing the pelvic floor muscles, are a great way to help students and clients of all genders become more present and aware in their bodies. Teaching the basics of Kegel exercises is easy to do with individuals in a therapeutic setting and can be a great exercise for group presentations, too. Talking clients and students through the squeeze and release of a Kegel can help direct their attention to their pelvic floor in a way that may be different than the pressures they feel when trying to be sexual; not expecting any particular reaction, but rather noticing whatever they experience in that moment. Some clients and students respond well to the idea of building muscle strength and control, especially those who have not previously felt strong or in control of their sex lives.

For students or clients who experience genital pain and muscle tension, the squeeze part of the exercise may not be appropriate. If they are seeing a pelvic floor physical therapist (and they likely should be), this could be a great question for them to ask their PT. However, they may enjoy taking a deep breath and relaxing their pelvic floor as they exhale. Many clients have told me they were unaware of the tension they were carrying in their pelvic floor muscles until we took a deep breath and exhaled together. This is easy to do throughout their day and promotes body awareness and relaxation. Make sure to tell students and clients that whether or not they experience pleasure from these exercises is not the point. This is a no-pressure exercise. However, cultivating a greater awareness in the pelvis and genitals is often one of the building blocks to experiencing and increasing pleasure. Even these simple exercises are setting them on the road to good feelings in the future.

What Feels Good in Your Body?

Increasing sexual pleasure can often start with identifying more general pleasures. In fact, sometimes starting with sexual pleasure is too threatening or too difficult. Clients and students who have never had a pleasurable sexual experience may feel that pleasure is impossible for them and they have no knowledge to draw on. Starting with experiences of nonsexual pleasure can be more approachable and less triggering. It also proves their ability to identify and experience general pleasure in their bodies, which is likely to lend confidence if and when they decide to explore pleasurable sexual experiences.

The exercise on the following page may help clients to identify and define their experiences of pleasure, both sexual and nonsexual.

Make sure to slow down during this exercise and draw out the specifics (adjectives and reasoning) of the client's answers. The point is to help them remember the feeling of these experiences and draw them into greater body awareness in a way that feels safe and low-pressure. Asking them to describe what they like about their answers can give you important information and help them clarify the feeling in their own bodies. Further exploration deepens, "I love apple cider," into, "I like the warmth of apple cider in the fall when it is cold outside. I like how it is both sweet and spicy. I like how it feels on my tongue." By the time they have said this much, your client or student is likely feeling those good feelings in their body and connecting them with the concept of pleasure.

Details about why these activities and experiences are pleasurable to your students and clients will provide greater insight into what they need to create a situation that facilitates pleasure (safety? sexiness? risk taking? quiet? privacy?). "I love how powerful I feel in my suit," may help identify feeling powerful as an important part of their experience of pleasure. It may also give insight into gender expression or how they like to be perceived sexually. But of course, you will always need to ask them to know for sure. By exploring these issues, you are helping them define their sexual selves and identify the elements that will help them create more sexual pleasure.

Exercise: What's Your Pleasure?

Inspired by the work of Jennie Hilleren, MA, LMFT, CST, CSST

Can you think of times when you have felt pleasure in the following situations?

Delicious food or drink
(examples might include crisp apples, cool lemonade, rich, creamy chocolate)

Clothes
(soft knit socks, a leather jacket that fits just right, a nightgown that feels silky on the skin)

Outdoors
(the way the sunlight feels on my face in the summer, the feeling of freedom as I ride my bike on a trail)

Exercise/Movement
(my morning run, dancing in a big crowd where I don't think anyone is looking at me, lifting more weights than I have been able to before)

Temperature
(the crispness of the air while ice skating in winter, the warmth of a cup of coffee in my hands on a cold day)

Favorite items
(my softest blanket that I grab when I am sick, the ring I wear that I enjoy playing with because the stone is so smooth)

Nonsexual body pleasures
(massage, getting a good shave or haircut from the barber, putting on lotion, getting a manicure)

Nonsexual body pleasures with a partner
(holding hands, a hand cupping my cheek, playing basketball together)

Sexual pleasure in your body
(For people who struggle with this, any small feeling of pleasure counts. Tingling, a memory of feeling comfortable while naked, and of course orgasms or other "showy" signs of sexual pleasure are great as well.)

Sexual pleasure with a partner
(Starting small is just fine. Feeling a tingle of excitement while holding hands, enjoying a kiss. Again, "bigger" signs of pleasure are great information too.)

Supporting and Amplifying Small Experiences of Sexual Pleasure

Sometimes I talk with clients or students who tell me they are unhappy with their sexual response and unable to orgasm. When we talk further, they can usually identify some experiences of sexual pleasure in their body, but feel these experiences are too small. Sometimes this is a situation that requires education about common experiences of orgasms. For example, it is not common to experience an orgasm that lasts 5 minutes, or even 2 minutes. Certainly, some people achieve high arousal states where they feel orgasmic for long periods of time, but many people's experiences of orgasm are much shorter, often less than 30 seconds long. When clients and students have elevated expectations of pleasure in their body it can be a struggle to feel happy for what they do have or even recognize it as pleasure.

Lindsey Says

I was once approached by a woman, probably 40 years old, after a class. She indicated that she needed to speak with me privately, and seemed very ashamed about what she was about to say. Finally, she confessed, "I can only have orgasms when I press on my thighs. What is wrong with me?" She was so focused on trying to have an orgasm the "right" way that she was missing out on enjoying the ones she was already experiencing. Whether they come from the clitoris—or the elbows—we can allow ourselves to appreciate all of the good feelings our body can create.

Encouraging Reasonable Expectations

The What's Your Pleasure exercise described earlier offers a way to put into context what sexual pleasure might feel like in the body by comparing it to the pleasures of everyday life. Clients and students probably don't expect that wearing their favorite warm, fuzzy sweater will be so pleasurable that all other worries will leave their minds as they are overwhelmed with ecstatic feeling, but they might expect sexual pleasure to be this immediately all-encompassing. They may be waiting for sexual pleasure to overtake them in a way that makes the work stress, dirty laundry, or worries about grandma's health disappear. This isn't a realistic expectation in most people's daily lives. Think about the way desire often "reappears" for long-term couples on vacation. Once they get the day-to-day concerns out of the way and put themselves into a situation where it is socially sanctioned to focus on pleasure, they magically find more of it! What if that capability is always there under all the daily life stress, waiting for someone to give it attention? Establishing awareness of small pleasures is necessary to enjoy them and is a great first step toward creating more intense pleasure.

The Emotional Side of Pleasure

Pleasure is not just a sensation in the body; it is often connected with emotions. Sexual pleasure is frequently associated with happiness, joy, and love. Of course, it is also very commonly linked to guilt, shame, or ambivalence. It is important to explore with students and clients which emotions they connect with pleasure. People are often surprised by what they find.

Deandra came in to see me because sex with her fiancé had "dried up." She told me while the two had started their relationship passionately, she struggled to find desire to have sex anymore. Deandra was dedicated to her job as a high school teacher and while she loved devoting a lot of time and energy to the young people she worked with, it left her exhausted by the end of every day. One session, while we were discussing her struggles, I asked Deandra what emotions she associated with sexual pleasure and desire. She thought for a second and said, "It's frivolous." "Really?" I said, "Frivolous?" "Yeah! I have so much to do for my class, so much to do at home. If I spend time trying to figure out 'my pleasure,' when will I get my lessons done? I have 35 faces looking up at me every period. That is a lot of kids to disappoint and it seems frivolous to take time out for pleasure."

Other answers I have gotten include, "Fear. Pleasure has been pretty out-of-control in the past. I am a little scared to feel that again." "Anger. I don't feel like I've had much pleasure, but my partners sure have." "I feel so sad because sexual pleasure was so easy in my last relationship. Since they left I have trouble thinking about giving myself any of that." "Freedom. When I orgasm I can leave everything else behind for a little while."

With Deandra, once I understood that pleasure felt frivolous we could start to explore how this emotion interacted with her belief systems around pleasure. I asked her why she came to therapy to work on pleasure issues if she felt they were frivolous. "Well, they are important to my fiancé, so that is one reason." It was tougher for her to value pleasure for her own sake. Deandra and I talked about how she was raised to value being of service to others and how sex and pleasure didn't seem to be compatible with that. To address Deandre's values around being of service, I brought up the topic of self-care: "If you burn out, what good will that do your students? How much do you take care of yourself so that you can do your job well everyday and be the person you want to be in your relationship?" I asked. I was curious whether taking time for sexual pleasure could be part of taking good care of herself, a bit like pressing a reset button when she was feeling mild anxiety or stress. She (somewhat skeptically) agreed to think about it.

When Finding Pleasure Is Difficult

Other more overwhelming sensations in the body can make it difficult to tune in to pleasure. For example, depression can make it very difficult to find feelings of pleasure. Pleasure may not be as "loud" as anxiety, and so it can quickly get drowned out. However, both sexual and nonsexual pleasure can be a great way to remind clients and students of what "good" feels like. It can also be a way to begin changing their day-to-day quality of life by adding or appreciating small daily pleasures. As mindfulness is effective in treatment of depression and anxiety (Hofmann, Sawyer, Witt, & Oh, 2010), cultivating pleasure awareness can also be a valuable part of working with these issues.

When clients struggle to identify even small nonsexual experiences of pleasure in their lives it may indicate that something else is going on. Clients who have a history of unprocessed trauma often struggle to tune in to their bodies. Frequently, the discomfort they feel when they do try makes it very difficult to remain aware and present in their bodies. When this happens there is a great need for the practitioner to go gently and slowly.

Pleasure and Trauma

It is a sad reality of our world that when sex comes up, so does trauma. The two live together for many, many people. Not all sexual health professionals are trained in treating or working with trauma. It is up to you to decide your scope of competence and refer if needed.

Often, addressing trauma takes priority and it is assumed pleasure does not need the professional's attention, that it will happen "naturally" as trauma is processed. However, I have found it is helpful to address the two in tandem. There may be times when one aspect needs more attention than the other, but leaving out pleasure altogether means forgetting to include the healing power of the positive. Pleasure can be a reminder of the good things to come, a tool to bring people out of pain or despair. Pleasure can be a way to build confidence in their ability to self-soothe and take good care of themselves. Knowing how to create pleasure in their body can offer clients and students the kind of control over their experiences that they may not have had in the past.

Be cautious of going too far, too fast. Remember, this is supposed to be about pleasure, not pressure. Nothing shuts down sexual pleasure like fear, or expectations to have pleasure in a certain way, at a certain time. However, if you and the people you work with can leave some space open for pleasure, it can often deepen and accelerate healing from trauma. Scaling questions can help you understand client's levels of discomfort so you can be a better ally and guide in their process. I frequently ask questions like, "On a scale of 1 to 10, 1 being completely relaxed and 10 being intense anxiety or panic, how do you feel when I start talking about sexual pleasure? Scale of 1 to 10, where are you at when we talk about masturbation? How intense is the fear that just came up for you, scale of 1 to 10?" Practitioners can always back up, slow down, and validate strong emotion as it comes up.

Exploring Connections and Separations of Sex, Pleasure, and Relationships

It is easy to assume sex and pleasure are connected, but often they are not. People have sex for a variety of reasons. Even sex that people have with the intention of seeking pleasure, and that follows a pattern that has been pleasurable to them before, may not feel good this time around. As professionals, we shouldn't make assumptions about what kind of situations might have been most pleasurable for the people we work with. Many people have the experience of having non-pleasurable sexual experiences in otherwise positive, loving relationships. Sometimes people have had the most pleasurable sexual experience of their lives with someone they really disliked or who treated them badly. Some people may have had more pleasure with themselves than with any partner they have had, or vice versa. A pleasure timeline can be a great way to help students and clients focus in on what their personal experiences of pleasure have been like.

Box 6.1   Exercise: Pleasure Timeline

The purpose of a pleasure timeline is to identify patterns of people, actions, or environments that inhibit pleasure, encourage pleasure, or where pleasure was perhaps expected but absent.

On an extra long piece of paper, small poster board, or any kind of surface that gives you lots of space to work with, draw a line lengthwise across the page. This will be the pleasure timeline.

The far left point of the line is labeled "birth," and time progresses across the page to the far right side, which is present day. Divide the line into sections: childhood, young adult, adulthood. From there, make note of important life events such as relationship beginnings and endings, marriage(s), divorce(s), miscarriage(s), birth of children, medical issues, body changes, and so on. Once you have recorded the client's history of sexual experiences and relationships, move on to pleasure questions. Make notations at the appropriate time period on the line about the experience they had at that time ("Very close emotional relationship, not sexually pleasurable," "Lots of sexual pleasure at this time but not feeling comfortable in my body," "Very hot experience, but I had mixed feelings about it later").

Asking clients about their history with pleasure can be confusing at first. Most people are not used to conceptualizing their lives based on when they felt pleasure or when they did not. Following are some questions that can help with the process.

Childhood

- Think of your early childhood, as far back as you remember. Do you remember anything you particularly loved the smell or feel of? A teddy bear? A favorite blanket?
- What kind of pleasurable touch (if any) did you get growing up? Hugs? Wrestling? Someone doing your hair?
- Can you remember feeling pleasure in your body? Climbing on the playground? A cozy bed at night? Figuring out your body through masturbation?
- Were there experiences that "should have" been pleasurable but were not? For example, someone you did not like to give hugs to? Playground activities your friends enjoyed but you disliked?

Young Adult to Adulthood

- How did you feel about your body through puberty? Were you excited or dismayed about the changes taking place? Did you feel good in your body as it matured? Did puberty take away some activities you found pleasurable (growing breasts getting in the way of sports, feeling "too grown up" to cuddle with parents)?

- Did you have pleasurable, nonsexual, physical experiences with friends? Team sports? Practicing hair and makeup on each other?
- What were first sexual or romantic experiences with others like? Pleasurable? Awkward? Fun? Frightening?

Adults/Elders

- Have your sexual or romantic experiences with others been pleasurable? Are there people with whom sex was always pleasurable? Never pleasurable?
- In relationships where sex was sometimes pleasurable and sometimes not, do you know what factors helped or detracted from the experience?
- Do you have pleasurable experiences (sexual or nonsexual) currently in your daily life? If so, what are they?
- Do you have pleasurable nonsexual touch with friends, family, or loved ones? (Hugs, putting arms around shoulders, etc.)
- Do you get massage, chiropractic, salon services, acupuncture, tattooing, or other professional services that involve touch or caretaking? If so, are these pleasurable for you?
- Has pleasure changed as your body has changed (menopause, pregnancy, childbirth, aging, injury, illness, erection changes, changes in fitness or health)? If so, in what ways?

Once you have finished the questions, you and the client can look back at the timeline and draw more information from it. Notice how pleasure and sex connect or are separate events. Do pleasure and relationships coincide or are they separate? Was there a certain time of life that had more or less pleasure? What other connections can you find? What meaning does the client make of this information?

While I use this exercise often in therapy, I have also given it as a handout for students to take home and work on. I have had clients who wanted to add pictures or art to their timelines and enjoyed processing in this more kinesthetic way. One particularly visual client chose different colors for sex, relationships, and pleasure and added color to their timeline. This created a lovely visual depiction how pleasure interacted with sex and relationships in their life. There are so many possible ways to do this exercise; give your clients and students free reign to use their creativity.

The Importance of Masturbation/Self-Pleasure

Masturbation is one of the best ways people can learn about themselves sexually and connect with sexual pleasure in their body. Self-pleasure is sexual self-expression, a vital part of sexual identity for many people, and a way to be good to oneself. Clients and students who are seeking to increase pleasure in their lives frequently need to focus in on masturbation first. However, this is often one of the areas that professionals struggle to talk about.

Talking About Masturbation/Self-Pleasure

It can be easy to freeze up around the topic of masturbation because it feels too personal or too directly sexual. Many educators who work with young people or in school settings may feel masturbation is a risky subject that could get them in trouble. However, if we go back to the goalposts of factual and appropriate, it becomes clear there are many ways to address this very important topic in a professionally.

Explaining that masturbation is normative and extremely common is important for people to hear when they feel nervous or have been told otherwise. Students and clients sometimes feel they are taking a big risk if they attempt masturbation and they need to know that this is not a "weird" or harmful behavior. In fact, between 67% and 94% of men and between 43% and 84.6% of women report they have masturbated at some point in their lifetime (Herbenick et al., 2010). Self-pleasuring is a behavior the vast majority of people do and it has the possibility of great benefits to health and sexual enjoyment. Even the adults I work with frequently need to hear this information to reassure themselves and will tell me, "I figured that was probably true, but you hear all kinds of things. It is nice to know how common it is."

Lindsey Says

When masturbation comes up, generally people (of all ages) start giggling. I usually like to mention that though people joke about it, it is pretty common, nobody would ever know if you do it or not, and it is something that most doctors/medical associations say is healthy. I ask participants what they think might be healthy about it and have them generate a list like this:

You don't get pregnant or STDs.

You get to let off steam.

It is exercise.

It helps you relax.

It helps you sleep.

It feels good.

You only have to think about yourself.

You get to know your body.

It is good for your immune system.

The tension in the room changes notably during this conversation, and by the end, the blushing cheeks have returned to normal as everyone relaxes their worries about whether or not people will suspect them of masturbating. This seems to dramatically legitimize this healthy, normal sexual behavior in the span of just a few minutes. My hope is that those in the room who felt shame about their masturbatory practices approach their next solo session with a smile and a sense of pride that they are taking good care of their bodies. I hope that people feel more comfortable discussing masturbation with any sex partners they may have, as this may lead to better communication and better shared pleasure between them. I also hope this helps those who are interested in masturbating but are holding back (for whatever reason) gain a little confidence and maybe decide to give it a try, if they choose.

How Do I Work This Thing? Addressing Concerns About How to Self-Pleasure

Often, when I was selling sex toys, people would buy a toy they liked the look of, then look at me and say, "I don't even know where to start. What do I do with this?" For people who are intrepid sexual self-explorers this may seem like a silly question, but for many people, figuring out where to start causes much trepidation. Imagine if you had never seen a bicycle before and you only had a vague sense of what they were supposed to do. Maybe you had even received some wrong information about bicycles that sounded kind of scary. Then someone hands you a bike and says, "Have a fun ride!" Is that likely to sound fun or totally overwhelming?

Telling people that masturbation has many positive benefits and they should try it can sound much the same way. Clients and students are likely thinking, "Where do I start?" The bravest of them might ask, but most will just quietly wonder and then either have an experience that is unnecessarily filled with anxiety or just avoid it all together. When educators teach about masturbation or therapists give self-pleasure as an assignment, it is essential to give the client or student some education and instruction. Again, draw on what is appropriate and factual for the situation.

I might say, "People self-pleasure in all different kinds of ways. We are all different people and enjoy different things. So think of this as an exploratory mission, less about getting results and more about just trying things and paying attention to what happens in your body. You are gathering information about yourself." Notice that all of this is based off the fact that people like different kinds of stimulation. Another helpful fact is about concentrations of nerve endings: "Some body parts have a lot more nerve endings than others. That means they have a lot of capacity to give you sensation but it also may mean that they are so sensitive they need to be touched or stimulated in a different way. Again, everyone likes different kinds of touch and stimulation, so it will be a process of experimentation to see what works well for you."

Listing specific body parts that have high concentrations of nerve endings can be helpful: "The clitoris, head of the penis, and the anus are all body parts that have a lot of nerve endings." I almost always give clients information about a variety of body parts and not just the ones I may assume they have. They may have partners with different genitals than they have, or a friend who needs some sex advice down the road. This also helps in situations where your client is gender diverse, intersex, or has a nontraditional genital configuration.

Other helpful facts that make good jumping-off points for explaining masturbation in a professional way might include:

- The importance of oxygen ("The way people breathe can change their experience of arousal. Pay attention: Are you holding your breath in certain moments? Does breathing deeply change the sensation you experience?")

- The role blood flow (engorgement) plays in arousal ("One part of arousal is that blood flows to the genitals. That might mean these body parts appear to deepen in color, and usually it means these parts engorge. Basically, that means they get bigger and usually more sensitive. With penises this might look like an erection; with vulvas, the clitoris gets bigger and might be more visible. The labia and all the other outside-the-body parts might get bigger and more sensitive, too. Noticing these body changes is great. Many people think it looks really exciting, whatever you are doing sexually is likely to feel even better at this point, and it means your circulatory system is doing a great job.")
- Common differences in the amount of time it takes to become aroused and orgasm ("Some people progress quickly from the first moment they feel arousal to the time when they can orgasm and others need more time and stimulation before they even start to feel pleasure and arousal. You might even find the time you need differs depending on the day. The important part is to know that it may take longer to get to orgasms than many people assume. It is not uncommon for people to need 20–40 minutes of pleasurable stimulation before they can have an orgasm. It is also helpful to remember that while not everyone has orgasms, especially in every sexual experience, everyone has the capacity for pleasure.")
- Safety facts about any sex toys that might be in use (see Chapter 8)

The Important Role of Fantasy

Sexual health professionals shouldn't forget fantasy's role in experiencing pleasure. As important as body awareness is, it is also true that the brain is one of the most important erogenous zones. Fantasy plays a key role in experiencing sexual pleasure. Often, it seems, fantasy activates desire. When people experience sexual arousal in the body without connection to desire or fantasy, it is sometimes not perceived as pleasurable (spontaneous erections or seemingly random lubrication would be some examples).

Many people I have worked with say they tried Viagra or Cialis and "nothing happened." When asked if they did anything to help arousal along, such as fantasy or sexual touching, they report they expected the pills to just "make it happen." In these situations, and many more, fantasy can be the missing component.

Lindsey Says

Taking time to practice fantasizing is both practical harm reduction (even abstinence friendly) and hopefully inspires some future creativity and fun between the sheets. A really fun activity is to instruct students to come up with the sexiest thing they can imagine that doesn't include touching. Depending heavily on your setting, this may be an OK activity to do out loud, but is likely more appropriately done individually. This activity will certainly elicit a bunch of giggles, blushes, and amazing ideas. It will also likely be a memorable experience that demonstrates that it is fun to try a variety of things, that each person is going to be turned on by something completely different, and that there is so much more to sex than "sex."

Helping clients and students access a sexual fantasy life that makes them happy and turns them on can be a difficult task. I like to encourage clients to explore lots of different avenues to develop fantasies. Some people like to read, some like to listen, and some like to watch. Movies (both mainstream or pornographic), written or pictorial erotica, erotica read aloud, romance stories, music videos, art, or vintage photos are all possibilities to explore.

Five Types of Fantasy

So many of the people I work with are nervous about their fantasies; it is important to normalize fantasizing and let clients and students know that lots of people enjoy thinking about behaviors they would never want to pursue in real life. Fantasy is often a way of playing sexual make-believe and it is a vital component to experiencing pleasure. I explain it this way:

> I think there are five types of fantasies. The first type is the kind you know you want to do in real life. Maybe you've done this before and enjoyed it, or you just know you would like to try it someday. The second are the "maybes." Maybe you would want to try that fantasy someday in the right situation, in the right mood, or with the right partner(s). You might not be sure if you actually want to do it or you just want to fantasize about it. That's OK. That's what makes it a "maybe."
>
> The third type is the kind you know you don't want to do in real life. You know you like to think about it but you would never want to actually do it. Maybe because it would be a really bad idea, maybe it wouldn't be fun in real life, maybe it would be too messy or take way too much time. Whatever the reason, it is one you keep just for fantasy.
>
> The fourth type reminds us that human beings are amazingly creative creatures: sexy aliens, vampire stuff, dinosaur/human romance novels, giant vaginas you imagine stuffing yourself into, whatever. It might not be physically possible and it might make you think, "Well where did that one come from?" But really, it's just fine because it's just fantasy.
>
> The only kind of fantasy that I tend to worry about is fantasy number five: fantasies about activities that have caused you trouble in the past, or that would get you into trouble in the present *and* that lead to thoughts about how to actually do them in real life. For example, if you are a sober person, it may not be super helpful for you to constantly fantasize about sex while high, or if you have fantasies about sexual behavior that would victimize another person and it is starting to creep beyond fantasies into thoughts about "How could I make this happen?" These are great times to talk with a professional.

Setting Pleasure Goals

Don't forget to ask your clients and students about their pleasure goals. When professionals phrase goals only in the language of treating pathology, we are missing an opportunity to envision our clients as happy humans who have a wealth of pleasure in their lives. Setting pleasure goals helps people understand that they are working not just away from pain or anxiety, but toward pleasure.

Often, when I ask clients what kind of goals for pleasure they would like to set, I hear something like, "I'd like to have sex two times a week." I usually ask, "OK, and would you like that sex to feel good?" Clients sometimes tell me they think that is too much to wish for, an unreachable goal. Clients sometimes laugh and say, "oh yeah, I forgot about that." Clients sometimes tell me that pleasure is a secondary goal to restarting their sexual relationship. No matter what, this always leads to me learning more about my client and having important conversations with them.

It can often be hard for clients and students to give themselves permission to prioritize pleasure. By encouraging them to define their personal pleasure goals, you are not only giving them permission, you are also letting them know that you, a professional, view pleasure as an important part of the process.

The next exercise is a great follow-up to the What's Your Pleasure? exercise, or it can be used alone. If clients struggle to come up with answers for the goal-setting portion, you can always go back to the What's Your Pleasure? exercise to help generate ideas. The following goals can be specific to sexual pleasure or they can be broader, depending on what seems most appropriate for your client.

Box 6.2 Exercise: Defining Personal Pleasure Goals

How much pleasure do you have in your life?

What do I experience daily or weekly that is pleasurable?

How many pleasurable experiences do I notice or try to have daily? Weekly?

Am I happy with that amount or would I like to make changes?

Recognizing pleasure in your life:

Are there daily or weekly experiences that could be enjoyable that I am not paying attention to or that I rush through and forget to enjoy?

If so, what can I do this week to enjoy and experience more of the pleasure I already have in my life?

Increasing pleasure in your life:

What pleasurable experiences with myself could I incorporate or be more aware of?

What pleasurable experiences with a partner/in my relationship could I incorporate or be more aware of?

What would I like my pleasure goals to be?

References

Herbenick, D., Reece, M., Schick, V., Sanders, S. A., Dodge, B., & Fortenberry, J. D. (2010). Sexual behavior in the United States: Results from a national probability sample of men and women ages 14–94. *The Journal of Sexual Medicine*, 7(s5), 255–265.

Hofmann, S. G., Sawyer, A. T., Witt, A. A., & Oh, D. (2010). The effect of mindfulness-based therapy on anxiety and depression: A meta-analytic review. *Journal of Consulting and Clinical Psychology*, *78*(2), 169.

McCabe, M. P., Sharlip, I. D., Lewis, R., Atalla, E., Balon, R., Fisher, A. D., . . . Segraves, R. T. (2016). Incidence and prevalence of sexual dysfunction in women and men: A consensus statement from the fourth international consultation on sexual medicine 2015. *The Journal of Sexual Medicine*, *13*(2), 144–152.

Rosenbaum, J. E. (2009). Patient teenagers? A comparison of the sexual behavior of virginity pledgers and matched nonpledgers. *Pediatrics*, *123*(1), e110–e120.

Chapter 7

Guilty Pleasure

Helping Students and Clients Work Through Guilt and Shame

In the last chapter we discussed many ways to help clients identify and increase pleasure in their lives. However, two of the biggest roadblocks to enjoying pleasure are guilt (the feeling that you have done something bad) and shame (the feeling that you are bad). Many people feel guilty prioritizing pleasure in their lives or have shame about what they find pleasurable. US culture has words for people who put sexual pleasure in a place of importance and the vast majority of them are derogatory. Guilt or shame can easily kick in for clients based on societal messaging alone. When you add in religious beliefs, cultural norms, prejudices, and experiences of being shamed by friends, family, or partners, it is easy to understand why these issues hold so much power over our clients and students.

Guilt may help people recognize when they have acted in ways they regret. However, the helpfulness of guilt is limited. If it causes amends for hurts that have been caused and change in future actions, guilt may have served a positive purpose. However, guilt is often present even when no one has been hurt. Clients and students frequently feel vaguely guilty for actions that when consciously examined fit just fine into their moral code or value system. The vague creep of guilt most often serves no helpful purpose and shame almost always causes more harm than good. Believing that something intrinsic to ourselves (not our actions or behaviors) is wrong often eats away at people and pulls them away from their positive goals into behaviors they feel bad about. Clearing away guilt and shame can clear a path to greater pleasure. Feeling good in our bodies and with partners can help loosen the hold of shame and guilt. How fabulous is that?

A Note on Guilt, Shame, and Sexual Trauma

Experiences of sexual trauma often create intense feelings of guilt and shame. Working with victims/survivors can be a complex process. While the exercises in this chapter may be helpful for people who have had traumatic sexual experiences, they are only one piece of a likely multifaceted healing process. These exercises are more likely to be appropriate for clients or students who have already done some work in processing and healing from their experience(s) of sexual violence.

Skills for Working With Guilt and Shame

This chapter introduces five main skills for helping students and clients address feelings of guilt or shame that may be blocking progress toward their pleasure goals:

initiating conversations about belief systems, normalizing sexual pleasure, legitimizing sexual pleasure, addressing negative consequences from the past, and encouraging further exploration and processing.

Initiating Conversations About Belief Systems

Many factors may affect students' and clients' beliefs about pleasure: religion, culture, past experiences, social judgment, as well as perceived or actual conflicts between value systems and sexual pleasure. When working through guilt and shame issues, these are likely to come up. Conversations about cultures, religions, and values can be a vital jumping-off point for clients and students who are trying to figure out how they want sexual pleasure to fit into their life. If they have beliefs that make the topic of sexual pleasure a concerning one to them, or cause guilt and shame, it is important to talk about those beliefs.

Students and clients may have never been asked questions about their beliefs around pleasure. Whether it is a conversation over multiple therapy sessions or one class period that inspires someone to continue their exploration at home, there are appropriate ways for professionals of all kinds to introduce conversations around belief systems. The following exercise is meant to start some of these conversations. It can be adapted to fit many purposes: a one-on-one discussion in therapy, a take-home writing activity for therapy or class, a prompt for large- or small-group discussion, and more.

Box 7.1   Sexual Pleasure: What Does Everybody Say?

What do my cultural values or traditions say?
What do my religious, spiritual beliefs, or morals say?
What does society say?
What did my sex education say?
What did my parents or family say?
What do my kids say?
What do my friends say?
What do(es) my partner(s) say?
What do I say?
What do I do?

The final questions, "What do I say?" and "What do I do?," can lead to important discussion of whether their beliefs match their behavior. If there are areas where the two diverge, how do they feel about that? If their individual beliefs differ from belief systems they have been taught, how do they feel about those differences? These conversations will sometimes lead to talk about guilt or shame, which is great as it gives you the opportunity to process those issues with them.

Depending on the people you are working with, you may want to add in other questions:

What does Alcoholics Anonymous say?
What does the queer community say?
What do community elders say?
What do third-wave feminists say?

When processing these questions in a group, it can be interesting to see that people who share religious denominations or cultural backgrounds often hold differing ideas of what their religion or culture says about sexual pleasure. If you had a whole group of people who identified as "Midwesterners," there would likely be many differing opinions on what Midwesterners say about pleasure. Starting this conversation can encourage students and clients to continue exploring and shaping their own interpretations of their beliefs as well as seeking space in their communities to discuss them with others. Professionals who encourage continued exploration of belief systems and how these interact with sexual pleasure can spark a lifelong process of evaluation and change for their students and clients.

Providing Pleasure Education for People With a Variety of Belief Systems

It can be easy, when you work with enough people struggling with guilt and shame induced by their belief systems, to view certain sets of beliefs as "the enemy" of sexual pleasure. Sexual health professionals who contend with censorship, protest, and anger from certain groups could easily hold some of their own anger, or at very least trepidation, toward these groups. Because of these challenges and conflicts, it can sometimes seem easier to avoid the topics of religion, values, or culture altogether; to avoid "rocking the boat." However, silence around these issues does nothing to help the people we work with explore how their belief systems interact with sexual pleasure (or the lack thereof) in their lives.

A common question I get asked when people find out I am a sex therapist is, "How do you work with Christians?" It seems to be a frequent assumption that people who identify as Christian would be difficult for sexual health professionals to work with, or less receptive to sexual health information. To be honest, I had some of those same prejudices when I was training to be a therapist. However, my experience has been that I very much enjoy my Christian clients. They have frequently been deep thinkers about sexuality, grappling with issues such as how to blend their religious beliefs, the science of sexuality, and the needs of partners in a way that feels ethical to them. They have overwhelmingly been concerned with the happiness, pleasure, and well-being of their partners. They have made me realize I had a lot of biases and stereotypes about people who identify as Christian that were wrong.

I am thankful to have (so far) worked with people who identify as Quaker, Hindu, Jain, Unitarian Universalist, Jewish, Muslim, Spiritual, Pagan, Atheist, and many denominations of Christian. Experiences with these clients and students have widened my views and challenged my own prejudices. All of these people have had important concerns about sexual pleasure. All of them were kind to me and respectful of the information I provided (even if they sometimes disagreed or declined to try certain suggestions). I hope they feel I was kind and respectful of their beliefs as well.

Hostility toward specific groups can easily convince students and clients who belong to these groups that sex education or therapy is "not for them," which is both untrue and a loss to everyone. Anti-pleasure views will never shift if we avoid engaging in conversation, and as professionals we are much more likely to inadvertently push our own values and cultural biases (we all have them) onto the people we work with if we are not asking respectful questions about our clients' and students' belief systems. It is not my job to convince someone to "see it my way." Instead, I want to give them information about bodies, relationships, and pleasure and strive to provide a safe, non-judgmental place to talk about the ways they fit with their belief systems and ways they may struggle with them.

Judgment or Shaming Messages

Lindsey Says

Remember way back in Chapter 2 when I was talking about how in my classes with parents, they overwhelmingly say they want to teach their children that sexuality is natural, normal, and beautiful? Surprisingly, when I ask young people (even the children of those same parents) to tell me what their parents have taught them about sex so far, they say things like "It is bad," "It is nasty," "It is a sin," "I should be ashamed of myself," etc. There is clearly some disconnect here! When parents have the opportunity to see this, their first reaction is shock: "I never said that!" After time for contemplation, though, parents begin to realize that yes, though they may believe all of these positive things in their hearts, what leaves their mouths is typically laced with shame—likely messaging that they absorbed from their own upbringing. It seems that many parents find it difficult to find a way to say the positive things, because they feel awkward and don't know the appropriate way to say something good about sexuality to a child. Instead, kids just hear "Don't do that!" or "That's inappropriate!" over and over again. Once they become more aware of the ways they are teaching children—even toddlers—messages around guilt versus pride in bodies and sexuality, parents are usually eager to make a purposeful switch in their language.

People get judgment messages about sex from many different sources: family members, friends, partners, cultures, and societal perceptions. Social judgment is a powerful force, and shame can be internalized from the statements of others even when the person being shamed believes their actions are just fine. Clients and students often feel that their sexuality is wrong, too big, dangerous, should be toned down, shouldn't take priority, or must be put last. Sometimes they are unaware of these thoughts or unsure of where they first heard these negative statements. The following exercise can help students and clients examine what judgments they may be internalizing and where they might be coming from.

When the Judgment List is completed, you can have your students or clients do it a second time, but this time flipping their perspective.

Exercise: Judgment List

As you read these statements, fill in the blanks with any judgments that may come to your mind. These could be judgments you make about yourself or that you hear from other people. The italicized answers below the questions are to help start your thoughts, but feel free to write whatever answers fit for you. Fill in the blanks with short answers or write longer responses if you like.

If I sought out pleasure it would mean _____.
(I am selfish. I am greedy. I am slutty.)

If I sought out pleasure _____ would be disappointed in me.

If I enjoy sex _____.
(Sex might take over. I would make bad decisions. My family wouldn't respect me.)

If I am a sexual person I cannot be a _____ person.
(smart, good, happy)

If my partner(s) saw me experience sexual pleasure they would _____.
(think I look funny, lose respect for me)

If I had a overwhelming feeling of pleasure in my body, like an orgasm,
I might _____.
(make an ugly face, move in an odd way)

_____ is too many sexual partners.

If I prioritize pleasure it would mean I would not be able to prioritize
_____.
(my sobriety, being a parent, getting work done)

If _____ found out about my sexual thoughts/
activities, they would be upset or disappointed in me.
(my family, my church, my peers)

If I were to pursue sex or pleasure I might be kicked out of or in trouble
with _____.
(my culture, my religion, my friends)

Exercise: Approval List

As you read these statements, fill in the blanks with any positive statements that may come to your mind. These could be thoughts you have about yourself, you wish you had about yourself or that you would like to hear from other people. The italicized answers below the questions are to help start your thoughts but feel free to write whatever answers fit for you. Fill in the blanks with short answers or write longer responses if you like.

If I sought out pleasure it would mean _____.
                        (I take good care of myself. I love my body. I value my happiness)

If I sought out pleasure _____ would be excited for me.

If I enjoy sex _____.
(I might be happier. My relationships might improve. I might know more about my body.)

If I am a sexual person I can absolutely be a _____ person.
                                 (smart, good, happy)

If my partner(s) saw me experience sexual pleasure they would think
_____.
  (I am beautiful. I am sexy. I am powerful.)

If I have had sexual experiences, some positive or important things I have learned from these are _____.

If I had a overwhelming feeling of pleasure in my body, like an orgasm, I might _____.
     (feel really great, get rid of some stress, feel relaxed and closer to my partner)

If I prioritize pleasure it would mean I would be better able to prioritize
_____.

(my well-being, time for myself, my other responsibilities because I would have more energy)

If _____ found out I was happy with my sex life, they would be excited for me.
  (my friends, my partner[s])

If I were to pursue sex or pleasure I might build new relationships with
_____.

  (my partner[s], local community or education groups)

Discussing these lists afterward can help advance the conversation about guilt or shame around sexual pleasure. Which list was easier for your students or clients to fill out? What was it like to imagine people approving of prioritizing sexual pleasure and happiness? Regarding the judgments they describe, are these things that have already happened or just guesses of how they feel people would respond? Is there any chance the people they fear judgment from would respond with approval, or even in a neutral way? What holds more sway for them, judgment or approval? This conversation could go in many directions and all of them can bring important realizations.

This exercise is great to do with couples, but you may get more honest answers if they do it separately, at least at first. Once each client has processed it on their own they may feel more ready to share their answers with their partner(s).

Normalizing Sexual Pleasure

It is a positive and normal instinct to seek pleasure. When we as professionals make this statement, we provide a viewpoint that is different from the guilt and shame purveyors in our students' and clients' lives. What clients and students often end up seeking is someone to tell them: "Yes, you are normal. Your struggles are common to other people's struggles. Your wants, needs, and desires are similar to what other folks are looking for." Many times, if clients can let go of the worry that they are "wrong" or "weird" through normalization, they see an improvement in their sexual function as well. Normalization is one of the easiest and most universal skills a sexual health professional can utilize. It can also be one of the most valuable and impactful. Isn't it wonderful when that happens?

One way to normalize the desire for pleasure is to point out that even babies value pleasure. I might say, "Babies are born seeking pleasure, whether from the comfort of being held, the good feeling of drinking milk, or the contented feeling of being warm and dry. When babies fall out of feeling good, because they need a diaper change, they are hungry, or they want a person to soothe them, they protest . . . loudly. As much as this seems annoying when you can't get a crying baby to calm down, it is a good instinct on the baby's part because it helps their caregivers keep them safe, healthy, and happy. Sometime between babyhood and adulthood we start to think that pleasure seeking is unhealthy or selfish. Pleasure as an adult has many of the same positive aims as when we knew we needed to feel better as kids. Sexual pleasure can be a way to seek connection with our important people, comfort or soothe ourselves, and feel good in our bodies again. It can be a really great way to take care of ourselves mentally, emotionally, and physically."

Lindsey Says

Young people are totally bombarded by talk of the "risks" of sex. I visit hundreds of different classrooms each year and witness the way that many teachers introduce sex education. Students are usually warned about physical and emotional pain, regret, unplanned pregnancy, STIs, and ruined reputations. Teens are told they are too young to be thinking of sex right now, that they are making "wrong decisions," that someone who wants to have sex with them is probably just using them, that their parents would be angry at them, and when the sex is over they will feel discarded and ashamed. It is a pretty grim picture overall, and not one that realistically portrays healthy sexual encounters. However, this is a popular approach to sex ed.

One thing I try to work into most sex talks is that sex is supposed to be good. This is not to say that it always feels good, because that isn't always the case. More specifically, what I say is, "People should be able to feel good about what they are doing before, during, and after." Boy, does this get their attention! I further explain: "Ideally, people should not have to feel scared or intimidated at any point. They should get to be comfortable and confident with what they decide to try, and afterwards, enjoy guilt-free feelings of happiness, relaxation, pride, and delight in their bodies. If at any point they are unsure or uncomfortable, they should have the right to express that and think about what changes they would like to make. Overall, healthy sex should be a pretty good experience."

Now, I realize there are a lot of "shoulds" in there. That is typically a word I purposefully avoid, as it is not my place to tell anyone what they should do in bed. In this case, I believe it works, because what I am really saying is that one "should be able to," in that they have the right to, if they so choose. Of course, all of this would rely on consent and open communication.

This part of the conversation—where I tell young people that sex "should" be good—has been really powerful. One particular student, a 16-year-old in a chemical dependency treatment program, stands out in my memory. He was not particularly engaged with class at first, head down on his desk. After hearing my declaration, his head snapped up: "Whoa. Nobody has ever said that to me before. That is amazing. It makes so much sense." Of course, he actively took part in the rest of class.

Normalization for the Not-So-Normal: Healthy Uniqueness

Normal is often overrated, and "getting to normal" should be a goal only if your client states that it is. Using normalization as a tool is not intended to deny or devalue people's uniqueness. However, sometimes it makes all the difference in the world for people to hear the words, "you are not alone." Even for situations that might be a bit more unusual or unique, hearing, "Yes, many other people feel this way too," can go a long way to combat shame. This is why I tend to look for the "normal" in my client's concerns.

For example, if someone comes in concerned that they have a fetish and expressing worry they are "weird," I can say, "If the Internet has taught us anything, it has taught us that people are into lots of different things." Even if their fetish is a bit unique, they may benefit from knowing that the experience of having a fetish is one that many people share. This is one way I try to help people view themselves through the lens of healthy uniqueness rather than isolation or pathology. This approach can also help encourage people to seek out communities of like-minded people. Having community is a great way to combat guilt and shame.

Legitimizing Sexual Pleasure

Many people feel guilty about prioritizing sexual pleasure in their lives. However, the positive effects of pleasure in the body, on relationships, and on health outcomes (as discussed in the first section of this book) are great evidence that pleasure is a legitimate thing to prioritize. Often, when clients and students see the positive benefits to their health and relationships, they feel less guilty about cultivating more pleasure and less shameful for wanting sexual pleasure.

Teaching about the positive effects of masturbation is a powerful way to legitimize pleasure. Often, masturbation is sexual pleasure that is specifically self-centered, meaning it is not sought for the enjoyment of or to satisfy the desire of anyone but the person engaging in it. It is self-directed rather than other-directed. As people see improvements in their self-esteem and way they feel about their bodies because they have positive, guilt-free experiences of masturbation, they may begin to legitimize sexual pleasure just because it feels good.

When masturbation is portrayed as a selfish act, we miss the reasons it can be important, not only to the self but also to relationships. People who enjoy masturbation are more likely to be able to convey information about their likes and dislikes to a partner. Each person in a relationship needs to be able to take responsibility for their own pleasure (through masturbation and communicating needs/wants to partners). When one person in a relationship is struggling to have partner sex due to trauma, pain, or body issues, they often want their partner to masturbate. Some of my clients in this situation have said, "It is a lot of pressure to be responsible for all the sex in this relationship and that is how I feel when you don't masturbate." If one partner can self-pleasure while the other is working on the issues coming up for them, this often provides more space to heal. Sex then retains the future possibility of being a fun, exciting opportunity to connect with their partner rather than a responsibility they can't uphold or some way that they are failing the relationship.

Many people consider the desire for sexual pleasure legitimate in others while simultaneously feeling guilty for their own desire. Clients will often tell me they understand that their partner wants pleasurable sex even if they do not. Often, they even value this trait in their partner(s) and name it as part of what attracted them in the first place. In this case it can be helpful to explore why it is legitimate for their partner(s) to want pleasure but not legitimate for them to want the same. Seeing their own desire as similar to their loved ones' can help them question any guilt or shame they may have.

Of course, there are also clients who do not value their partner's desire for pleasure and instead find it threatening, immoral, or "gross." For these clients, exploring the Judgment List exercise may be helpful for understanding where their negative feelings are coming from. Normalizing and legitimizing their partner's desire for sexual pleasure, while also discussing their concerns, can help to begin the conversation of how to find a solution that works for both of them.

One way to help legitimize sexual pleasure seeking is to seek out a sexual pleasure role model. Finding examples of historical figures; TV program, book, or movie characters; or other people whom students or clients identify with can help clarify goals as well as dispel guilt or shame for what they want.

Box 7.2   Exercise: Find a Sexual Pleasure Role Model

Find your sexual pleasure role model. Who do you admire? Who personifies your goals for sexual pleasure in your own life? Obviously, you may not know what kinds of sex your sexual role models are really having, and you don't have to. Pick your role model based on the traits they have that you would like to have more of in your sexual life (bravery, daring, sense of humor, confidence). If you want to have fun instead of feeling intimidated about sex, pick a famous adventurer who always seems to be having fun in the face of danger. If you want to be able to be more emotionally connected to partners, pick someone famous for their big heart.

You may want more than one sexual role model. Different people may represent different aspects of your sexual self. The most important thing to remember that is you are looking for people or characters who inspire you and embody your goals and values.

Depending on Your Goals, You Might Ask

Who has managed to seek sexual pleasure without becoming greedy?
Who has managed big desires without hurting themselves or others?
Who has been bold and fearless in their sexuality?
Who demonstrates that sexual pleasure (or pleasure in general) is a good way to take care of themselves?
Who is good at advocating for their needs?
Who embodies freedom to pursue pleasure?
Who has done a great job of being good to their partner(s) while seeking sexual pleasure?
Who do you perceive as sexy in the way you would like to be seen by others?

Places to Look for Inspiration

Sexual history makers: People known for changing the way we think about sex, our bodies, or pleasure
Musicians, actors, performers
Characters in movies or books
Activists in sexual communities that you identify with
Historical figures you find inspiring

Clients and students can do this exercise in many ways. They may just answer the questions listed and come up with a few ideas. Some people may want to write down who they picked and their reasons why. Some might want to make collages or art about their sexual role models.

When Pleasure Has Had Negative Consequences

A major source of guilt or shame can be when sexual pleasure has been linked with past difficulties, regrets, consequences, or negative repercussions. When people have lost relationships due to infidelity, struggled with out-of-control sexual behavior, or been convicted of a sexual offense, it can be very difficult to see sexual pleasure as anything other than dangerous or regretful. However, while students or clients may need to change their behavior or act within new limits, this does not mean they should avoid sexual pleasure completely. In fact, while complete avoidance of sex and or pleasure provides no skills for managing risk of reoffense or guidance about pro-social sexual expression, careful exploration of sexual pleasure as a positive and protective force can provide a blueprint for channeling desires into consensual and legal behavior (Williams, Thomas, & Prior, 2015).

Sexual health professionals can normalize the experience of "too much of a good thing" for clients and students if we compare sexual pleasure to eating too much of something we enjoy, exercising too much, or sleeping too much. All of these are examples of things that can be healthy for the body and that feel good when they are in balance. However, doing too much of them can cause problems. However, if we tried to cut eating, exercising, or sleeping out of our lives entirely we would end up with other serious problems. How can the client or student factor sexual pleasure into their lives in ways that will maximize the benefits and avoid the negative outcomes? How did the previous issues occur? Can the client see ways to be sexual that could be different or avoid those pitfalls?

As your students or clients begin to define their idea of healthy, positive pleasure in their lives it can be helpful to contrast this with past actions they do not want to repeat. Setting pleasure goals that are different in focus and intent then past actions can help steer away from shame. Pointing out the ways in which their current goals could have a positive effect on their lives and partner(s) lives can counteract guilt that may come up around sexual pleasure seeking.

I was working with a longtime couple who had come to therapy to increase their connection and restart their sex life, which had been tapering off over the years. The tipping point that brought them into therapy was when Jon overspent on Internet porn, and Debbie noticed this on their credit card bill. Debbie had mixed feelings about porn to begin with and was very upset that Jon was not only watching a lot of it, but spending too much money and keeping it a secret. Jon's sense of shame and guilt came up frequently as we worked to improve their connection and sex life.

One session Jon came in solo and told me he had been thinking about buying a sex toy for Debbie as a present. He was excited about the idea of getting her a toy and really wanted them to use it together: "We're trying to get our sex life going, right? That's why we are here. So she'll appreciate it, right?" However, he was feeling guilty about the idea of buying something sexual and he wondered if it would remind Debbie of his troubles with overspending on porn.

I encouraged Jon to think about how buying this sex toy lined up with his new goals around what healthy sexual pleasure looked like for him. We brought out his specific goals that he had set and also shared with Debbie, which included the following:

1. My fantasy life is my own and it is OK for that to be private.
2. I want to share more of my sexuality with Debbie through greater honesty and inviting her to be more involved in the things I like.
3. I do not have to feel guilty for my interest in sex.
4. I will not spend more than $40 on sexual materials without checking in with Debbie first.

So I asked Jon, "How does your plan to buy this sex toy fit with your goals?" Jon pointed out that buying the toy for Debbie could fit with his goal of sharing more of his sexuality with her. I agreed but asked him, "If this is a present, is it really a present for Debbie or is it more of a present for you?" Jon laughingly agreed it was more of a present for him and he wasn't really sure if Debbie would like it. I pointed out the toy he was thinking about would likely be over the agreed-upon $40 budget. I suggested he might talk to Debbie next session about his wish to get her the toy and see how she felt about it. Jon said, "I'm afraid she is going to be upset or just not want to try it at all." As we talked through his concerns it became apparent he was avoiding talking with Debbie because he didn't want to feel ashamed about wanting to use the toy or embarrassed about the toy he had chosen. So we discussed goal number three, "I do not have to feel guilty for my interest in sex." I asked Jon if he would be able to hold firm inside himself on this goal even if Debbie reacted in a way that felt shaming. Jon wasn't sure but felt better reminding himself that he did not need to feel guilty just for wanting to be sexual with Debbie or being intrigued by a sex toy.

The conversation between Jon and Debbie had mixed results. Debbie was embarrassed when Jon brought up the toy and, at first, she did respond in a way that felt shaming to Jon. However, when I pointed out how Jon had made a good effort to stick to his goals and present this toy as a way for them to connect sexually together, Debbie softened a bit. Praising Jon's current behavior of openness, honesty, and vulnerability as contrasted with his past behaviors of secrecy and closing off sexually helped Jon to combat the shame and guilt he could have so easily fallen into. A few weeks later I heard from the couple. They had not bought the sex toy that Jon had picked out. Instead, they had gone shopping together and picked out a toy they both were interested in. They both felt good about this compromise. Jon and Debbie likely would not have had that positive experience together if Jon had held himself back from having the conversation due to guilt about past behavior or shame about the toy he suggested.

When the Risks Are Greater

In the earlier couple, the risks around sexual pleasure seeking were relatively low. Overspending had occurred, but not enough that it caused significant financial damage. The couple was not on the brink of a breakup over these issues. With some clients or students, the risks may be greater. Sober clients may risk relapse if they seek sexual pleasure in the same ways they did while using. Students or clients may risk losing relationships, repercussions in their professional life, or being outed if they pursue pleasure with abandon. There may be times when you are working with people who have significant limits put on them, such as conditions of probation or in the context of a set treatment program. For people who must function within very strict limits of behavior, shame and guilt are very important issues to explore. No matter what boundaries your students or clients need to maintain, unprocessed feelings of shame and guilt around sex are not helpful.

When working with people who have a history that indicates higher risk associated with seeking pleasure, it is important to go slowly and encourage as much safety as reasonably possible. Safety planning—creating a plan that helps clients and students identify warning signs that might indicate they are headed toward behavior that will have negative consequences—can be helpful. Safety plans can include whom they can contact for help or support, and what they can do if they find that they need to get out of a situation. Safety plans should be specific to each client's or student's individual needs. Here is a guide to creating a safety plan that I use with clients in therapy and as a handout in classes.

Box 7.3   Exercise: Sexual Safety Map

Get a big piece of paper and separate it into four sections; X Marks the Spot, Maybes, Triggers, and Danger Zone. Add a drawing of a compass and instead of "North, South, East, West," write "People, Situations, Behaviors, and Goals." As you add to each section of the map, use the compass as a reminder to include examples of people, situations, behaviors, and goals as appropriate.

X Marks the Spot

These are sexy behaviors, sexual goals, dreams, or values, anything you can think of that is part of your healthy sexuality that holds little to no risk for you and are likely to have positive effects on your life.

Examples may include:

Orgasms/pleasure
Feeling safe with partners
Your safer sex rules
Sexual behaviors you love

Maybes

These are behaviors or fantasies you might like to try someday. These may be situations or behaviors you enjoy only sometimes. You might not know how you feel about the things you put in your "maybe" category. It is OK to still be figuring that out. "Maybes" could be great topics of discussion with a therapist, counselor, or your trusted support system in order to figure out whether they support your healthy sexuality goals.

Examples may include:

Sexual acts you might want to try
Fantasies you are not sure if you want to act out
Things that have gone well in the past sometimes, and have not gone well
    at other times

Triggers

These are people/places/behaviors/situations/sensory experiences that may trigger anxiety, intense emotions, memories of past traumatic incidences, or use of substances.

Examples might include

Feeling intimidated
Alcohol or chemicals present in the situation
People you have had a negative sexual relationship with in the past
Certain smells, sounds, or situations that have negative associations from the past

Danger Zone

These are people/places/behaviors you know are not a part of your healthy sexuality: They may be bad for you or perhaps you dislike them. They might be opposed to your goals or values. They might have caused trouble in your past. These can also include warning signs that you are on a risky path, such as finding yourself suddenly being dishonest or keeping secrets from trusted loved ones.

Examples might include:

Noticing you are starting to omit information from what you share with your therapist, counselors, or trusted support circle
Unsafe sex
Sexual behaviors you don't enjoy

Sexual Safety Plan

Using the factors you identified in the Triggers and Danger Zone sections, create a sexual safety plan about what to do when you notice you are triggered or are in a dangerous situation.

Safety plans sometimes include:

Ways to calm your body down or de-escalate yourself when triggered
People you can call in a dangerous situation to pick you up
Friends or professionals you can talk with if you are unsure whether you are making plans that may be triggering or unsafe for you
Carrying safer sex supplies with you at all times

Encouraging Further Exploration and Processing

While starting the conversation about guilt and shame is incredibly valuable, these are issues that are likely to come up more than once in people's lives. Clients and students may have further realizations down the line that shame or guilt is showing up again, perhaps in a slightly different form or situation. It can be helpful for students and clients to hear that they can continue to process these issues as time goes on. Encouraging the people you are working with to keep examining these issues beyond a class or outside of therapy can empower them to engage in this important ongoing process.

Reference

Williams, D. J., Thomas, J. N., & Prior, E. E. (2015). Moving full-speed ahead in the wrong direction? A critical examination of US sex-offender policy from a positive sexuality model. *Critical Criminology, 23*(3), 277–294.

Chapter 8

Lube Changes Lives

What Every Sexual Health Professional Needs to Know About Lubrication

Sexual lubrication changes people's experiences of sex in important ways. Using lube makes a variety of activities wetter, slipperier, sexier, safer, and much more pleasurable. Lubrication can increase pleasure during hand sex on any type of genitals. It can help with unwanted friction or chafing during vaginal or anal penetration. Lube makes a wide range of anal play possible as the anus and rectum do not produce their own lubrication. While the vagina and vulva do produce lubrication, they may not produce enough for comfortable and pleasurable sex play. There are many factors influencing vaginal lubrication, and sometimes vaginas and vulvas do not get wet even when a person is aroused. Lube can be fantastic during masturbation. It makes sex toys more fun. It is helpful for dryness or chafing not just during sex play but also in day-to-day life. Lube helps to make sex safer by preventing condoms, dental dams, and gloves from breaking.

Sexual lubrication is a tremendous tool for students and clients experiencing pain during sex. I have worked with clients who have 10-, 15-, or 20-year histories of vaginal pain during penetration that have had their pain disappear through use of the right lube. This seemed miraculous to my clients, and I shared in their excitement that sex didn't hurt anymore. However, it made me incredibly sad that they had suffered through years of pain, frustration, and conflict with partners when there was such a simple, easy, affordable intervention available to them. Of course, some people's pain issues are not resolved so easily, but for many students and clients, learning about lube significantly increases sexual pleasure and possibilities. Lube changes lives.

Sexual health professionals need to know the ins and outs of sexual lubricant to be better able to answer student and client questions, as well as help them avoid possible hazards (breaking latex barriers by using oil based lubes, or choosing lubricants that are irritating to their bodies). Sixty-five percent of women and 70% of men report having used lubricant at some point in their life, and 20% of women and 25% of men say they have used a lubricant within the past 30 days (Herbenick, Reece, Schick, Sanders, & Fortenberry, 2014; Reece, Herbenick, Schick, Sanders, & Fortenberry, 2014). Ninety percent of gay and bisexual men report using lube in their lifetime (Dodge et al., 2014) and 21.9% of lesbian and bisexual women reported they had used lube in their last sexual encounter with a female partner (Schick et al., 2015). These statistics indicate that no matter who you might work with, they likely have questions about lubrication.

All the populations mentioned stated they used lubricant in order to increase pleasure or comfort in their sexual activities (Dodge et al., 2014; Schick et al., 2015) and lube was associated with significantly higher reports of sexual pleasure and satisfaction for women (Herbenick et al., 2011). It is exciting that so many people are using lubricant to increase pleasure, but how much better might their experience become with some education on the pros and cons of the different types of lubricant available? Sexual health professionals are in a perfect position to spread the word about lubrication, but often have received no training on what lubrication is, the strengths and drawbacks of each kind, and how they work with people's bodies. Many of the current concerns about lube's interaction with the body (hyper or hypo-osmotic lubricant causing damage to the epithelial walls, body sensitivity to various ingredients, whether plant-based oils encourage bacterial growth) are just beginning to be explored and understood. This chapter will bring you up-to-date with the most cutting-edge knowledge and research that may be revolutionary in understanding lube, so you can educate your students and clients.

Lube Off the Beatin' Path

As wonderful and important as sexual lubricant is, not all lubes are created equal. Teaching about lube is not as simple as recommending your students and clients go to their corner store and pick some up, as the most easily found brands are often the worst for your body. Most lubricants found at drug stores, big box stores, and sometimes even the doctor's office, are made with irritating ingredients like glycerin and sugars, and are not created with the mucous membranes of the body in mind. These products can create more problems than pleasure. The best places I know of to buy lubricant are education-based sex toy stores that have whole displays devoted to lubricants. Often, they have tester bottles so people can put the lube on their hands and see if they like the feel, smell, and taste.

The people you work with may have had bad experiences with lube in the past. They may have noticed irritation, burning, itchiness, or maybe it was just sticky or unpleasant to use. It is helpful to let them know that finding the right lube for their body is likely to result in a very different experience. While it may take a little time and research for students and clients to understand what kinds of lube work best for their needs and where to find high quality, nonirritating brands, once they do, their sex lives are likely to be changed for the better, forever.

Silicone, Water, Oil, and Hybrid Lubes

There are three main types of sexual lubricants: silicone, water, and oil-based. There are also "hybrid" lubes that combine water and silicone. All the types have advantages, disadvantages, activities they are especially good for, and possible concerns when using them. Table 8.1 lists the basics of each.

Silicone-Based Lube

Pros: Silicone lube does not dry up, so it stays slick for a very long time. This makes it a great choice for handjobs or masturbation with a penis, as other lubes can get sticky during these high friction activities. Silicone lube can be great for use as a hypoallergenic massage "oil," and then users can transition to sexual play without having to wash their hands (as can be a good idea when using oil-based lubes; see

Table 8.1 Types of Lubricants and Their Properties

Lube Type	Ingredients Will List:	Is Super Great At:	Possible Concerns	Can I Use It With Silicone Sex Toys?	Can I Use It With Latex/ Polyisoprene Safer Sex Supplies?	Possible Concerns About pH and Osmolality?
Silicone	Dimethicone, dimethiconol, other ingredients that end in "cone"	Staying slippery for a long time. Very few people have sensitivities to silicone lube.	May bond with the surface of a silicone toy and ruin it	Maybe, but it could also ruin your toy. Do a spot test.	Yes	No
Water	Water is very likely to be one of the first two ingredients.	It will never ruin, degrade, or break anything.	People may have a reaction to ingredients, pH, or osmolality issues.	Yes	Yes	Yes
Oil	Coconut oil, other plant based oils, shea butter. Note: Petroleum-based or other non-plant based oils may be problematic when used inside the body and should be avoided when possible.	Outside-the-body stimulation, activities that don't involve latex or polyisoprene safer sex supplies.	Can degrade latex and polyisoprene safer sex supplies; not enough studies to know whether it could promote bacterial infections when used internally.	Yes	No	No
Hybrid	Water, and types of silicone (dimethicone, dimethiconol, or usually end in "cone")	Very smooth and slippery, lasts for a long time.	Could have irritating ingredients (as in water-base lube); could possibly stick to silicone sex toys	Maybe, but it could also ruin your toy. Do a spot test.	Yes	Yes

the Oil-Based Lube section). Silicone is safe for use with all safer sex supplies (condoms, FC2, dental dams, gloves), any body part, and is great for use in the shower or bath as it doesn't immediately wash away. You might want to have some sticky ducks on the floor of your tub, though, because it is super slippery and you might fall and hurt yourself! Silicone leaves a light silky feeling on the skin. While it does not add moisture, it can provide a somewhat protective barrier to the skin that helps to seal in the moisture of the body. Many people in menopause who experience dryness or chafing will find that applying silicone lube to their vulva in the morning helps them avoid soreness that can occur from regular daily movement. Athletes use it on various body parts to avoid chafing.

Some people wonder about the safety of a synthetic, but evidence indicates that silicone does not absorb into the skin in any significant way, is not irritating, and people are not likely to develop sensitivities to it (Johnson et al., 2011; Nair, 2002). In the meantime, it protects the surface of the skin from irritation from sexual friction and leaves your cells undamaged. Silicone does not encourage the growth of bacteria or yeast, and so it is a great choice for people who frequently get bacterial vaginosis, UTIs, or yeast infections. While more research is needed, it currently appears to be the safest lube for those who have multiple sex partners or are otherwise at risk of STIs, specifically HIV and herpes, as it does not cause any cell damage that could increase risk of transmission (Fuchs et al., 2007; Gorbach et al., 2012; Nicole, 2014).

Cons: The main downside to silicone lube is that it can stick to silicone sex toys and ruin the surface of the toy. Liquid silicone molecules sometimes bond with solid silicone molecules: If this happens, a toy's surface will be sticky forever. The situation becomes more complex as only certain kinds of silicone bond with other certain kinds of silicone, and so this won't happen with every silicone lube and every silicone toy. However, it is very disappointing (and expensive) when it does happen. If students or clients want to use silicone lube with a silicone toy, they can conduct a spot test with a small amount of lube on a part of the toy that is not likely to touch the body (the underside or base might be good spots). If it gets sticky and won't wash away, you know that this a toy and lube cannot be used together. Silicone lube can stain sheets or clothes, but generally these marks come out easily by adding a little white vinegar in with your laundry soap.

Another possible drawback of silicone is that some people don't like the way it lingers on the skin. However, some people love it precisely for that feature. People like all kinds of different things when it comes to lube, and the best way to discover what their preferences are is for them to try a few different kinds.

Water-Based Lube

Pros: Water-based lube is safe for any sex toy and all safer sex supplies. It is very slippery at first and when it starts to dry up on the skin it can be reactivated with a little water or saliva. Water-based lube is a great all-around lube for anyone whose sexual activities are not putting them at risk for STI transmission.

Cons: When the water in the lube begins to absorb into the body and evaporate off of the skin, what is left behind can feel pretty sticky. Silicone- and oil-based lubes tend to stay slick longer than water-based lubes. Water-based lubes tend to have the most ingredients and additives. Because of this, the vast majority of water-based lubes on the market contain ingredients that can be irritating or contribute to yeast infections (Nicole, 2014). Water-based lubes have both pH and osmolality. When their pH and/or osmolality are not formulated well for bodies, users may encounter problems such as irritation to mucous membranes, damage to sperm, and increasing the risk of transmitting or contracting certain STIs. People whose activities place them at higher risk for STI transmission, people who experience pain or sensitivity of their genitals, and people trying to get pregnant might want to consider other kinds of lube or look for specific, nonirritating brands of water-based lube. In-depth information on osmolality, pH, and irritating ingredients is included later in this chapter.

Oil-Based Lube

Pros: Oil-based lubricant has some great properties. It feels creamy and smooth on the skin and can double as a moisturizer. It is great for use on the outside of the body, such as general body massage and stimulation on a penis. Oil is thick and provides a good cushion for penetration, which makes it great for anal play and larger penetration such as fisting (it is important to note that oil does degrade latex and polyisoprene safer sex supplies so this isn't a good choice when using latex gloves, condoms, or dental dams). Many people who do not have frequent bacterial infections choose to use it vaginally and don't notice any adverse effects.

Cons: Oil-based lube has been avoided by many sexual health professionals in the past, because it's downside is that is can degrade, compromise, and break latex and polyisoprene safer sex supplies. This means that oil-based lubes are *not* recommended for anyone who is depending on condoms or other latex/polyisoprene barriers. People have also thought that using oil vaginally could possibly cause bacterial infections since oil could provide bacteria a hospitable environment to grow in. However, coconut oil is antibacterial (DebMandal & Mandal, 2011) and some sources show coconut oil to have significant effects against yeast infections (Ogbolu, Oni, Daini, & Oloko, 2007) and the herpes virus (both 1 and 2) (Lieberman, Enig, & Preuss, 2006). It seems likely there is a difference between plant-based and petroleum-based oils, with plant-based oils (i.e. coconut) being less associated with bacterial vaginosis, and petroleum (i.e. Vaseline, baby oil, mineral oil) being more problematic, but research on this topic is lacking. Existing research doesn't offer much differentiation between different plant-based oils (i.e. avocado oil, shea butter, etc.) though it seems likely they may also have different properties. Oil-based lubes can stain sheets or clothing. Pretreating the stains with dish soap that is formulated to remove grease can usually save your sheets and favorite sexytime outfits, but it is good to be aware of the risk.

Lindsey's oil-based tip:

Someone once told me that they use a mini-ice cube tray to chill little cubes of coconut oil in the refrigerator. When she is ready, she simply pops in a "lube cube" and is ready to go! Another tip is to stick with refined coconut oils in order to avoid the small crystals that are often in the unrefined type—those can hurt!

Hybrids

Pros: Hybrid lubes include both water and silicone in their ingredients. Because of this, the have the feel of a water-based lube (which many people like) and the ability to stay slippery for a very long time, like silicone lubes.

Cons: People love hybrid lubes because they have the benefits of both silicone- and water-based lubes all rolled into one. Unfortunately, they also have all the drawbacks of both silicone- and water-based lubes.

A Note on Safer Sex Supplies

Safer sex supplies may include gloves, oral sex barriers (also known as dams or dental dams), condoms for penises, and the FC2 (sometimes referred to as the female condom, receptive condom, internal condom, or bottom condom). Gloves, condoms for penises, and dams/oral sex barriers are frequently made of latex. However, safer sex supplies such as gloves, condoms for penises, and oral sex barriers also come in other materials such as nitrile, polyisoprene, and polyurethane. The FC2 is made of nitrile. Some condoms are made of lambskin, but these are for pregnancy prevention only, not for use preventing STIs. Oil-based lubes will degrade latex and polyisoprene but work just fine with nitrile and polyurethane products. Between non-latex safer sex products and the wide variety of lubricants available, hopefully no one needs to choose between making their sex safer and enjoying the sex they are having.

The Importance of Reading the Ingredients

Each client and student has different needs that will influence what kind of lubricant is right for them. Many people have allergies. Sensitivities to fragrance are very common (and fragrance isn't a good thing to be putting on the mucus membranes of your genitalia anyway). Glycerin, the second ingredient in many water-based lubes, is a sugar alcohol. I recommend people prone to yeast infections avoid this ingredient because I have heard so many glycerin yeast infection stories from people I have worked with. Some lubes actually include straight-up sugar or honey (to add a sweet taste) but again, any form of sugar is likely to lead to irritation or a yeast infection when used vaginally.

Some water-based lubes may include ingredients that kill the helpful bacteria of the vagina, thus leading to bacterial vaginosis (Dezzutti et al., 2012). Several ingredients common to water-based lubes (including glycerin and propylene glycol) have been found to increase transmission rates of HSV 2 in mice (Moench, Mumper, Hoen, Sun, & Cone, 2010). L-arginine, an ingredient in some lubes and stimulating gels, may increase herpes symptoms (Griffith, DeLong, & Nelson, 1981). Spermicides, though not nearly as prevalent as they used to be, are still used; many people are not aware that they are likely to increase the risk of STI transmission (Wolf, 2012, World Health Organization, 2012). Propylene glycol is a common ingredient in water-based lubes that indicates high osmolality (World Health Organization, 2012).

While all this can sound overwhelming, it doesn't need to be. For one thing, silicone lube is unlikely to have any of the ingredients mentioned here and thus may be a helpful option that avoids the issue of potentially irritating ingredients.

If clients or students are using silicone sex toys or just do not like the feel of silicone lube, helping them gain awareness of lube ingredients and the factors around osmolality (covered in the next section) can greatly benefit their ability to make informed choices.

How will you, the professional, or your clients and students know what is in a lube? By reading the ingredients. A good rule of thumb is to look for lubes with few ingredients. I encourage my students and clients to read the ingredients in every lube they try. Over time they notice patterns, either ingredients they feel they might be sensitive to or ingredients that are in all the lubes they enjoy. I love watching students and clients gain knowledge about what works with their bodies so they can make better informed choices that increase their pleasure.

Osmolality and How Lubes Interact With the Body

Recently, The Smitten Kitten, the sex toy store in Minneapolis, Minnesota, where I got my start as an educator, has compiled some very important research on how the common ingredients in water-based lubrication interact with the body. Sarah Mueller, the sex educator heading up this project, sat down to talk with me about "osmolality." She has a lot to say about this confusing word and what it means for the mucus membranes of our genitals. "Lube is something I've always cared about a lot," Sarah told me. "I'm diabetic and I've always really struggled with finding lubricants that work for me because glycerin is just immediate yeast infection [in my body]."

While working with customers in the store, Sarah realized many of them expressed sensitivity to glycerin and propylene glycol, so she decided to research lube ingredients. She quickly discovered the difficulty of trying to piece together information from studies that never tested lubricants on human bodies and didn't take into account the various kinds of sexual activities in which lubes are actually used:

> That's been tricky and it's also just been . . . kind of depressing in a lot of ways. I don't think science is asking the right questions and I think it is sad that it doesn't seem like anyone has sexual pleasure in mind when they are designing these studies.

Besides a newfound understanding of the possible irritants in water-based lubes, some of the most important and compelling information Sarah has found regards osmolality. Osmosis is the diffusion of water across a membrane from a region of high concentration of water to one of lower concentration of water (Debnam, 2005). If, like me, you need that explained again, Sarah described it to me this way:

> Osmolality . . . it sounds like it shouldn't be a word. The simplest way to describe osmolality is the concentration of particles dissolved into a solute, or water. So osmolality only applies to water-based lubes. You can't take the osmolality of silicone or oil-based lubes because nothing is dissolved into water.

Sarah pointed out, "every fluid that is water based has an osmolality, so that [also] applies to the fluids of your mucus membrane." Remember, the mucus membrane we are talking about here can refer to the inside of the vagina, rectum, urethra, and some parts of the vulva. Sarah explained:

> The cells of your body want to maintain a level of homeostasis when it comes to their osmolality. Water can flow freely in and out of the cell wall of mucus membranes, and because that happens your cells are always trying to maintain osmotic pressure so the inside of the cell and the outside of the cell have an equal amount of water pressure pressing up against the membrane. So when the mucus of the body, say vaginal mucus, comes into contact with a lubricant, if that lubricant has a higher osmolality than the mucus, the mucus is going to push water out of its' cells to try to balance it out. It's essentially going to try to water down the lubricant and then the mucus cells become dehydrated.

I was able to relate to this through the example of using contact lenses: You need saline solution because regular water will dry out your eyes. While this is not an exact parallel (contact solution is more about the salt-to-water ratio than osmolality) it is one I have started using when I have only 30 seconds to explain this complex topic for students and clients. Sarah continued, "If the osmolality of the lubricant is so high that they become totally dehydrated, then those cells die."

.While cell death sounds extreme, our cells are dying all the time. So what actually happens to genitals when these cells die due to lubricant with high osmolality?

> It basically turns the mucus that is already on your skin into a stickier substance. Then it dehydrates the skin cells of the epithelial layer, the outermost layer of skin on the mucus membrane, and those die and slough off. Those cells die and slough off all the time, just like any other skin cells do, but with this rapid dehydration and cell death, *sheets* of epithelial cells come off. It's not something you could see with your eyes, but in the research I have found when they look through a microscope they say, "this is concerning and extraordinary." Several studies have found that hyperosmolar lubricants cause epithelial damage (Begay et al., 2011; Dezzutti, 2012; Fuchs et al., 2007).

When Sarah told me this I thought of my clients who experience pain during penetration. It seems to me that the last thing they need is mucus that is stickier, causing more friction, or significant cell loss that may cause extra sensitivity. My second thought was that the rectum is more delicate than the interior of the vagina, and the osmolality of lube used anally might make a big difference in the safety and comfort of anal play. In fact, this is true, as researchers have found epithelial sloughing in the rectum due to the use of hyperosmolar products (Begay et al., 2011). Sarah pointed out something I hadn't even considered: increased risk of STI transmission. This is what the majority of the research is investigating and studies seem to show:

> [Epithelial sloughing] leaves the mucus membrane more vulnerable because it doesn't have that protective layer of skin. [The cell death] also increases the autoimmune response cells and makes them more available to whatever other fluids are there, meaning retroviruses have more target cells available to infect.
> (Fernández-Romero, Teleshova, Zydowsky, & Robbiani, 2015)

It seems we are just beginning to understand the implications of how the osmolality of lube interacts with the body. Research that directly focuses on the realities of how lube is used for various forms of sex in the human body is in short supply. However, even at this early stage the information appears to have significant implications. For people using water-based lube who do not experience discomfort and are not at risk for STI transmission, this information may not be as important. One study suggests the epithelial lining could be back to normal within 8 hours (Phillips, Taylor, Zacharopoulos, & Maguire, 2000).

However, for people experiencing compounding issues, this information could be quite important. For example, people at risk for STI transmission, people who have thinning of mucous membranes such as postmenopausal people or people going through chemotherapy, and sex workers (or anyone else) who may be applying lube several times a day, are some of the groups who may be at greater risk for adverse effects. As many people use hyperosmolar water-based lube frequently without experiencing pain or discomfort, I have to guess that cell death and damage to the epithelial layer of skin is not always something that people can feel. Whether people who already experience sexual pain or discomfort find their symptoms increase when using hyperosmolar water-based lube is not something that I could find evidence about—but, in my opinion, it doesn't seem worth the risk when there are other good lube options available.

The way sexual health professionals talk and teach about lubrication needs to take into account these new emerging factors. One way to do so may be to recommend silicone lube for clients or students who need a lubricant for frequent use or who are at higher risk for STI transmission, as silicone lube has been found to be safest in these areas. There are also some water-based lubricants that are iso-osmolar—close enough to the osmolality of the mucus membranes that they do not cause cell damage (Dezzutti et al., 2012). Some of these include Aloe Cadabra, Good Clean Love, Sliquid, and Yes water-based lubes.

Currently, it is difficult to know the osmolality of lubes. This is not information you will find listed on the bottle. A 2012 study from the World Health Organization lists the osmolality of some lubricants—and luckily, much of Sarah's research is available online at www.badvibes.org, a consumer advocacy website run by The Smitten Kitten, designed to help people make informed decisions when purchasing sex toys and lube.

Conception-Friendly Lube

When people are trying to become pregnant, they often do not even think about the lube they are using. Unfortunately, the lube that may be fabulous for increasing pleasure in sex may also be decreasing their chances of pregnancy. There are two main factors in determining whether a lubricant is conception friendly: pH level and osmolality.

Lubricants that are off in pH and osmolality are likely to decrease sperm motility and damage the sperm itself (Agarwal, Deepinder, Cocuzza, Short, & Evenson, 2008). One difficulty is that vaginas and sperm prefer different pH levels. So lubes with a pH that is closer to vaginal levels (3.8 to 4.5) may not be sperm friendly. Lubes that have a pH closer to sperm's preferred levels (7.1 to 8.0) may be irritating to the vagina. Choosing a lube that is formulated to be sperm friendly in pH and osmolality, and that does not use ingredients that may interfere with sperm motility, can help (or at least not hinder) conception. Yes Baby and Pre-Seed are two conception-friendly lubricants.

Lube and Safer Sex/Pregnancy Prevention

As mentioned earlier, lubes that are hypo- or hyperosmolar or that use irritating ingredients can increase the chances of contracting STIs such as Herpes Simplex Virus (HSV), Chlamydia, and HIV (Begay et al., 2011; Cone et al., 2006). At this point, studies seem to indicate that silicone-based lubricants and iso-osmolar water based lubricants are the safest choices to avoid cell death that could lead to increased risk of STI transmission, yeast, or bacterial infections (Nicole, 2014; Dezzutti et al., 2012; Sudol & Phillips, 2004).

While the information about osmolality may make it seem like lube is risky in terms of STI transmission, lube actually helps to prevent STI transmission as it decreases the likelihood that condoms, dental dams, and gloves will break from friction (World Health Organization, 2012). Lube also makes using condoms and other barriers much more enjoyable, and pleasure is a big factor in getting people to actually use condoms and other barriers. In fact, it may be the biggest factor. In a nationally representative sample of 2,328 heterosexually active, unmarried 15- to 24-year-old young adults, pleasure-related attitudes had stronger associations with lack of condom use than all other variables. Young women who said condoms were almost certain to reduce pleasure were 8.7 times as likely to not use a condom and young men were 9.1 times as likely not to use a condom (Higgins & Wang, 2015).

Teaching and Talking About Lube for Safety and Pleasure

Lindsey Says

When talking about condoms, gloves, and dental dams, I always need to have a bottle of lube in my bag of props! Obviously, the first complaint most people give about condoms is that sex feels better without them. It is absolutely critical that we sex educators help people understand how to make latex feel great so that it is welcome in the bedroom. When I am teaching about condoms, it may sound a little like this:

"What is this slippery stuff all over the condom called? Lube, or lubrication. Yep, you want lots of lube on a condom. My motto is "The Wetter the Better!" (Everyone laughs, which is perfect. We are all getting comfortable.) Dry latex rubbing against your sensitive skin can feel a little irritating and reduce the amount of sensation you want to be getting, as well as add to friction that might make the condom pop. Here is a pleasure tip: Unroll the condom an inch or so and squirt some lube right into the tip of the condom, or on the tip of the penis. Then squeeze out any remaining air and roll this right down over the shaft of the penis. What you should see is a snugly fitting condom (you don't want lube all over the shaft!) with an inch or two of loose latex filled with lube, but no air bubble, hanging down past the tip of the penis. This gives the head of the penis lots of nice slippery room to move around, and this helps give you much more feeling!"

I can easily use my thumb and forefinger to show how well the condom can slide around the tip of the wooden penis model, and am very casual with the lube that inevitably drips off, showing that it isn't icky, but rather kind of fun. If it is water based, I just wipe it on my pants and remark that it won't leave a stain. Silicone is better wiped off on a Kleenex than your pants, because it can leave a mark. Sometimes I will just rub it around on my hands and arms, mentioning that it feels silky and it is usually in lotions and soaps, and even rub a little into my hair and note that it tames frizzy fly-aways. This gets a giggle, but I am working to demonstrate my comfort and reduce the eww-factor.

Note that FC2, also known as the female condom/receptive condom/bottom condom, comes with some silicone lube already on it, but it can feel a little on the sticky side. I recommend adding some more, which could be done by applying it to the penis/toy that will be going inside, using fingers, or just putting it in the condom itself at the opening of the vagina/anus and it will travel in on its own when penetration starts to happen.

When demonstrating dental dams, people always ask if you can feel anything at all through them. I ask everyone to stick out their hand, and I place a dry dental dam on it and rub with my finger (or they can rub with their own—whatever seems the most appropriate given the setting). Of course, this doesn't feel great. Then I come around with a bottle of lube and give everyone a little squirt. I invite them to rub it around with their finger and just notice how it increases the sensitivity on their skin, and then I come by with the dental dam again and put it on their now-slippery palm. Rubbing this now slippery dental dam illustrates without a doubt that feeling goes through them! The crowd is convinced, and suddenly enthusiastic about lube! I will usually say "Of course, this will probably feel different than if there were no dental dam at all. But it should still feel really awesome!"

I also have a fun activity that I love doing with gloves and lube. Everyone puts a latex or nitrile glove on their hand, dry, and then shakes hands with a similarly gloved partner. It feels dry and a little weird. Then we put lube on the palms and fingers of the gloves, and it feels much, much better. People start smiling and recognizing how useful lube would be in their bedrooms. Next, we take the gloves off, put lube on our hands, and then put the gloves back on, and again shake. The gloves are slippery inside and out, and they feel great. Now people are laughing, enjoying the experiment, and definitely interested in trying lube next time they have sex.

Another fun activity is to have people roll condoms over their hands, so it looks like they have little flippers. Put some silicone lube into one of their palms and then have them rub their hands together vigorously. This can go on for many minutes. Repeat with a little baby oil, and the condoms typically pop almost immediately!

I try to normalize lube as much as possible to combat the assumption that it is something you only need if there is something wrong with you. I will mention that having lube on hand takes some of the pressure off of a person who might be concerned about whether or not they are going to get "wet enough" on their own, that even if you do get wet, you might want to add more after you have been going for a while, and sometimes you just don't have time to wait for your body to lubricate on its own. Lube is on-demand "Awesome Sauce," ready to go at a moment's notice, and lots of people like to use it for partner sex and even when they are touching their own bodies because it can make the sensitive skin feel great. I sincerely hope that I am helping people find better, healthier stuff to use during masturbation and sex, and that they skip the hand lotion, baby oil, and hair conditioner that are so often irritating and damage not only mucous membrane skin cells, but condoms as well.

When I teach adults about lube, either in a class setting or with clients, I think it is important to have lubricant available for them to touch, taste, and smell. Explaining lube without having some in the room is a bit like teaching a cooking class and trying to explain the ingredients to people who may never have seen, tasted, or touched them before: You can do it, but a lot may get lost in the translation and somebody is probably going to end up frying their chicken in powdered sugar instead of flour. Just like in Lindsey's examples, I find it important to demonstrate the slipperiness of lube on my own hand to it normalize and make lube fun rather than intimidating. For people who have only used lubes that contain glycerin and other ingredients that easily become sticky, lube without these ingredients often feels very different in a way they notice immediately.

I start by passing out paper towels or tissues and I usually joke, "because slippery is good but we don't want to be slippery all day, right?" I follow this with, "I am excited to show you this because lube is amazing. If you have never used it before, prepare to have your mind blown. If you have used it, this is a great opportunity to learn about a few different kinds and get a better idea of what you might like best. Yes, there are different kinds of lube. They are all good for different things. You know that game people play, 'If you were stranded on a desert island and could only take three things with you'? When I play that game I usually try to persuade them to let me take at least five things and all of them are lube. That is how important lube is, in my opinion."

I take out the silicone-based lube. While I give them information about it, I open the bottle: "Now you'll see that I am going to put a little bit on the back of my hand. As you pass the lube around, please feel free to do the same on your hand. Then take the fingers of your other hand and rub back and forth on the lube. See how nice it feels?" (If it is a group, usually there is laughter or small side conversations of participants talking with each other about their impressions of the lube. This is a great sign that people are feeling comfortable.) "Before you wipe your hands off, take a minute to smell and taste the lube. You don't want to be in the middle of a fun sexy situation and suddenly realize you don't like the way your lube tastes or smells, so this is an important thing to check when you are lube shopping."

Then I go through the same process with water, oil, and hybrid lubes. It is great to watch people who were nervous at the start make confident statements by the end about which kind they preferred.

Troubleshooting With Lubrication

There are many situations in which it is important to ask whether the person you are working with is using lube and if so, which kinds. Clients or students who are experiencing pain with penetration may find their pain lessens or goes away completely with lubrication. If they are already using lube but it contains glycerin, irritating ingredients, or is hyperosmolar, they may be creating discomfort instead of helping make sexual play more enjoyable. I have had clients who get repeated yeast or bacterial infections and blame their partner (or their own body), only to later realize it is a reaction to the lube they are using. Many people are sensitive to the lubes that are used in doctors' or gynecologists' offices and may not understand why they keep getting infections after their doctor visits. In this case, they can easily bring their own lube with them to future appointments. Students or clients who think they may have a latex allergy might actually be experiencing chafing due to a lack of lube on their safer sex supplies. With clients who describe their sex lives as "just not going well" but have trouble articulating why, suggesting lube can sometimes make quick improvements in their relationships, self-knowledge, and pleasure. Lubricant is my favorite low-to-no-risk experiment for increasing people's pleasure during sex. It is amazing how many times it makes a huge difference.

Lindsey Says

I was once working with a woman who shared this story: "I hate the lube my husband buys. After using it, my skin itches and I want to run right off to take a shower, and then I always spend the rest of the week with a yeast infection. It makes me not even want to have sex. I don't want to hurt his feelings by turning down the lube, though, because he likes it." This type of discomfort is common, but not something to ignore! Especially since a different lube would likely solve the whole problem. In this situation, I was able to show her some examples of silicone lube, and she really liked it. She agreed that her husband might like this even better. She felt like she could bring it home to him as a "surprise" and he would be excited about it, so she wasn't concerned about hurting his feelings. This simple change was key in changing the frustrating and painful pattern her sex life had taken on. One of my favorite things to say about lube is, "Change your lube, change your life!"

This story is a great example of how sex education, sex therapy, and lubrication information interact. There might be a further communication issue within this couple that could be addressed. Educators and therapists may do this in different ways, depending on what they judge is appropriate and within their scope of practice. However, if we don't have the lubrication information to give to the client, she still ends up itchy and miserable even if she is better able to tell her partner about it. No matter what branch of the field you are in, asking questions and providing information about lubrication is an important part of the job.

References

Agarwal, A., Deepinder, F., Cocuzza, M., Short, R. A., & Evenson, D. P. (2008). Effect of vaginal lubricants on sperm motility and chromatin integrity: A prospective comparative study. *Fertility and Sterility, 89*(2), 375–379.

Begay, O., Jean-Pierre, N., Abraham, C. J., Chudolij, A., Seidor, S., Rodriguez, A., . . . Fernández-Romero, J. A. (2011). Identification of personal lubricants that can cause rectal epithelial cell damage and enhance HIV type 1 replication in vitro. *AIDS Research and Human Retroviruses, 27*(9), 1019–1024.

Cone, R. A., Hoen, T., Wong, X., Abusuwwa, R., Anderson, D. J., & Moench, T. R. (2006). Vaginal microbicides: Detecting toxicities in vivo that paradoxically increase pathogen transmission. *BMC Infectious Diseases, 6*(1), 90.

DebMandal, M., & Mandal, S. (2011). Coconut (Cocos nucifera L.: Arecaceae): In health promotion and disease prevention. *Asian Pacific Journal of Tropical Medicine, 4*(3), 241–247.

Debnam, E. S. (2005). Osmolarity and partitioning of fluids. *Surgery (Oxford), 23*(6), 190–194.

Dezzutti, C. S., Brown, E. R., Moncla, B., Russo, J., Cost, M., Wang, L., Uranker, K., Kunjara Na Ayudhya, R. P., Pryke, K., Pickett, J. & LeBlanc, M. A. (2012). Is wetter better? An evaluation of over-the-counter personal lubricants for safety and anti-HIV-1 activity. *PLoS One, 7*(11), e48328.

Dodge, B., Schick, V., Herbenick, D., Reece, M., Sanders, S. A., & Fortenberry, J. D. (2014). Frequency, reasons for, and perceptions of lubricant use among a nationally representative sample of self identified Gay and bisexual men in the United States. *The Journal of Sexual Medicine, 11*(10), 2396–2405.

Fernández-Romero, J. A., Teleshova, N., Zydowsky, T. M., & Robbiani, M. (2015). Preclinical assessments of vaginal microbicide candidate safety and efficacy. *Advanced Drug Delivery Reviews, 92*, 27–38.

Fuchs, E. J., Lee, L. A., Torbenson, M. S., Parsons, T. L., Bakshi, R. P., Guidos, A. M., . . . Hendrix, C. W. (2007). Hyperosmolar sexual lubricant causes epithelial damage in the distal colon: Potential implication for HIV transmission. *Journal of Infectious Diseases, 195*(5), 703–710.

Gorbach, P. M., Weiss, R. E., Fuchs, E., Jeffries, R. A., Hezerah, M., Brown, S., . . . Cranston, R. D. (2012). The slippery slope: Lubricant use and rectal sexually transmitted infections: A newly identified risk. *Sexually Transmitted Diseases, 39*(1), 59–64. Retrieved from http://doi.org/10.1097/OLQ.0b013e318235502b

Griffith, R. S., DeLong, D. C., & Nelson, J. D. (1981). Relation of arginine-lysine antagonism to herpes simplex growth in tissue culture. *Chemotherapy, 27*(3), 209–213.

Herbenick, D., Reece, M., Hensel, D., Sanders, S., Jozkowski, K., & Fortenberry, J. D. (2011). Association of lubricant use with women's sexual pleasure, sexual satisfaction, and genital symptoms: A prospective daily diary study. *The Journal of Sexual Medicine, 8*(1), 202–212.

Herbenick, D., Reece, M., Schick, V., Sanders, S. A., & Fortenberry, J. D. (2014). Women's use and perceptions of commercial lubricants: Prevalence and characteristics in a nationally representative sample of American adults. *The Journal of Sexual Medicine, 11*(3), 642–652.

Higgins, J. A., & Wang, Y. (2015). The role of young adults' pleasure attitudes in shaping condom use. *American Journal of Public Health, 105*(7), 1329–1332.

Johnson, W., Bergfeld, W. F., Belsito, D. V., Hill, R. A., Klaassen, C. D., Liebler, D. C., . . . Andersen, F. A. (2011). Safety assessment of cyclomethicone, cyclotetrasiloxane, cyclopentasiloxane, cyclohexasiloxane, and cycloheptasiloxane. *International Journal of Toxicology, 30*(Supplement 6), 149S–227S.

Lieberman, S., Enig, M. G., & Preuss, H. G. (2006). A review of monolaurin and lauric acid: Natural virucidal and bactericidal agents. *Alternative & Complementary Therapies, 12*(6), 310–314.

Moench, T. R., Mumper, R. J., Hoen, T. E., Sun, M., & Cone, R. A. (2010). Microbicide excipients can greatly increase susceptibility to genital herpes transmission in the mouse. *BMC infectious diseases, 10*(1), 331.

Nair, B. (2002). Final report on the safety assessment of stearoxy dimethicone, dimethicone, methicone, amino bispropyl dimethicone, aminopropyl dimethicone, amodimethicone, amodimethicone hydroxystearate, behenoxy dimethicone, C24–28 alkyl methicone, C30–45 alkyl methicone, C30–45 alkyl dimethicone, cetearyl methicone, cetyl dimethicone, dimethoxysilyl ethylenediaminopropyl dimethicone, hexyl methicone, hydroxypropyldimethicone, stearamidopropyl dimethicone, stearyl dimethicone, stearyl methicone, and vinyldimethicone. *International Journal of Toxicology, 22*, 11–35.

Nicole, W. (2014). A question for women's health: Chemicals in feminine hygiene products and personal lubricants. *Environmental Health Perspectives, 122*, A70–A75.

Ogbolu, D. O., Oni, A. A., Daini, O. A., & Oloko, A. P. (2007). In vitro antimicrobial properties of coconut oil on Candida species in Ibadan, Nigeria. *Journal of Medicinal Food, 10*(2), 384–387.

Phillips, D. M., Taylor, C. L., Zacharopoulos, V. R., & Maguire, R. A. (2000). Nonoxynol-9 causes rapid exfoliation of sheets of rectal epithelium. *Contraception, 62*(3), 149–154.

Reece, M., Herbenick, D., Schick, V., Sanders, S. A., & Fortenberry, J. D. (2014). Men's use and perceptions of commercial lubricants: Prevalence and characteristics in a nationally representative sample of American adults. *The Journal of Sexual Medicine*, *11*(5), 1125–1135.

Schick, V. R., Hensel, D., Herbenick, D., Dodge, B., Reece, M., Sanders, S., & Fortenberry, J. D. (2015). Lesbian-and bisexually-identified women's use of lubricant during their most recent sexual event with a female partner: Findings from a nationally representative study in the United States. *LGBT Health*, *2*(2), 169–175.

Sudol, K. M., & Phillips, D. M. (2004). Relative safety of sexual lubricants for rectal intercourse. *Sexually Transmitted Diseases*, *31*(6), 346–349.

Wolf, L. K. (2012). Studies raise questions about safety of personal lubricants. *Chemical and Engineering News*, *90*(50), 46–47.

World Health Organization. (2012). *Use and procurement of additional lubricants for male and female condoms.* Retrieved January 13, 2016, from http://apps.who.int/iris/bitstream/10665/76580/1/WHO_RHR_12.33_eng.pdf?ua=1

Chapter 9

Toys as Tools

What Every Sexual Health Professional Needs to Know About Sex Toys

Imagine a construction site. Today is the day when a new construction worker is going to learn how to build a house. However, instead of walking the worker onto the site and showing them how to use the tools available to pour the foundation or frame out the walls, the foreman meets the worker in a coffee shop two blocks away to explain the process to them. This is the way sexual health professionals often work with clients and students. Many of us try to explain how bodies work while maintaining a prescribed ethical distance from the bodies of everyone we work with. As sexual health professionals, we may talk with clients in exhaustive detail about what happens when they are sexual: feelings, sensations, body reactions, partner reactions. However, we gather and give our information from a distance. While there may be valid reasons for this separation, it does complicate the job.

Now imagine the new construction worker sitting at the coffee shop, asking the foreman, "What kind of equipment do you have at the site?" and the foreman replying, "Well, you need to dig out a basement so you should probably consider looking for some kind of digging machine." Or, "I'm really not sure. I was never trained on the equipment." Many sex therapists and educators do not receive training about sex toys. This can put them in the position of the foreman who knows tools are available but doesn't know what kind. Sex toys are important tools. Educators and therapists need knowledge of what kinds of toys are available, as well as the possible benefits and safety information their clients and students need to consider.

Whether you choose to call them toys, tools, aids, or something else altogether, there are many products available that can enhance arousal or sexual response. These products can help people reach sexual goals, cope with body changes, express identity, and increase pleasure. I have seen vibrators boost low desire, cock rings help clients have penetrative sex again, and packers help clients feel more "right" in their bodies. While these "quick fixes" don't happen all the time, there are many occasions when sex toys make a dramatic difference in clients' and students' sexual pleasure and satisfaction quickly and easily. This chapter will discuss basic information about sex toys and how sexual health professionals might incorporate this information into their work.

Who Uses Sex Toys? Everybody!

Teaching classes and working with clients, I've heard all kinds of stereotypes about who sex toys are supposedly for (or not for). They often contradict each other. "I don't need a vibrator, I'm in a relationship right now," would be followed by, "I don't need a vibrator, I'm not in a relationship right now." If there is one thing I learned while working in a sex toy shop, it is that people from all walks of life, of all ages, in all different kinds of situations buy and enjoy sex toys. I loved interacting with the wide range of people who came into the store: people of varying ages, backgrounds, lifestyles, orientations, relationship situations, cultures, genders, body sizes, and degrees of ability and mobility. They all had different wants and needs when choosing sex toys or equipment. I think of a lady, probably in her 70s, who purchased a toy from me and said, "I bet you don't see people like me in here very often." To which I replied, "Oh yes, I do." I always tell the people I work with: "Everyone and anyone might want to use a sex toy. Or they might not. Sex toys are for people who have bodies and want to feel good."

Lindsey Says

You can imagine that talking about sex toys with young people might be a little tricky. It is not typically part of sex ed curriculum! However, this information is still valid to share and is definitely an area of interest. Mostly, I find ways to include sex toy education by making the most of "teachable moments" in response to direct questions. If someone asks a question, even if they seem too young to know about something, it shows us clearly that they do have at least some information and they need assistance in learning what is true and what it all means. My policy is to always honestly answer any question that is asked.

"Is that a dildo?" a student asks as they point to the condom demonstration model.

"Nope, this is just for condom practice. A dildo is something people use to put inside their body for pleasure. Sometimes they are hard like this, and sometimes soft and bendy. They might look exactly like a penis or like something else entirely!"

"Ooh, have you heard about that fire and ice stuff?" asks a student when I mention lube.

"Yes! Some people really like feelings that are cool, or warm, or tingly, on their sensitive skin! A nice thing about stimulating gels like that is that they can really increase your blood flow, which is good for your sexual body parts and can even increase pleasure. That might be really useful if, for example, someone was trying to figure out how to get some extra feeling when using condoms, to make them more fun. They can also be irritating to sensitive skin, though, so they don't work for everyone."

Though I have never been asked to visit a school to talk about sex toys, I am frequently invited to speak on this topic with out-of-school youth groups that are doing a sex ed unit. In fact, the most common groups that invite me are church groups! I typically show examples of the various items described in this chapter, and answer questions that students ask aloud or in the anonymous question box. Of course, I have 100% of everyone's attention! Laws on sex toys and minors vary by country and state, and I feel so lucky to live and work in a place where I am allowed to discuss with young people about these tools that many people will grow to find necessary and helpful in their futures. I think this opportunity to ask questions and see things in person goes a long way to demystify and de-stigmatize sex toys.

Toys/Tools

People use different terms when they talk about sex toys. I tend to use either "sex toy" or "tool." I have chosen these terms because "sex toy" sounds fun and non-threatening when dealing with a subject that is intimidating to many people. It also conveys the message, "Using this could be fun!" as toys are seen as fun and playful. Increasing fun and playfulness is likely to increase pleasure. I also like the term "tool" because it conveys the idea that these objects are here to work for the client or student. It encourages them to think from a problem solving/pleasure increasing point of view. "Tool" conveys value and usefulness, which contrasts the perception that sex toys are perverted or juvenile.

Sometimes choosing professional language around sexual products can be difficult. For example, toys commonly known as "cock rings" can be tricky to present in more formal settings. If I am in a setting where using slang may push my listeners to the point of being offended or too nervous to hear my message, I have at times presented them as "penis rings" or even just "rings." However, for people who don't like medical language, "cock ring" may actually feel more reassuring or welcoming. It can be tough to know when presenting to a group of students or talking with a client you don't know well what language would make them feel most comfortable. Whatever words you choose when talking about sex toys, make sure you know why you are making the choices you make and that concern over language is not preventing you from sharing important factual information. Remember that hearing the word "cock" isn't actually going to harm anyone. You give your subject matter credibility by the way you present yourself. If you can stand in front of a group and say "cock ring" like a total professional, your audience is likely to perceive it as professional.

What Are Sex Toys Made Of?

It would be easy to assume if a toy is made to be used on or in the body that there must be guidelines for the materials used, or a government agency to inspect it and ensure it is safe for the body. However, in actuality, there are currently no guidelines or rules regarding the materials sex toys are made of (Reynolds, 2013). Because of this, the burden of judging a product's safety is passed on to the consumer.

Our cultural tendency to devalue anything associated with sex or shroud it in shame means that many people buy sex toys with a "get in, get the toy, get out quick before someone sees me" attitude. Consumers often do not ask important questions about the products they are buying such as, "How can I clean this toy? Can I sterilize it? What material is this made of and is that safe for the body?" Sometimes they do ask and are given misinformation. Information on sex toy materials is not readily available and tracking down accurate information is time consuming. Well-intentioned people often get this info wrong and sometimes have even been given incorrect or misleading information from manufacturers.

Here is how I explain sex toy materials to students and clients:

"There are two factors to consider when thinking about what you want your toy to be made of: Does this toy potentially contain chemicals I don't want in my body, and how can I clean or sterilize this toy? Let's start with the question of chemicals. There are currently no regulations in place about what toys can be made of. There is a lot of debate right now about the chemicals that are in some toy materials and whether they are healthy for the body or not. If you ever get a toy that has a smell, anything from a 'new shower curtain' type smell to toys that have been scented or perfumed, you are dealing with a toy that is porous and what you are smelling is the chemicals in it off-gassing. These are the toys you probably want to avoid. If something has no smell, it is likely made of body-friendly materials.

"If you are using a toy on or inside your body, you want to make sure you can clean it well. It could be possible to transmit STIs or bacteria through sharing toys if they aren't properly cleaned. Even if you are the only one using a toy, if it isn't cleaned well it could grow bacteria and cause an infection, unless it is made of non-porous materials. When a material is porous, that means it has spaces or small holes that substances can pass in or out of. Sometimes these holes are too small to see. If a toy is porous, you can do a great job cleaning it and it still might not be clean all the way through because bacteria can hide out in the pores. It may also mean that chemicals in the toy can pass out of the toy into your body. Silicone, hard plastic, acrylic, glass, and surgical steel are great materials to look for because they are nonporous and they are also won't be leaking or off-gassing any of the concerning chemicals I mentioned earlier.

"Cleaning your toys should be fairly simple. A nonporous toy can be simply washed with soap and hot water. If you would like to sterilize a silicone, glass, or metal toy that doesn't have a vibration mechanism or any electronics inside, you can boil it. For toys that do have electronics, make a solution of one part bleach to 10 parts water, spray it on the toy, let it dry and then wash it off with soap and water. Some sex toy companies sell special cleaning solution for their toys. This gives the companies more proceeds and conveys a sense of reassurance to their customers that they are cleaning their toys properly. However, these cleaners are often necessary because the toy is made of material that will degrade if cleaned with soap. If that is the case, it means the toy is also porous and virtually impossible to thoroughly clean or sterilize, even with that special cleaner."

When you start down the rabbit hole of information about sex toy materials you can easily keep going for a long time (see www.badvibes.org and www.dildology. org for more information). However, it doesn't need to be complex. In fact, it is probably best to keep it simple for your clients or students to make sure they don't feel overwhelmed. You can always have further research on hand for people that are more interested, or encourage them to do their own research on the subject.

Types of Sex Toys

Styles and aesthetics of sex toys change regularly, and improvements in technology mean that new exciting products are always entering the market. However, toys can be broken down into some basic categories that remain constant and will allow you to convey valuable information to clients or students, no matter what the "in" color pallet for dildos is this year.

Vibrators

Popular myth states that vibrators are meant for use with vulvas, vaginas, and of course, the clitoris. However, it is important for sexual health professionals to get the word out that anyone with nerve endings may enjoy vibration. People like vibration on all kinds of body places: the back, the shaft of the penis, anus, clitoris, nipples, inner thighs, perineum, inserted vaginally or anally, and probably other places I haven't even thought of. Everyone has different preferences about vibration: While some people love it, some don't like the sensation. Each individual has to do their own experimenting to figure out what works well for them.

When talking with clients or students about vibrators (and sex toys in general) it is important to remember that people often feel overwhelmed and clueless as to how to use a toy and figure out what feels good to them. It is important to find professional ways to give your students or clients some guidance about how to start. The tricky part is doing so while not making assumptions about what might work for them. It is also important to normalize sex toy use and emphasize that this should be fun, not a chore.

At the therapy clinic where I work, SkyHill, we carry a few basic sex toys and lube options so that we can have these essential tools on hand for clients to buy. We also think it is important to give clients good information with these tools, so I developed informational handouts for clients to take home. Here is our informational handout on vibrators that attempts to give guidance without dictating any one "right" way to use them:

How Do You Use a Vibrator?

The best answer is to use your vibrator however you feel inspired to use it. Choose a time and place where you feel comfortable and ready to experiment. Vibrators can feel good when used on many places on the body, so you don't need to concentrate on or start with the genitals, but you can if you want. If you are using a vibrator with a partner you might take turns giving each other massages with the vibrator and seeing where you enjoy the sensation the most. Vibrators do not always create immediate pleasure. If you are having difficulty creating arousal or pleasure with the vibrator, consider doing anything else you usually find arousing and adding the vibrator in once you have reached a higher level of arousal. Vibrators can be used on their own or while engaging in other forms of sexual play you already enjoy. Vibrators can be used solo or with partner(s). Have fun!

Vibrators can be important tools for many of the issues clients or students may bring to sexual health professionals. They are often helpful with issues like low desire, difficulty creating arousal, difficulty reaching orgasm or for people who have not yet had an orgasm, when orgasming becomes difficult due to medication, learning to orgasm in different positions or situations, increasing blood flow to the genitals, learning to orgasm with partner(s), adding fun to solo or partner sex, and exploring the sexual self. What's not to love about that?

Outside-the-Body Vibes

Vibrators come in many shapes and sizes. Some are safe to use for penetration and some are not designed for this purpose. Of course, in order to make a decision about what kind of toy they want, students or clients will need to determine how they want to use the toy. Do they want the possibility of penetration or are they content with outside-the-body stimulation? This is a great conversation to start as it can help people clarify their preferences and needs.

I encourage clients and students to look at the shape of the vibrator to determine whether it is an outside- or inside-the-body toy. I'll say something like, "You'll know a vibrator is not meant for penetration if it is a shape that doesn't easily go into the body (like a circle or an oval), if it has small parts that could come off inside someone, or if it has a cord that would end up inside the body if inserted. While some of this may sound obvious, remember that both arousal and anxiety can shut down common sense." Students and clients usually laugh at this joke, but it is true. It can be important for sexual health professionals to give information that sometimes borders on the obvious, since people are likely to have their mind on other things in the moment.

Outside-the-body vibes come in a wide range of shapes and sizes, from small enough to fit onto a finger to big enough to plug into the wall and be mistaken for a *Star Wars* prop. Bigger vibes can work well as back massagers and smaller vibes may be able to fit between two bodies during partner sex. Some vibes are "hands-free" and are meant to sit in a lap, on a chair, or a bed. These options may be helpful for people who have arthritis, mobility issues, or want their hands free to do other things. Again, it is up to the client or student what is appealing to them and meets their needs.

Inside-the-Body Vibes

Inside-the-body vibrators are shaped to facilitate penetration and are usually some kind of oblong shape. They are available in varying textures, and some are curved at the end, which would make them useful for g-spot or prostate stimulation. It can be helpful to remind the people you work with that penetrative vibrators can also be used for outside-the-body stimulation. While the shape may not be specifically designed for this, it often works anyway and is a great way to get more versatility from a toy. The main thing to convey to clients and students about penetrative vibrators is that they should be designed to facilitate penetration safely. What is "safe" will also depend on what part of the body they want to use the toy on.

Safety Concerns for Vaginal and Anal Penetration

Because the vagina is capped at the end by the cervix, it is not possible for a toy that is inserted vaginally to get lost or "float away" into the rest of the body. However, this is a genuine fear that many people have, so it is an important point to address. The rectum does not have a definite end point, so toys used anally that fully enter the body can become difficult to retrieve. Any toy used for anal penetration should have a flared base (a base that is big enough in size that it will prevent it from slipping all the way into the body) to prevent these issues.

Dildos

The term "dildo" basically refers to any toy that is meant for penetration. Many dildos do not vibrate but some do have vibrators that can be inserted into them for extra stimulation. When does a vibrating dildo become a penetrative vibrator? That is a mystery for the ages, much like the question "Why can't we find something better to call them than 'dildo'?" Dildos come in many shapes and sizes. Some look like biological penises and some have textures and colors that do not occur in nature. If the dildo has a curve at the end it may be helpful for stimulating the g-spot or prostate.

People may use dildos vaginally or anally. However, it is important to choose a dildo that is safe for anal play—one that has a flared base or a handle to make sure it does not fully enter the body. Dildos can be used in many ways: to gradually increase ability to envelop/experience greater length or width of penetration; to experience penetration in multiple body parts at once (double penetration); for use with a harness (strap-on-sex); for penetration with differing shapes, sizes, and textures; for solo or partnered play; and to increase fun and pleasure. In addition, dildos can help people stimulate body parts that may be difficult to reach with fingers or without the help of a partner, such as the g-spot or the prostate.

Dildos Versus Dilators

Sexual health professionals often recommend dilators for people experiencing vaginal pain that prevents or hinders penetration, as well as anyone who may be experiencing loss of vaginal elasticity (such as people in one of the stages of menopause, who have had gender confirmation surgery, or who have had cancer treatment). Having worked with many people who felt they were handed a dilator and told "use it or lose it" without getting any further information, I strive to create an atmosphere of positivity and empowerment when advising people about dilators. It is so important to talk with clients or students about the positive effects that practicing penetration (with a good lube) can have for their body, rather than just handing them a dilator assuming they will figure it out. Making sure to save time for concerns or questions they might have can mean the difference between the client or student having a positive experience or a painful, difficult experience.

Dilators are often quite expensive and some clients I have worked with have gotten a very medical, "something is wrong with you" connotation from them. While there are a few dilators out there that come in different colors and look a bit more "cheerful," the options are limited. Students and clients don't have to buy something specifically labeled "dilator" unless that is the product they feel drawn to. Dildos or penetrative vibrators that are smooth and gradually increase in size can be more affordable, more attractive, and can shift the focus from "fixing what is wrong" to "finding pleasure in my body." Many of my clients have told me their attitude predicts their results. If they feel like they are buying a medical device, they think about what is "wrong" or "unhealthy" about their bodies. If they find a product that is designed for pleasure, they give themselves more permission to explore what might be fun and sexy in their changing body. Of course, for some people, the idea of a dilator as a medical device that their professionals have recommended for them can be very comforting. They may never feel comfortable going to buy a vibrator or dildo, but they will go get a dilator if recommended. As with most things, the only way you will know what the person you are working with prefers is by having a conversation with them.

Here's an example of how I might talk through how to use a dildo/dilator with someone who is recovering from cervical cancer.

"So after your surgery, did you get to have any conversations with your doctors about what body parts they removed?" *(Often clients do not know what body parts may have been removed and this is an important empowerment piece for them to clarify what has happened to their body. For the sake of this example we will say the client knows that their cervix was removed.)*

"OK, so how much do you know about what the inside of the body looks like as far as your reproductive or pleasure organs?" *(This might be a good time to get out a drawing, model or chart.)*

"So when the doctors removed your cervix they sewed up the end of the vaginal canal. So in many ways your vaginal canal is like it was before surgery; it is still like a tube with a definite end so that nothing can enter the rest of your body. If you were to put a toy inside you there is no way for it to float up and poke you in the liver or something." *(Usually, they end up laughing at this. I often use humor to help people feel relaxed and take away the sense of severity that talking about medical issues can often have, but I always make sure that the humor is well received. I wouldn't want to come across as being disrespectful if this is something that feels very serious to them.)*

"Some differences you might notice could be that the end point of your vagina may feel different. If you ever touched your cervix with your fingers you might notice that the new ending to your vagina may feel different than your cervix did. Other changes might be that your vaginal canal might be shorter, or feel less elastic or flexible. Those are some of the things that practicing penetration might help with. Just like yoga or stretching any part of your body, the more often you practice, the easier and more relaxed it will be and the further you may be able to stretch." I find the comparison to yoga or stretching makes trying penetration less intimidating and normalizes the need for regular practice.

"Lubrication is so very important in this process. Even if you have not used lubrication in the past, it is very important to use it now. Lube will cut down on friction, which could help your body relax, and it will help protect your tissues, which might feel more sensitive than they used to. Lube can feel very sensual or sexy. Let's talk about what lubes might be best for you and how you want to apply the lube: to the dildo/dilator, to your body, or, to both."

"It is important to create an environment that will help you relax and feel good when you are trying this. What do you imagine that would look like for you? What might help you enjoy this experience? Can you imagine that this might even feel good? In fact, combining using your dilator/dildo with things that you know feel pleasurable to you or create arousal would be really helpful for the process. Clitoral stimulation or using a vibrator if you enjoy those can make the whole process easier and just more fun."

"Pushing through an experience that is painful or frustrating is probably not going to be helpful in the long run. Going slowly is absolutely OK and it will get easier over time so please don't feel the need to rush yourself. Can you think of any signs from your body that would be a signal that it might be time to stop for the day and try again another day? Next session we can talk all about how this went for you, whether it was difficult, fun, or both."

Obviously, this is a long process and not every sexual health professional has the ability to talk through this in detail with every client or student. However, it is so important to take enough time to explain lubrication, why this is important to the body, to normalize, and lighten the mood while acknowledging there may be struggle involved. When people feel like they have a good idea of how this might go and what to do, they feel comfortable enough to try. When they feel confused, lost, or scared they often don't.

Strengthening Balls/Barbells

Kegel exercises are a way to strengthen the pubococcygeus muscle: the hammock-like muscle that stretches across the pelvis, from the pubic bone to the tail bone. A strong pubococcygeus muscle (PC muscle for short) has many health benefits, including possibly increasing pleasure and sensation in the genitals. There are many different toys available that are designed to make Kegel exercises pleasurable and fun. While some of these may be used anally (strong PC muscles are important for people of all genders), many are not designed in a way that is safe for anal penetration, so make sure to reference the "Safety Concerns for Vaginal and Anal Penetration" section when making these determinations. Many people like these toys not just for exercise but for pleasure, especially people who are interested in using toys but do not like vibration. They can also be very helpful for people in the following situations: increasing bladder or bowel control, preparing for or recovering from vaginal childbirth, becoming more in touch and aware of the PC muscles, and strengthening/toning PC muscles to increase orgasm intensity. These are likely not the best choice for students and clients who experience pain or tension in their pelvic floor muscles. When in doubt about strength of PC muscles or whether they PC muscles are tense, referrals for a consultation with a pelvic floor physical therapist may be helpful.

Butt Toys

Just about everybody has an anus. That's why I like to call the anus "The Great Equalizer." Lots of people are also very nervous about talking about the anus, which is a reason I make that joke right off the bat during classes or when talking with clients.

Speaking of sensitive topics, the anus has a wealth of nerve endings, so it makes sense that this very sensitive area could be a source of great pleasure for many people. Sex toys that can be used anally come in a wide variety of shapes and sizes. The one constant should be the flared base that ensures the toy does not enter past the anus and into the rectum, as it could become difficult to retrieve. Some toys made for anal use vibrate and some do not. Again, this is up to the personal preferences of the buyer.

When talking with students or clients about toys for anal use, it is very important to let them know that the anus does not produce its own lubrication and so using lube for anal play is extremely important in order to avoid injury, not to mention to make things much more pleasurable.

Butt toys are made for different purposes. Some are shaped in a way that makes them useful for the back-and-forth movement of penetration. Others are shaped more like plugs; usually with a "neck" or less girthy area (right before the flared base) that is meant to give the anal sphincters an area to close around. The shape of plugs makes them more difficult to use for quick in-and-out movement. However, they are much loved by people who prefer a feeling of fullness to the back-and-forth movement of penetration. Another way people use butt plugs is to gradually and gently relax the anal sphincters so they can pleasurably receive larger penetration by using a series of plugs with gradually increasing neck size. A vibrating plug can be especially helpful in relaxing the anal sphincters.

Some of the situations in which anal toys have been helpful to my clients have been exploring anal eroticism, preparing the body for pleasurable anal penetration, learning how to relax the anal sphincters without the use of drugs or alcohol, playing with fantasies of multiple partners for individuals or couples who do not want to actually add in another person, and addressing pelvic muscle tension that affects the anal area. In the latter case, suggesting the client see a pelvic floor physical therapist as well is advisable.

Prostate Toys

The prostate is often overlooked as a sexual body part. In fact, the prostate is also frequently glossed over in reproductive health education, so unless your students or clients have had health issues with their prostate, they are likely to be generally uninformed about this important organ. However, the prostate can be an excellent source of pleasure for many people.

Prostate toys are mainly designed for use internally through anal penetration. They are likely to look like a butt plug or dildo, but with a curve at the end. Some prostate toys even incorporate movement; once the toy is in the body it can rock or rotate to provide stimulation to the prostate. There are some toys available that sit outside the body and stimulate by providing pressure to the perineum, so if you have a client or student who does not want anal penetration, these options may be a helpful choice.

Here's how I might explain the pleasure possibilities of the prostate: "Have you heard much about the prostate?" *(Usually this answer is "no" or "just some things about prostate cancer.")* "Well, the prostate is a body part that gives many people a lot of pleasure. The prostate in inside the body and to stimulate it people can either push up on the perineum, the flat space behind the balls and in front of the anus, or people can stimulate the prostate more directly by putting pressure on the front wall of the rectum. So that could mean a finger, a penis, or a toy goes into the anus and pushes or strokes gently on that front wall."

"Many people find prostate stimulation very pleasurable. People say it feels good even without leading to orgasm, and when it does lead to orgasm people often describe their orgasm feeling different; a more all-encompassing or prolonged experience. Some people find that prostate stimulation helps them get or maintain erections and some people enjoy prostate play specifically because they want to try something that is not as focused on sensation from the penis."

Usually at this point a client will address some kind of concern, such as cleanliness, fear of pain, embarrassment, or wondering how to talk with a partner about prostate stimulation. Sometimes people express excitement at the possibility for new pleasure. For more information about anal penetration to answer these questions, two excellent resources are *Anal Pleasure and Health* by Jack Moran or *The Ultimate Guide to Anal Sex for Women* by Tristan Taormino. Of course, the wonderful book *The Ultimate Guide to Prostate Pleasure* by Dr. Charlie Glickman and Aislinn Emirzian is a great place to get more prostate information.

I have introduced the idea of prostate toys to clients and students looking for a non-penis-centered way to find sexual pleasure, people having trouble getting or sustaining erections, people who have pelvic tension in the anal area (outside-the-body prostate stimulation can also function as a massage for tense muscles), and as a fun new way to explore individually or in a partnership.

Cock Rings

Whether you want to call them "cock rings," "penis rings," or just "rings," these toys can be useful and fun tools. Cock rings work by putting pressure on the veins that are right under the skin of the penis. The arteries that bring blood into the penis to facilitate erections are not affected by the pressure of the ring, so blood flows into the penis normally. However, the ring pressing on the veins that bring blood out of the penis causes blood to flow out much more slowly. This means erections can become firmer with a ring and possibly last longer. People using cock rings often report increased or intensified sensation. Some people love this and some find it irritating.

Cock rings are made of many different materials: silicone, elastomers, leather, rubber, metal, and more. Some have vibrators attached (for the pleasure of the wearer and/or any partner they might use the ring with), and some do not. Rings are put on in different ways. Some are a solid ring that the genitals must be gently pushed through. Beginners may want to avoid this type as it is the most difficult to get on and in order to get it off the erection must subside. Less tricky methods include rings that are very stretchy, and therefore easier to get on and off, as well as rings that open using snaps, buckles, or Velcro. When a client interested in penis rings expresses to me that they have anxiety, whether that is about using a cock ring, body anxiety, anxiety around closed spaces, or even sometimes more general anxiety, I will often suggest they look at cock rings that can open quickly and easily. This is an easy way to cut out at least one possible source of concern and create a better atmosphere for pleasure.

Sometimes rings are made to go around the shaft of the penis and sometimes they are intended to go around the penis as well as the entire scrotum. One important consideration: If a cock ring goes around the scrotum and pulls the testicles away from the body it is possible that the wearer will be slower to orgasm or in some cases, unable to orgasm. When a person nears orgasm, their testicles pull up closer to the body. This can be a helpful trick for clients and students who want to maintain an erection for a longer time period. I have had clients who orgasm earlier than they would like become able to hold off longer by choosing a cock ring that keeps their testicles farther from their body. Some people find they remain hard even after ejaculation while wearing a ring.

It is important to talk with students and clients about safety issues regarding cock rings:

"Remember that a cock ring is basically like a tourniquet. People use cock rings frequently without any problems, but if you use them in an unsafe way you could cause yourself permanent damage. While the penis may darken in color due to increased blood flow, if you notice any colors that look bluish or gray, it is time to take that cock ring off right away. Any feeling of numbness, tingling (not the sexy kind), or coldness are also signs that you need to remove the ring. When you first try wearing a ring you may only want to wear it for 1 minute, 5, or maybe 10. You may find that this amount of time is all you need or want, or you may like it so much you want to wear it longer. Either way, starting off slowly and building to longer times it a great way to take good care of your body and build knowledge about how your body reacts to wearing a cock ring."

Cock rings can be helpful for clients and students who want to hold off orgasm longer, to intensify the sensations in their penis, who find the look of a cock ring arousing, who want to try something new for their penis, and people who get erections but want to increase the firmness of these erections to facilitate penetration (these people should of course consult their medical doctor as well).

Penis Pumps

Penis pumps consist of a tube to put your penis in and a hand or electric pump that creates a vacuum in the tube. The exact anatomical way a penis pump works can be complex, but a simple explanation is that the vacuum created inside of the tube pulls blood into the penis, helping the user get an erection. Some pumps come with a cock ring to help maintain the firmness of the erection. Some people find the sensation pleasurable and use pumps as a masturbation tool or a fun addition to partner sex. Some penis pumps are sold in sex toy stores and some are available by prescription from a doctor. Clients or students buying their own may want to look for models that include a vacuum limiter to prevent pressure from increasing to the point of injuring the penis. Other concerns may include bruising or tenderness after using (especially if the user takes blood-thinning medication), but most people find they can avoid this as they get more familiar with their pump (Mayo Clinic Staff, 2015).

Students or clients may benefit from using penis pumps when they are experiencing difficulty getting erections, after prostate surgery, or to create more pleasure alone or with a partner. Consulting with a doctor is a good idea for any people you work with who are noticing changes in their erections, as these can indicate other health issues. In addition, asking their doctor if a penis pump is a good option for their particular medical situation is always wise.

Masturbation Sleeves

Masturbation sleeves are usually some kind of sheath that is meant to encompass the penis. The user can either thrust into the sleeve or use their hand to rub the sleeve around the penis. Often sleeves have added texture or a vibration mechanism to provide further stimulation. This is one type of toy in which care around choices of material is tricky. Unfortunately, many people tend to find silicone sleeves too firm to create the desired sensation. This means most sleeves that have the feel that people enjoy are made of materials that are at best not able to be sterilized and at worst give off irritating or harmful chemicals. Elastomers (various kinds of rubbers) seem to be a good material for masturbation sleeves since they have the light, stretchy feel people tend to prefer and usually do not contain the chemicals that are most concerning in other "jelly" type toys, such as phthalates. However, elastomers are porous materials and are not sterilizable. It is important to talk with students or clients about the ways they can minimize risks with elastomer toys including buying sleeves meant to be thrown out after a few uses to avoid bacteria growth and not sharing them with others to avoid the possibility of STI transmission.

I think masturbation sleeves are the unsung heroes of sex toys. They have so many possible clinical uses. For clients or students who have masturbated in a specific way for years and have trouble orgasming any other way, sleeves can offer a different stimulation that may help them broaden their orgasmic abilities. Practicing with sleeves can help people learn to orgasm in different positions or situations. For students or clients who are orgasming more quickly than they would like, using a sleeve can provide a way to practice holding off orgasm. For people who are taking longer than they would like to orgasm, practicing with a sleeve may help them orgasm more quickly. Being able to practice orgasm skills alone may decrease anxiety, so people may be better able to learn these skills through using a sleeve than with partner sex. Later, they can work on transferring their newfound skills to sex with their partner(s).

In addition, masturbation sleeves can be great fun for couples seeking ways to be sexual with each other that are not focused on penetration or avoid penetration all together. Sleeves can make handjobs even more fun. Some sleeves may be used as additional stimulation during oral sex on a penis. If the sleeve is short and has holes on both ends it can be used as a stimulation ring placed at the base of the penis while a partner provides oral stimulation to the head of the penis. If clients or students want to try this trick with a sleeve that is egg shaped and relatively thin material, they can cut off the top so the head of the penis is able to stick out of the end. This is especially helpful when the person giving oral sex does not want to take all of the penis in their mouth or has a strong gag reflex.

Harnesses

Harnesses anchor a dildo to a part of the body. The most common type of harness is made to fit the pelvis and position the dildo in relatively the same position as a biological penis. People who already have a biological penis can wear a harness that positions a dildo above their bio penis or on top of their bio penis while it is flaccid.

Pelvic harnesses can be helpful to clients and students in many different situations. They can facilitate penetration when neither partner has a biological penis or when a partner does not get erections that are firm enough for penetration. They can allow people to choose dildos that are different shapes, sizes, and textures for variety and fun. Harnesses can help people try double penetration with just one partner. They can provide an additional option for safer sex if partners want penetration but are concerned about STI transmission.

Other types of harnesses include thigh harnesses, chest harnesses, and hand harnesses. These can be used by anybody, but may be especially good options for clients who have negative associations with pelvic thrusting due to sexual assault, but who still wish to incorporate penetration into their sex lives. Thigh or hand harnesses can be helpful when the penetrating partner has physical limitations; such as back problems that interfere with thrusting, or arthritis that could prevent them from holding a penetrative toy. Thigh harnesses can be great for people in wheelchairs who want their partner to be able to straddle them for penetration. With a thigh harness, this can often be done while they are sitting in their chair. Harnesses can add versatility and fun for a wide variety of students and clients.

Packers/Pack and Play Dildos/STPs

Some toys may be more than just toys: They may be an important part of someone's identity. Packers look and feel like a flaccid penis and a scrotum. They are designed to be tucked (or "packed") into underwear to give the feel and look of a penis. Packers come in a variety of skin tones. For people who are trans or gender variant, a packer can be an important part of their identity, a part of their body. STPs ("Stand-To-Pee") are a kind of packer that have a tube inside that enables the wearer to pee through the packer while standing up. Pack and play dildos are soft or flexible enough to fit into underwear, under clothes, while still being hard enough for penetration. They may be worn with a pelvic harness or held in place by underwear and then pushed out the fly of the underwear.

Breast Forms

Breast forms come in several styles: breast adhesives, breast forms that are meant to be worn inside a bra, breast plates that are one-piece and attach around the neck, and adhesive nipples. They may be made of silicone, latex, or silicone gel in a plastic skin. Breast forms may be worn by trans women, people who have had their breasts removed, people who enjoy crossdressing, or anyone who wants to add breasts to their body.

Prosthetic Vulvas

Prosthetic vulvas are latex or silicone vulvas that can be worn over a biological penis. There are several styles of prosthetic vulvas, including shorts, v-strings, and briefs. Prosthetic vulvas are sometimes "closed" and sometimes have an opening to facilitate peeing or penetration. These are great for trans women, people who enjoy crossdressing, and anyone who wants to have a vulva.

Packers, Breast Forms, Dildos, Prosthetic Vulvas: Sexy Toys or Body Parts?

When working with clients or students that use packers, dildos, harnesses, prosthetic vulvas, or breast forms, you may want to ask about the relationship they have or the meaning they give to their equipment. Is it a dildo or is it their penis? Is it an important body part or is it something they put on to feel sexy? Is it part of their identity, the way they express their gender, a way to play with sensation, or just a fun toy they like to use? Their answers may be any or all of these but no matter what, understanding their answers will be important to your work with them.

Stimulating Gels

Stimulating gels are meant to add extra sensation to the genitals. Some are meant to cool and some to warm. Sometimes they are formulated for a specific body part such as the clitoris or the penis. They might be water based or oil based. They are meant to intensify sensation, either used by themselves or with other kinds of sexual stimulation. Lots of people swear by their tingly power. Other people don't enjoy the sensation they provide. While it is important to be aware of the ingredients in stimulating gels (see Chapter 8), usually people are using such a small amount of these that they don't have to be quite as careful of ingredients as when they are picking a lubricant. That said, if the person you are working with has sensitivities, the same guidelines for picking lubes should apply to stimulating gels.

I often talk to students and clients about stimulating gels when they are having trouble finding desire for sex because daily worries or anxieties keep them from getting in the mood. These gels can draw their attention away from daily worries and to their body. The arousal that stimulating gels facilitate is often enough to spark the desire to be sexual that was hanging out under all those other thoughts or needed some extra time and encouragement to develop. Stimulating gels are also great for a hands-free (at least after it is applied) option for boosting sensation. If your hands cramp holding a vibrator or you have trouble getting a toy to stay in place between your partner's body and your own, a stimulating gel can be a great way to intensify the tingle.

Partner Toys and How to Talk About Them

There are many great toys that are meant to be used with a partner. These might be small vibrators that can sit between two bodies, penetration toys that can be shared between two people, or many other varieties of toys.

While any sex toy can be used with (or at least near) a partner, many students or clients conceptualize using toys as something people do by themselves. This is a shame since toys are tools that can often be helpful for partner sex. Many people struggle to figure out how they might bring up the idea of using a toy with a partner. They worry their partner will feel intimidated or like the toy will "replace" them. I like to remind people that while toys are wonderful, you probably aren't going to take your vibrator as a date to your friend's wedding. Your dildo doesn't make you laugh when you are frustrated or hold you when you cry. No toy can replace a partner. Using a toy with a partner can be an experience you share together (and would likely be different than if you were to use it alone). Reminding clients and students that toys can sometimes do what human bodies cannot can take away the perception that "we should be able to do this on our own."

People don't usually feel threatened by other fun things that can add arousal and pleasure to their sexual relationship. We don't generally hear people say, "Having sex in this fancy hotel room just feels like taking the easy way out. I need to be in our messy bedroom to really feel like I've earned it," "When you wear those special underwear that we both like I worry that it means you don't find me arousing enough to just be naked," or "If you were to have an orgasm while I was whispering sexy things in your ear I would feel like the words gave you the orgasm instead of me." Reassuring students and clients that using sex toys does not mean there is anything deficient about them or their relationships can be just what they need to hear in order to have the confidence to try something new.

And More!

There are so many kinds of sex toys and equipment that a full description would need a whole book of its own. However, there are many great products out there that may be beneficial to the people you work with. Positioning tools (firm, shaped cushions) can be very helpful for people with mobility issues. BDSM toys are so various and complex, it could take years to study them all.

Taking a trip to your local sex toy shop can be a great way to learn more, especially since you will gain insight into what the experience might be like for any clients or students that also go to the shop. Pay attention to whether or not the sex shops in your area are staffed with trained educators. Ask them what their criteria is for the toys they decide to carry in the shop. If the answers you get are not reassuring, you may be better off finding a more reputable store online.

References

Mayo Clinic Staff. (2015, January 15). *Tests and procedures: Penis pump.* Retrieved March 18, 2016, from http://www.mayoclinic.org/tests-procedures/penis-pump/basics/how-you-prepare/prc-20013151

Reynolds, R. (2013, December 10). *Maybe the FDA should regulate sex toys, huh?* Retrieved February 18, 2016, from http://www.vice.com/read/maybe-the-fda-should-regulate-sex-toys-huh

Chapter 10

Sharing Pleasure
Consent and Communication for Couples

The preceding chapters have focused mainly on how to work with individuals on developing their sexual selves, shedding guilt and shame, and talking about pleasure. However, most people want to express their sexuality with partners, at least some of the time. This chapter focuses on ways sexual health professionals can help people increase their ability to communicate about pleasure and cultivate greater pleasure in their partnerships. While this chapter frequently uses the word "couple," many of the exercises and skills presented in this chapter can be used effectively with people who have multiple partners and people in nonmonogamous relationships.

Pleasure and Consent

Consent is the foundation of pleasure. Nothing erodes pleasure and eroticism in a relationship as fast as not asking about, honoring, or attending to a partner's boundaries. In contrast, when people discuss, negotiate, and plan sexual play they are excited about, and when they quickly stop and reassess if something is going wrong for a partner (without giving their partner a guilt trip about it), pleasure most often follows. Teaching about consent includes encouraging people to check in with partners in a variety of ways (verbally and nonverbally) to make sure everyone is having a good time and to collaborate on decisions about "What should we do next?" or "Do you want to try . . . ?" When we encourage clients and students to have open and honest conversations about pleasure, before, during, and after all kinds of sexual contact, we are helping them navigate consent as well.

With Young People

Lindsey Says

Sex can be such a mystery when you haven't had it yet. I find that talking about consent can put some of the nervousness to rest and help young people feel more confident about how to approach such an exciting unknown. I love to discuss the idea that you could ask a person for a kiss before you do it. You've got your body really close to the person you like. You want to kiss them. You wonder if they want to kiss you too. You think they do, but what if you are wrong? I ask the students to tell me what they might be scared of, and usually hear responses like, "What if you go in for the kiss and they pull back suddenly, leaving you in an awkward puckery vulnerable embarrassing mess? What if you land the kiss and they are shocked, and say that they don't think of you like that?"

One strategy to make sure the kiss is going to turn out well is to lean in and softly say, "Can I kiss you?" If they are into it, they will smile, say yes, and then you can both prepare your lips, smile, and come in with your heads at the right angle. Success! If they say no, here is the ticket to saving face: You can say, "Well, I am so glad that I asked, because I would never want to make you feel uncomfortable" (Domitrz, 2003). DANG! What a good response! In the end, even if rejected, you look respectful and downright suave!

Young people love this idea. It is so concrete and simple, easy to use in real life, and you look cool in the end either way. This can lead into a great discussion of how things are set up to go better if both people sort of know what to expect and can get excited and prepared, rather than worry about possible failure. With a kiss, for example, if you know it is coming you can get your mouth ready (assess lip moisture and breathing) and get ready for a successful lip lock. If you are trying to just sneak in and plant one on your unsuspecting partner, though, you might end up with a super awkward moment where you bang foreheads as they try to duck away. Or maybe they even want the kiss, but their gum is malpositioned and it is going to be weird if they don't know you are about to swoop in. Consent helps you both look cool and achieve more pleasurable success.

It works for other sexual acts too ("Can I unbutton your shirt") and for all ages. Some students will worry that it sounds nerdy to ask. I then joke about not using a nerdy old teacher voice like mine to talk about sex in real life, but to use the sexiest voice, words, and body language you've got. This would be a place for slang that you use easily and that you and your partner enjoy, not necessarily the terms from a medical chart. Many people get really turned on by hearing their partner say sexy things, or by hearing someone say what they want to do. You can use this type of talking to turn a partner on, make sure things are pleasurable, and get good consent along the way!

With Adults: Spectrum of Consent

There is disagreement about how to teach about consent, even within communities of sexual health professionals. Some professionals take the position we should teach people to verbally ask for consent all the time and with every sexual action, even with established sexual partners. Some professionals think this method sounds cumbersome and takes a lot of the sexiness out of the relationship. Of course, every person has the right to say no to anything at any time. It also seems to make sense that established partners would be able to make some assumptions about consent as long as they pay attention to their partner's reactions and respond immediately to their partners' "no's". But then again, sometimes people freeze up or have trouble communicating their discomfort or "no" for a variety of reasons. How can we teach about consent in a way that addresses all these concerns? Pleasure can provide a road map through this dilemma. If each person is actively attentive to the other's pleasure it is less likely that they will continue a behavior their partner is not enjoying. However, while pleasure is the goal, aim, and guiding principle, professionals also need to be able to talk about the instances where pleasure didn't happen.

Figure 10.1 shows a tool I have used with clients and students to get the conversation started.

Figure 10.1 The Spectrum of Consent Can Be Used as a Tool for Educating About Consent Issues as Well as Defining or Processing Clients' or Students' Personal Experiences

---

Examples of how each of these might happen:

- **Enthusiastic Consent:** "Yes, I would be very excited to do this sexy thing!"
- **Interested Consent:** "I'm not sure if I will like this sexual behavior but I am interested in trying it." "I am curious about this sexual activity." "I am excited about giving this a try and there is also chance I might decide I don't like it." "I would like to try this but I have had some bad experiences with this kind of activity before, so we need to go slowly."
- **Non-enthusiastic Consent:** "I don't really enjoy this sexual behavior but I will do it because you enjoy it." "I don't mind doing this but it is really more your thing than mine." "This sexual behavior might be somewhat uncomfortable for me, but I will agree to do it until it becomes too uncomfortable." "I'm not really in the mood, but you are, so I will give it a try."
- **Boundary Aggressions:** "I was not asked for consent before this action took place." "This is an action that I have previously stated I do not like."

  In this case it feels like a partner is going right to the edge of what behaviors were agreed on and then trying to push past them a little bit.
- **Non-Consent:** "I said no but they did it anyway." "They didn't ask first and they didn't respond to my signs of discomfort." "I felt frightened and/or powerless to stop the situation."

  (It is important to note that this is not meant to be a legal definition of non-consent, but rather to refer to people's perceptions of their experiences. If people feel they did not have a say in a situation it is important to address that experience).

It is important to note a few things about this spectrum, especially when explaining it to clients and students. Most importantly, the spectrum is not static: A person may start out at one place on the consent spectrum and move to another place at any time. Starting out at one place on the spectrum does not mean you are obligated to stay there and (of course) people always get to say that they need to slow down, change, or stop a sexual experience.

Obviously, there are points on the spectrum of consent that are less desirable than others. Enthusiastic and interested consent are the kinds I encourage people to aim for. Boundary aggressions and non-consent should never be aimed for. Non-enthusiastic consent is tricky to navigate, and while it sometimes goes well, can also lead to feelings of resentment.

Why would I include non-consent, boundary aggressions, or non-enthusiastic consent on the spectrum if the goal is enthusiastic consent? Because these concepts describe experiences that people frequently have: Pretending they don't exist is not helpful. Many people enter my office believing that non-enthusiastic consent is the only thing they will ever experience. Maybe they have never experienced enthusiastic or interested consent. In these cases, telling clients or students to stop being sexual altogether until they or their partner experience enthusiastic consent often makes them feel hopeless and they may give up on the idea that you as a professional can help at all. Introducing the spectrum of consent helps them put words to their experiences and starts the discussion of where on the spectrum they and their partner need to be in order to feel good about engaging sexually with each other.

As they get comfortable with these concepts, I encourage them to wait for interested or enthusiastic consent before engaging sexually with a partner, even if that means missing some opportunities to be sexual. If a partner does not express interested or enthusiastic consent, it may be time to ask them if there is something you can do to ease concerns or increase excitement for them; essentially inquiring about what might help to move them up to interested or enthusiastic consent. This is a much better plan than going ahead with only non-enthusiastic consent.

Working With the Consent Spectrum

Non-Consent

Unfortunately, non-consent is a frequent occurrence for too many people. Non-consent exists on a range of accidental ("I thought you were awake when I started to touch you. When you woke up and told me to stop, I stopped right away.") to purposeful. Having experiences of consent being violated, broken, or ignored can often have lingering effects if the person is not able to process the experience in a safe and supportive way. This can greatly affect clients' and students' ability to feel safe enough during sexual experiences to cultivate pleasure.

Sometimes clients or students first realize they have had nonconsensual sexual experiences by hearing about what other forms of consent look like. When people don't have any frame of reference, they may not know that consent can be interested or enthusiastic. If they were unable to say "no," they may think that constitutes consent, or if they "only said no a few times" and eventually stopped saying no because someone was pressuring them, they may believe this is just how consent goes. Hearing about different kinds of consent can change their expectations of partners and their perceptions of past experiences.

Naming an experience as nonconsensual can be very powerful in both positive and painful ways. Clients and students (rather than the professional) should always be the ones to decide whether they feel a sexual experience was nonconsensual or consensual.

Boundary Aggressions

Many couples struggle with boundary aggressions. These often occur out of failed attempts at seduction or the intense sexual frustration of a partner. This kind of behavior could include touching a partner in ways they have requested not to be touched ("You still come up behind me in public and hug me in a way that lets you grab my boobs. I've told you I hate that!"), attempting to initiate sexual contact by involving the other person's body before getting consent ("I don't like it when we are cuddling and you take my hand and put it on your crotch"), or asking for sexual behavior that has repeatedly been declined in the past ("I've told you I don't like sex in the morning but every Saturday morning you ask me again as if I will have changed my mind"). These moments sometimes feel like minor incidents. However, sometimes they feel like a major overstep of boundaries. No matter where they fall on the scale, boundary aggressions create a feeling of disrespect and erode trust that sexual expression is a mutual decision between partners. They create annoyance, resentment, and sometimes even trauma. Because pleasure and consent are so closely related, boundary aggressions can often kill desire.

For the partner who is committing the boundary aggressions, questions might include, "Did you understand that your partner was uncomfortable? How do you feel when you initiate something and you know/suspect your partner is uncomfortable? What response are you hoping for when you (*try that kind of hug you know bothers them, ask repeatedly when they have already said no, kiss them in public when they have asked you not to*)? Now that you understand how your partner feels about your actions, how do you imagine changing your actions? What could help you remain clear about your partner's boundaries in the future so that you can respect them?" In therapy, this could be done during individual or couple's sessions, depending on the dynamics of the couple.

For the partner whose boundaries are being pushed, it can be helpful to explore situational questions such as, "How would you like your partner to suggest being sexual or come on to you? What actions or words would you like them to use? How would your partner know that you are annoyed or not enjoying their suggestions? How would you tell your partner with words that you want them to stop? How would it feel to say that to them?" It is important to explore how to say "no," or "stop," to a partner, and to create a plan for how to do so. So often, students and clients are afraid to initiate even the things they find pleasurable with their partner because they worry these will lead to sexual activities they don't find pleasurable and they will feel awkward telling their partner to stop or switch activities. Helping clients and students practice saying "No thanks," will help them feel more free to say "Yes, please!"

Non-Enthusiastic Consent

Non-enthusiastic consent can manifest as discomfort, dislike, indifference or, "I don't mind." Non-enthusiastic sex is not a negative experience in every situation. Many people in long-term relationships have "maintenance sex" (deciding to be sexual even though they are not feeling sexy) and feel just fine about it. Normalizing the experience of partners not being "in the mood" at the same time as their partner can sometimes help clients and students relax and take pressure off of themselves. However, when non-enthusiastic consent is the only kind ever given, when sex turns into a chore, becomes distasteful, uncomfortable, or painful, the couple is likely creating more harm than good by trying to push through these issues without addressing them. This would be a good time to discuss what might move the couple from non-enthusiastic consent up to interested or enthusiastic consent.

Un-enjoyable or painful sex is another obstacle many couples face. When partners give non-enthusiastic consent to various forms of sex they do not find enjoyable because they feel like they can "work through" pain, they feel bad telling their partner "this hurts," or they feel like they "should" enjoy it, they are very likely to develop negative associations with sex and cultivate resentment. While in this case everyone may be verbally consenting to the sexual activity, often times both partners notice sex is not pleasurable or fun, and does not feel mutual. I have heard from many clients who feel awful participating in sex if they suspect or know their partner is in pain or not enjoying it. They tell me "I know they said yes but I feel like a predator when we have sex," or, "They always tell me to keep going but it doesn't really seem like they are enjoying it. Honestly, I would rather just stop." These partners can feel the difference between active, excited consent and consent given in spite of reservations, and that is a good thing. This demonstrates their awareness of their partner and the importance they place on their partner enjoying the sexual experience.

Clients and students sometimes need encouragement to follow their perceptions and pause or hold off on sexual contact in these moments, as many (especially people who grew up identifying as male) have gotten the message from society that if a partner says "yes" you should plow through any feelings of discomfort from yourself or your partner and keep going. Sometimes partners feel this is the best opportunity they will get, especially if they never have had an experience where their partner is excitedly consenting. However, this is not a way to increase pleasure or enthusiastic consent in a relationship.

People who say "yes" to sexual contact that is painful or distasteful to them need validation from their sexual health professional that it is better to say "hold on" in those moments, reassess, readjust, or take a break. Pushing through actively unwanted sexual experiences almost never leads to "learning to like it" or pain magically going away. Denying signals from your body that something isn't going well (and witnessing partners disregard these signals as if they are not important) sets a precedence that the body's signals should be ignored. This often leads to less connection with the body, more numbness or distance from its cues, and associating sexuality with fear, pain, disrespect, disregard, and fulfilling the needs of other people.

Interested Consent

There are many sexual activities that people are interested in trying but aren't sure if they will actually like them or not. Imagine going to an amusement park and seeing a roller coaster that looks interesting to you. You may have a great ride but there is also a slight chance you might throw up. You can make a calculated guess based on how you have responded to roller coasters before, but you really can't know how you will respond to this particular one, on this particular day. The good news about being sexual with a partner is that unlike a roller coaster, you can signal that you need to slow down, take a break, or change directions.

It can feel disingenuous for people to express enthusiastic consent in situations where they may be interested, but not confident of how they might respond. The concept of interested consent may feel more accurate in these situations. It can also be helpful to their partner to know they are interested, but not fully enthusiastic just yet. That way, their partner can be careful of going slowly, checking in, and making sure they are enjoying the ride.

Enthusiastic Consent

What encourages pleasure more than knowing the person you want to be sexual with is also is super excited to be sexual with you? Not much. Knowing that your partner values your enthusiastic consent, and in fact, is checking in with you because they don't want to proceed without knowing they have your enthusiastic consent, is a great aphrodisiac as well. However, it is always good to remind students and clients that even if people start out with enthusiastic consent, this can change at any time. That is OK! It is also the reason why people need to continue to check in verbally and nonverbally with partners and everyone should enter into sexual experiences knowing they may be asked to slow down, change something, or stop at any time.

Pleasure and Communication

Communication is key to creating pleasure with partners. Sexual health professionals frequently work with communication skills, whether brainstorming ways to verbally check in about consent with a group of students, or creating a safe space for partners to share a fantasy with each other in a therapy session. This section presents ideas and strategies for helping your clients and students become expert communicators about pleasure issues.

Sharing Pleasure With a Partner: Vulnerability and Safety

What a student or client finds pleasurable can sometimes feel like the most vulnerable information to share with their partner(s). What they desire, enjoy, and fantasize about sometimes feels more personal and intimate than discussing boundaries, limits, or safer sex practices. It is like the difference between telling someone "I live in a house," and inviting them into your bedroom. The people I work with are often more comfortable telling their partners what they absolutely do not want from sex than what they think they might really enjoy. This is opposite of many other aspects of relationships where people tend to fantasize about what they most want to do with their partner(s): vacations they want to take together, what their dream home would look like, plans for having children or adorable pets. While some partner(s) fantasize the same way about the pleasure they want to have together, many find this idea intimidating.

Without a feeling of safety, couples are not likely to share intimate sexual information or desires with each other. If they share when they do not feel safe doing so, the experience may end poorly and shake trust rather than helping to build it. So, how does the sexual health professional help students and clients create the safety needed to share this vulnerable information?

Bringing up sexual pleasure in a gentle and supportive way can build a sense of safety around the topic. Whether in the classroom or in couple's therapy, setting the expectation that people's desires and questions will be respected and confidentiality will be kept is a good way to start. If I am working with a couple in therapy, I may schedule time with each of them individually to talk over what pleasure issues they would like to bring up to their partner. If they have worries about their partner's possible reactions we discuss how to build confidence in expressing sexual desires, even if their partner(s) end up saying "No, thank you."

Whether in therapy or in a class, providing examples of how to react to fantasies and requests in non-judgmental ways can give clients and students the words that may not come naturally to then when they are in the middle of a conversation. Responding positively to a partner sharing pleasure information does not have to mean they are saying yes to actually doing the things their partner brings up. I might say, "I think we have all had that feeling of nervousness about telling our partner(s) something that feels intimate to us. So even if your partner tells you something that you don't think is hot, you know you don't want to do, or something that brings up feelings of anxiety, you can always say, 'Thanks for telling me that. I think I need some time to think about it (or I don't think I want to do that one, or let's bring that one up in therapy so I can figure out how I feel about it). But I know it can be hard to tell someone a fantasy, and I am so glad you took the risk to tell me.' Even when the answer is no, there is no need to shame a partner for telling you what they want. In fact, that is the best way to shut someone down and ensure they won't be sharing their desires with you again any time soon."

Assessing the Couple's Pleasure Knowledge and Communication

Before you can help couples communicate about pleasure, you need to make sure they understand what they are trying to communicate about. It can be helpful to start by assessing their understanding of the basics that were mentioned earlier in this book: how pleasure works in bodies in general, dispelling any myths or stereotypes, and having realistic expectations of their bodies and their partner(s).

Next it can be helpful to find out how much each person understands about what creates pleasure in their own bodies. Are they aware of their own fantasies and desires, what kinds of stimulation they enjoy and in what contexts? Then, have they communicated this pleasure information about themselves to their partners? If your students and clients don't understand what gives them sexual pleasure they won't be able to communicate this to a partner, and so couple's communication skills are built on the self-knowledge of each partner. If you are working with a couple that is struggling to communicate, it may be worth considering going back to the skills presented in earlier chapters and working on building each individual's understanding of their sexual wants and needs.

Next, assess the partners' knowledge of each other and ability to communicate about pleasure. How well do these partners know what is pleasurable for each other? Do they check in during romantic or sexual moments in order to find out what is going well or what they might want to change or adjust? Do they talk afterward about what went well and what didn't? How do they decide what they want to do together when they want to be sexual? If they don't do any of this, they may not currently have much understanding and communication about pleasure and might be following a sexual script about what "should" be pleasurable that they picked up somewhere along the way.

Lindsey Says

The idea that sex involves a specific set of activities, some of which are better or more advanced than others, does us all a disservice. The idea that some acts count as foreplay, but real sex means penetration is not only a heterosexist norm, but also imagining that there is some sort of sex game plan that works for everybody is pretty ludicrous. We certainly can't take what worked in a previous partnered sexual experience and expect to do the same things in the same way with the next person we are involved with. Humans are not pre-programmed sex robots who all work by pushing the same buttons. We are much more creative and interesting than that!

My favorite thing to compare sex to is a buffet. You have about a hundred options! There are probably some things at the buffet (mashed potatoes) that you know you love and you want a heaping helping of each time. In fact, you might go just for those potatoes and not even want anything else. Sometimes you like egg rolls, but you might not be in the mood for them today, and that is fine. You may try a variety of new things from time to time. Maybe a little coleslaw, some crab legs if you're feeling extra fancy. You don't usually love the pasta salad, but sometimes you find yourself wanting a taste anyway. You know you love to finish up with some ice cream, but sometimes you pick a brownie instead. Sometimes you have both. Sometimes you don't care about dessert, because, damn, those mashed potatoes! You could even go to the buffet by yourself. There are no right or wrong choices to make. One food is not empirically better or worse than the next, they are all just different, wonderful options.

The focus in the buffet line is deciding what you are in the mood for and how much of that specific pleasure you want. Of course, if you were sharing your plate with someone else, you would definitely need to talk pretty openly about what you each wanted, and make those decisions together. You would probably want to discuss ahead of time which things you were really hoping for, or if there are any things you totally hate. You might find yourself trying something new, because your buffet-partner is excited about it, or you might skip one of your usual favorites because they dislike it. You will want to find things you both can enjoy. Moving forth without talking about it first would probably be pretty frustrating, as it is unlikely that you both have the exact same dinner in mind.

This analogy always gets some giggles, which is great. Humor is an excellent tool for helping people relax and open up on a sensitive topic. Invariably, people start pointing out other similarities they see between buffets and sex, all great points for discussion and usually pretty hilarious. Ultimately, we are having a good time together talking about sexual variety and deconstructing the notion that vaginal penetration is some kind of goal.

You Are Responsible for Your Own Pleasure, Even in a Relationship

The idea that everyone is responsible for their own pleasure is a revolutionary idea for many of the people I work with. When in a relationship, many people transfer responsibility for their sexual happiness onto their partner. It is easy for people to blame a partner for their sexual unhappiness if that partner wants to be sexual less frequently, experiences pain that limits sexual play, or may otherwise be viewed as the person limiting the couple's sexual expression. While it is true that the sex in a partnership will always be limited by either person's "no," blame is an unhelpful place to get stuck. When couples play the blame game, the partner who is struggling to enjoy sex or wants it less sometimes ends up feeling like "the problem." The partner who wants more sex or different kinds of sex often ends up feeling like they have no control or ability to change their situation.

By starting a conversation with students or clients about self-responsibility and pleasure, it is possible to find a new angle, a way out of the blame/shame cycle many couples find themselves in. If each member of the couple is responsible for their own pleasure, the focus shifts back to what each individual can do to help themselves. For many of my clients and students, focusing on themselves has actually helped their sexual life with their partner(s).

If partner sex is off the table for the moment, or very infrequent, it might be a great time to focus on individual sexual identity and expression. Masturbation can be very helpful, as can exploring and developing the individual's sexual self-concept and fantasy life. As each partner becomes more comfortable and happy with themselves, they often feel more comfortable sharing this new self-knowledge with their partner just for the sake of sharing and without the expectation that it will immediately lead to partner sex. This kind of sharing of the sexual self (to promote greater understanding and openness) can feel very different to the lower desire partner than previous requests for sexual contact that may have felt blaming or needy.

Sexual Self Work for Couples: Anika and Rae

Anika is a cisgender female who identifies as bisexual. Rae is genderqueer, uses "they" pronouns, and identifies as pansexual. When Anika and Rae came to therapy, they told me in the first session, "Rae wants to have sex and Anika doesn't. That's the basic problem." They were in a cycle of sexual pressure/blame (for Anika) and rejection/shame (for Rae) that had them both exhausted. In order to take pressure off of Anika, I suggested it might be a good time for Rae to do some sexual self work. I encouraged Rae to find the aspects of their personal sexuality that were not dependent on Anika wanting to be sexual with them. In an individual session, Rae told me they used to feel confident in their sexual self, knew what they liked to do, and felt good about what they had to offer as a sexual person. However, after this long cycle of not much sex and frequently feeling rejected, they weren't really sure what they thought about their sexual self anymore.

We started working on the sexual role model exercise (see Chapter 6) in individual sessions. When Rae had done a good portion of the exercise and was feeling positive and confident, I asked if Rae would be willing to present their work to Anika. Rae was nervous, worried that Anika would dislike the project and Rae would feel rejected again. So we set some ground rules on how to proceed, including that Anika was only to listen, not to comment. It turned out that Anika loved hearing Rae present about their sexual role models. To Anika it seemed like a way to engage with her partner's sexuality with no pressure of having to "perform" sexually (one of her fears). Anika said it felt a little like when she and Rae were first dating, when she was able to focus on the curiosity of getting to know Rae rather than the pressure and anxiety that sex often brought up for her. This exercise didn't have the couple immediately jumping into bed together, but it did give them a positive moment of focusing on Rae's sexuality without shame and a window into how pressure was really influencing Anika's desire. Anika liked the exercise enough that she thought she might want to identify her own sexual role models. Watching her partner's work helped her feel comfortable with the idea of trying it herself. She was excited about finding ways to talk about sex that weren't filled with the anxiety that she had been struggling with for so long.

The Masturbation Conversation

Talking to couples about their masturbation habits and their beliefs about masturbation is imperative. Many people I have worked with had no idea whether or not their partner(s) masturbated and made wrong assumptions about how their partner(s) might feel about them masturbating. We discover this only by having the masturbation conversation. Reminding partners that masturbation is a possibility can be a helpful part of work with couples. When each partner has the option of masturbation and partner sex is not the only option for sexual expression, it can lift the perceived burden of sexual responsibility from the partner who is struggling to be sexual at that time.

When I asked Rae and Anika about whether they masturbated or talked about masturbation in their relationship, they both got quiet and Rae blushed. "So, does that mean that you don't really talk about it?" I asked and we laughed. After a while I was able to gather that Rae had been avoiding masturbation because they thought it might upset Anika if they masturbated. Now Anika blushed and told us that she actually masturbated regularly on nights when Rae wasn't home. At first Rae felt hurt, "You are masturbating instead of having sex with me?" Anika said, "It's not that I don't want to have sex with you. But you know it gets me all anxious. I don't get nervous when I am all by myself." While I understood why Rae might feel hurt, I also reminded them, "Hey, in a lot of ways this is a good thing. If Anika is masturbating, it means she still enjoys being sexual and has desire. Those are two things you have been worried about, Rae, and now we know they are happening." I told Anika, "Pay attention to what you like about masturbation, what goes well for you, what makes you feel good. Maybe we can work some of that into partner sex when you feel ready for that."

Then I asked Rae why they thought Anika would be upset if they masturbated. Rae said, "I thought she would feel more pressure. That if I asked for private time or space that she would be reminded again that I want to be sexual way more than she does." I asked Anika if she would feel this way. "No way! I'd love it if Rae masturbated. It would take the pressure off me because right now I feel like if I'm not up for sex I am depriving Rae of everything. If they could have masturbation as an option when I'm not in the mood, I wouldn't feel so bad." Anika and Rae worked out guidelines about sexual private time around their house. In the end, they both felt relieved that they had finally talked about an issue that had felt so secretive for so long.

The masturbation conversation has been helpful to many of the couples I work with. In this example, Anika and Rae still had work to do on having the partner sex relationship they both wanted, but they had made a lot of progress regarding understanding their solo sexualities and finding ways to communicate about sex in which each took responsibility for their own pleasure. This was an important stage on the way to building the partner sex relationship they want to have. While sometimes people get frustrated, feeling that self work and masturbation are slow steps when they are longing for sexual connection with a partner, I see them as vital basic skills for constructing the sexual relationship they want. Just like most things in life, taking time to build proficiency in the basic skills means progress toward complex goals goes much faster later on.

Counterbalancing Cultural Baggage by Putting Pleasure Center Stage

Society feeds people many stories and myths about the way sex is "supposed" to happen in relationships and the fantasies or desires that are "normal." When I work with couples I always encourage them to put pleasure (as defined by them) as their guiding principle instead of trying to fit their sex lives into societal expectations. Helping students or clients develop their definition of pleasure as a couple is a great way to start. The exercise that follows can be used in classes as a handout that couples can complete at home. When using it in therapy it may be helpful for each partner to share their answers privately in an individual session before sharing them in a couple's session. You are more likely to get honest answers if they have that privacy. If anyone is nervous about sharing their answers with a partner, an individual session provides time to talk over their concerns and develop strategies for how to share this information.

Box 10.1   Couple's Pleasure Questions

To be completed as individuals first, then couples can share their answers and see how they can combine to find mutual goals.

Are you happy with the ways you are sexual in your relationship?

What kinds of sex are you currently having in your relationship (hand sex, oral sex, penetrative sex, use of sex toys, other activities)?

Of these, which are your favorite activities?

Are you happy with how often you and your partner get to do your favorite sexual activities? If not, what changes would you like to make?

Are you happy with the frequency with which you and your partner are sexual together? If not, what changes would you like to make?

Are there any sexual activities you would enjoy adding to your sex life with your partner? If so, what are they?

Do you find your sexual activities with your partner pleasurable?

Do you have orgasms when you are sexual with your partner? If so, are you happy with how often you have orgasms or would you like to increase this? If not, is having orgasms with your partner a goal you are interested in working towards?

What makes sex pleasurable to you? Is it specific activities, body pleasure, emotional connection, intimacy, something else entirely? Feel free to have multiple answers.

How can you increase the factors that give you the most pleasure with your partner? For example, if emotional connection is important to you, explore what circumstances create emotional closeness and how to have these more often. If you know you love spontaneous sex, how can you create more circumstances to allow for that?

Negative Perceptions of Pleasure in a Relationship

It is important to know what each member of the couple believes about pleasure. What negative perceptions of pleasure might they be bringing to the table? Some people believe pleasure is a selfish goal, that physical pleasure is about objectification rather than connection, or that their needs will be disregarded in their partner's search for pleasure. For people who hold these beliefs, setting goals around increasing pleasure may not be appealing. When one member of a couple holds these beliefs they may be upset with a partner who values pleasure. These perceptions need to be addressed or the couple will likely struggle to find goals they can both feel good working towards.

For Natalie, a cisgender female who identifies as straight, any sign that her husband was sexually attracted to her was distressing. Any time he would tell her she looked great, she would find a way to change the subject and put some physical distance between them. When I asked her what she thought about pleasure she said, "I don't think you can trust it. Pleasure makes people make bad decisions." When I asked her if pleasure had made her husband make bad decisions, she thought for a moment and said, "Not yet. But I think it could." Natalie told me one of her goals was to have fun and fulfilling sex in her relationship, but she was really struggling to find her way around her dislike of his arousal and distrust of pleasure in general.

When I asked Natalie when she first remembered distrusting pleasure, she thought back to one of her first relationships. Her boyfriend was very attracted to her and very interested in being sexual with her. At first Natalie found this to be a turn on; it felt daring to her in a way that she really liked. However, this boyfriend became more and more controlling and abusive as the relationship went on. Natalie described how he would flirt with baristas at the coffee shop while Natalie stood next to him, waiting to order. If she complained, he would tell her she was being ridiculous and jealous. This boyfriend also continually pushed Natalie's established sexual boundaries, using his arousal as an excuse, and told her, "Once I get going it hurts to stop." No wonder Natalie was suspicious of pleasure.

For many people healing from trauma or abuse, it can be important to establish positive motivation in order to go through the fear and discomfort that will likely accompany the healing process once they are in a safe, consensual, and mutual relationship. Perceiving their (well-intentioned, non-abusive) partner's sexual desires as demands that are put upon them is not good motivation and is likely to foster resentment or worse, feel re-traumatizing. However, if they can find a definition of pleasure that they like, even if it is hard for them to imagine in that moment, they have a positive incentive to work towards. I like to ask my clients, "What about pleasure would make going through the healing process worth it? This has to be worth it for you, and mean something to you. It can't just be for your partner."

For Natalie, this meant focusing on her desire to have a satisfying sex life with her husband, even if that was hard to imagine at the moment, and we began crafting a definition of pleasure that was very different than her prior experiences. Natalie liked the idea that pleasure could add intimacy and closeness to her relationship. She had some positive experiences of pleasure in her own body and could imagine what it might be like to have similar experiences with her husband. As Natalie became more confident and comfortable, she even decided she wanted to bring back some of the sexual spontaneity and passion that had felt so good to her in the beginning of her past relationship. In order to do that, she needed to hear from her husband that he was OK stopping sexual activities at any point in the process and that he wouldn't shame or guilt her about it. He agreed and affirmed to her that while he also wanted them to have a great sexual relationship, he wasn't interested in pressuring her or pushing for things she wasn't excited about. This couple now had shared pleasure goals they both felt good about. Having a shared pleasure goal can make the couple feel like a team rather than feeling like they are playing for different sides. Progress moved quickly from there.

Couples Pleasure Will Look Different Than Individual Pleasure

Even the best-matched couples will have differing ideas of what pleasure looks like. By normalizing these differences, we can help students and clients realize there is no "perfect match" for anyone. Instead, each couple gets to find where their shared ground is. I like to use a metaphor about chemistry when normalizing differing desires: "Chemistry happens when individual elements come together to form something new. Hydrogen and oxygen are both important by themselves. Hydrogen is the atom the universe was built on. We need oxygen to breathe. But when these two combine, they make something completely different and equally as amazing: water. They are still hydrogen and oxygen, but they function completely differently because they are together. Chemistry in your sex life can work the same way." Chemists may tell me this isn't completely scientifically accurate, but it gets the point across.

The following exercise works well in a variety of settings such as couple's therapy, small or large groups, or classes.

Defining Pleasure in Your Relationship

Choose from the following list of words or add your own to describe your definition of pleasure in this relationship. Each person should do this separately.

Happy
Fun
Safe
Unplanned
Risqué
Affectionate
Carefree
Spontaneous
Emotional
Romantic
Uncomplicated
Connected
Hot
Sensual
Edgy
Cozy
In the Body
Spicy
Slow
Explosive
Mellow
Organized
Fiery
Action-Packed
Seductive
Shared
Steamy
Considerate
Naughty
Ecstatic
Loving
Casual
Easy
Low pressure
Orgasmic
Attentive
Sexy
Effortless
Cuddly
Flirtatious
Feel free to add your own words.

Now compare your answers with your partner(s). What is similar and what is differ-ent? Can you find a way to combine your lists to compile a profile of what pleasure might look like in your relationship? Since each person's individual lists will look different, some words may end up on your mutual list that were not on your individual lists. This is great as long as all partners agree to all the words on the mutual list. When you have compiled your list of what pleasure looks like in your relationship you now have goals you can work toward. Have fun!

Partners With Differing Wants and Needs

No two people are ever going to have their wants and needs line up perfectly. How-ever, couples sometimes panic if their sexual wants and needs diverge. For monog-amous couples, sexual differences can be more intimidating than other possible differences, such as if one person loves to go running and the other would prefer video games. While people often participate in hobbies with friends or attend social events specific to activities they love, sexual expression in a monogamous couple is very dependent on finding a common ground between each partner's wants and needs. Sexual health professionals are in a helpful place to normalize differences in eroticism, fantasy, and what people find most pleasurable. This can help take the pressure off of the couple and give them more room to negotiate what would feel pleasurable for both of them.

Celebrate What the Couple Has in Common and Encourage Respect for Each Other's Differences

One great place to start is by identifying and celebrating the ways the couple does work well together. Have they had pleasurable and fun sexual experiences together? Exploring these may reveal ideas for how to capitalize on the couple's sexual successes and build more of these experiences in the future. Even small moments of pleasure together can be built upon. Even one experience of pleasure together shows that it is possible. Now the task becomes how to make that happen again.

What about the areas where partners may have differing sexual wants? Just because the couple doesn't share the same turn-ons doesn't make either person's turn-ons wrong. It can be easy for one member of a couple to vilify the desires of the other if they are feeling threatened by those desires. Sexual health professionals can create an atmosphere of acceptance by demonstrating respect for all consensual sexual practices, including curricula/information that acknowledges that couple's desires are not always in sync, and (when appropriate) working with couples to better understand why this desire is exciting for one of them. Sometimes the other partner decides they might be interested in trying this turn-on when they hear it described in positive, exciting ways. Sometimes partners still do not want to engage with this request, but they can understand their partner's desires better and decline without shaming them.

When the Differences Matter

Sometimes a monogamous couple's sexual differences are so divergent that they have a tough time reconciling them. Asking a partner to refrain from engaging in their desires may not be a viable option. For example, in a monogamous couple, if one person identifies as kinky and the other does not want to engage with kink in any way, the kinky person may feel like they are being asked to give up a part of their identity. Professionals can support clients or students in valuing their sexual selves and help them to explore possibilities for pleasure both in their partnership(s) and also in their solo sexuality. Here are some possibilities:

Self-Exploration, Masturbation, and Solo Fantasy. Sometimes a client or student can feel fulfilled if they explore a desire on their own and engage in this desire solo. This may include developing fantasies including their desire, buying erotica or pornography depicting their desire, or incorporating elements of their desire into their masturbation practices.

Fantasy With Partner. Some partners don't want to engage in a certain sexual behavior, but they are willing to engage in fantasy about it. This could be played out through erotic talk during other sexual activities, or being willing to explore erotica or porn with their partner.

Finding Community. There are communities of people who bond through shared desires or lifestyles. BDSM, leather, fetish, nonmonogamy, and swinging, among others, all have communities where people can learn, socialize, and be in the presence of people who understand their desires. Depending on the community, there may be opportunity to meet people to be sexual with (if the couple is nonmonogamous) or possible friendships for those who are looking for self-expression but not sexual connection. Sexual communities can be found online and many places have local, in-person, community events as well.

Consensual Nonmonogamy. Some couples find consensual nonmonogamy to be a helpful solution for differences in desire. There are many varieties of relationship arrangements within nonmonogamy. Options might range from permission to chat sexually with people online but never to do anything in person, to exploring long-term committed relationships with others. There are many great resources available for people considering nonmonogamy, including books, online forums, and community organizations.

When Relationships End Over Sexual Expression

When a person discovers they cannot be their whole selves in a relationship due to conflicts around sexual expression, it is not uncommon for them to feel selfish about the idea of ending the relationship. However, people frequently end relationships over conflicting goals, values, or experiences they know they want to have. "I know I want to be a parent and you know you don't; I'm not sure we can work this out," or "I know I want to move across the country for this job opportunity and you want to stay here, close to your family," are two examples of similar conflicts over wanted experiences. However, when the experiences involve sex or pleasure, people sometimes feel selfish or guilty about their choice.

Sometimes when relationships end over sexual differences, people begin to view their sexuality as a liability or something that keeps them from having the relationships they want to have. When professionals validate the importance of sexual expression and pleasure (in balance with their other life goals), clients and students are more likely to have confidence expressing their desires honestly and openly as they seek future relationships. Rather than viewing this important part of themselves with shame or anger, they may be able to honor their sexual desires and seek partnerships that honor these parts of them as well.

Communication Skills and Exercises

Pleasure feels wonderful, but it does not make people psychic. Couples often want to make each other feel good but struggle to figure out how. As people all have different ways they communicate best, they will need different strategies for communicating about pleasure. Here are some ideas that I have used in classes and with therapy clients.

Verbal Communication

Verbal sexual communication can be fun and sexy. However, sharing pleasure information or making a request of a partner isn't always easy. Here are some guidelines to help set up a more positive conversation about pleasure.

For partners bringing up the subject or request:

- Always present ideas in a positive light. The way you say something makes such a difference, especially with the things that feel risky to say. Telling a partner, "I've always thought spanking was a really hot idea. I've been nervous to try it but I think it would be really exciting to try it with you, if you want to," feels much more appealing and less intimidating than, "I know you will probably think it is weird and I hope you don't freak out, but I think I am into spanking."
- Lighthearted attitudes and humor can help nervous partners relax. Avoiding a deadly serious tone makes it feel like there is less pressure and conveys a sense of confidence from the partner bringing up a request.
- Let your partner know how you need them to respond during this conversation. For example, "This is embarrassing for me to say, so please don't joke around," or, "I have something I want to talk with you about and I was hoping you would just listen at first and not interrupt. I want to be able to get it all out."
- Remember that a "no" doesn't mean you were wrong for asking. Sometimes the answer will be "no.". While this can be disappointing, "no" does not mean that your desires are wrong.

For partners who are listening to information or responding to a request:

- Let your partner know you would love to hear about what they would find pleasurable. Actively telling them you would like to hear their desires can help them feel safe to do so.
- There is always a positive response you can give your partner, even if you choose to say "No" to whatever they are asking for. You can always say, "Thanks for telling me that" or acknowledge that it takes guts to share.

- When your answer is "No thanks," that may be all you need to say. Making a big deal out of things is not necessary and can feel shaming to your partner. However, sometimes you or your partner may want to have a continued conversation about why the answer is no. It can be helpful to talk about what parts of the idea are unappealing, why they are unappealing, and if there are any ways the idea could be adjusted so that everyone would be excited to try it. However, these conversations should have respect for the original "no" and not be about pressuring someone into giving a different answer. If you and your partner become locked in a never-ending conversation about sexual activities one of you wants to try and the other does not, that is probably a good time to go talk to a counselor or therapist to try to find some resolution.
- Take risks of your own by sharing your own pleasure requests. Pretty soon you will have a great conversation going.

Communicating Through Sexy Sounds

One great way for partners to communicate about what feels pleasurable is to verbalize through affirmative noises. Of course, this does not always give partners all the detailed information they might need, but it is a great way to communicate in the moment and it doesn't break the mood the way intricate instructions sometimes might. Partners often enjoy hearing their partner's sounds of breathing or moaning, and find it intensifies the sexual connection. In addition, making noises encourages people to take deeper breaths, which may heighten arousal by increasing oxygen in your body.

Having a conversation with people you work with about whether they make noise during sex, or how they feel about sexual noises, can bring up varied thoughts and perceptions about pleasure ("I don't want anyone to hear me and know. If I am too loud my partner will get nervous. I love hearing my partner . . . it's so sexy."). These thoughts can be important areas to explore.

"Hotter, Colder" Exercise

Challenge your partner to pick up on what you like during sex through the noises you make. Before you start, have a conversation about the guidelines of the game as well as any important boundary or safer sex issues. Tell your partner you will make more enthusiastic noises the more pleasure you feel from their actions. Inform your partner before you begin how you will indicate a request for faster/slower, stop/more. Some people use indications like shushing noises, sighing, or small but helpful phrases like, "Yes! Yes!" or "Just like that!" to help guide their partner. Sexiness and connection may be intensified if you make eye contact during this exercise.

Visual Communication

A picture is worth a thousand words. Sometimes clients or students may be nervous about the idea of describing in detail what they like. In some circumstances, it may be more helpful to show a partner what they want. Obviously, they need to be able to talk through this enough to obtain consent and not surprise their partner with something unwanted.

Visuals are one of the clearest ways to communicate touch requests. One example of this might be encouraging couples to watch each other masturbate to learn what feels good to their partner; a plus to this method is the couple might have pleasure or orgasm while they are communicating. Here is another helpful exercise.

The Goldish Rule Exercise

The Golden Rule teaches us to treat others the way we want to be treated, but what if the touch you want is different than the touch your partner likes? The Goldish Rule exercise is a chance to communicate to your partner the ways you like to be touched. Take a minute to find a comfortable environment to be sexual with each other and establish your sexual boundaries or safer sex procedures. Then take turns showing your partner the ways you would like to be touched. You can do this by demonstrating the touch you like on their body or by touching your own body in the way you prefer. Ask them to watch or put their hand on top of yours so they can feel your movements. Take turns doing this for each other and notice how the touch your partner likes may be different or similar to the touch you like.

Sharing Pleasure Information Through Media

A subtle but effective way of communicating pleasure preferences is to use media that pops up in daily life: movies the couple may attend together, books they are reading, porn or erotica they seek out. It can be easy to comment on images or fun fantasies as they come up. Saying something simple like, "Sexy!" or "Hot!" during a love scene or a music video can convey a preference or turn on.

Some couples prefer some individual time to process the information their partner gives them. In this case, it might be helpful to encourage the couple to trade DVDs they enjoy, share a hot picture they found, or highlight a sexy scene in a book. Perhaps they want to attach a note to tell their partner why they picked this scene. Then their partner can watch or read it privately and process it before they need to respond. This can provide more time to decide how they feel and craft an answer.

One difficulty with this method is the majority of the representations easily found in pop culture are likely to be heterosexual, cis-gendered, dyadic paired, and Caucasian. However, more diverse resources can be found with a little bit of effort. While you don't need to have a vast collection of erotic media in your office, it shows awareness of these societal dynamics when sexual health professionals take the initiative to find photo books, zines, movies, or other resources that offer a wider variety of representations. While it is not our job as professionals to find the perfect sexy images for each client, widening our knowledge of the resources available expands our professional understandings. It can also show that you are paying attention to your clients' or students' identities and that you understand that they may not always see their experience reflected back to them in the world. Initiating a conversation with students and clients about whether it is struggle to find positive, sexy representations of their identities, bodies, cultures, or relationships is an important thing to do as well.

For couples who struggle to share their turn-ons or people who can't convey this information to a partner because they don't have a clear understanding of their own turn-ons, the following exercise can be helpful.

Nightly Erotic Share Exercise

Every night for a week each partner will each pick an image, video, piece of writing, or piece of art that they find erotic in some way. Examples might be erotic stories, music videos, art books, porn, love poetry, or magazine ads. The couple will sit together and take turns sharing their find. Couples with a higher comfort level may want to have a conversation about what they like about the piece, and why they picked it to share. These couples may lead the conversation to elements they would like to incorporate into their own sexual play based on the pieces they both find erotic.

For couples who are more nervous, agreements might be made that certain mediums will be avoided ("I don't know if I will be OK with videos, but still images are OK"). If discussing the chosen pieces seems too intimidating, each partner can commit to sharing silently, without an explanation of why they enjoy the piece. Partners who are nervous about responding can always say, "Thanks for sharing this with me." Instruct the couple that they are not to be disrespectful of what the other shares, even if they do not find the piece to be erotic themselves. If the piece their partner presents brings up big emotions or fears for them, they may want to share how they are struggling (in a respectful way) or they may want to talk about it together in therapy.

This exercise is helpful in increasing each member of the couple's understanding of their own turn-ons, their partner's turn-ons, and where their interests overlap. It can also increase their understanding and comfort of the idea that they and their partner will always have erotic differences and that is OK. There is almost always common ground to build on.

Written Communication

Writing can be a more comfortable way of communicating about pleasure for students or clients who like to have time to choose their words carefully and think about their statements thoroughly. Writing also offers the option of privacy to the partner reading the letter. They have time to decide how they want to react, which is important to many people, especially people who feel nervous about communicating about pleasure. Writing a letter for a partner can be intimate and sexy. It can be a gift (a love letter) and a request ("I'd like to . . .") all in one.

Writing about pleasure can be simple. Clients and students don't have to be great writers to get their message across. The guidelines for verbalizing pleasure requests listed earlier could be helpful in finding phrasing that will make their request appealing to their partner. Some people find inspiration by reading published love letters or erotica. Or, for people who need a template and have a lighthearted sense of humor, the following exercise would offer one way to easily write about pleasure for their partner(s).

Erotic Mad Lib

Dear,

One thing I just love about you is _____. It really turns me on when you _____. Sometimes I fantasize about _____.
My favorite way for you to touch my _____ is when you _____ my _____ very _____. I can't wait until _____ when we could _____.

Your _____,

_____

(Your Name Here)

Of course, when people write down something sexual there is always the risk that it could be seen by someone they did not intend to see it. Initiating conversations with students and clients about what precautions they might want to take around privacy for their sexual writings or images is an important part of the discussion.

Final Thoughts: Consent, Communication, and Pleasure

The more comfortable clients and students feel saying "No, thank you," to what they don't want, the freer they will feel to say "Yes, please," to what they do want. In order to do this seemingly simple task they need to have a multitude of skills, including knowing how to navigate consent, communicate wants and needs, and figure out what they might find pleasurable to try. Consent, communication, and pleasure are intertwined and the work of sexual health professionals needs to incorporate all of them.

Reference

Domitrz, M. J. (2003). *May I kiss you? A candid look at dating, communication, respect & sexual assault awareness.* Greenfield, WI: Awareness Publications.

Epilogue

Creating a Pleasure-Positive Culture in Your Office, Your Classroom, and the World

Pleasure-positive culture: What does that mean? It means believing that pleasure is a key component of health; that pleasure education creates better health outcomes, improves self-esteem, and is beneficial to relationships. It does not mean all pleasure is good for everyone all the time. Certainly there are ways that seeking pleasure can have negative outcomes. Pleasure can become out-of-balance or detrimental (just like everything in life). However, pleasure-positive culture maintains that pleasure can be a powerful force of health and empowerment. It asserts that we are all capable of experiencing pleasure and that all human beings have a right to get the information and education they might need to create pleasure for themselves. Pleasure-positive culture has great potential to fight rape culture because it fights the myths that support rape and consent-violating behavior, and the shame that discourages victim/survivors from speaking out. When pleasure is no longer stigmatized, people will have more freedom to develop their sexual agency without negative repercussions, to say "yes" to the sexual contact they want and "no" to what they don't want.

Our world needs pleasure-positive culture. Who will create this change if not sexual health professionals?

How can we do that? Bit by bit. Day by day. Seemingly small actions can create big changes. Care around language to not equate penis-in-vagina penetration with "the one true kind of sex" will be a revolutionary thought for many of your students. The couples therapist who asks their clients not just how frequently they are having sex but whether everyone is enjoying themselves shifts their clients' expectations about sex to be more pleasure centered. The medical professional who asks their patient "Do you ever have pain with sexual activity?" and follows up with, "Pleasure is often a sign of health. How's pleasure going for you?" starts a conversation that patients may never have been invited to have before. The educator who teaches from a pleasure perspective captures students' attention, creates more inclusive lessons, and increases the chances their students will use safer sex practices.

Advancing pleasure-positive culture means not making assumptions about who may or may not want pleasure in their lives based on age, race, culture, ethnicity, body type, religion, STI status, ability/disability, orientation, gender expression, or relationship status. It also means learning to talk and teach about sexuality in a way that includes a wide range of sexual behaviors and expressions.

Selling lube and sex toys in your clinic or office is one way to promote pleasure-positive culture. Sometimes people who are told they could benefit from lubrication, a vibrator, or a cock ring, hit their embarrassment limit before they can get themselves to a shop that has the tools they need. Seeing toys and lube in a medical, mental health, or educational establishment may give people permission to believe that these items are valuable and "appropriate" for them to use. Whether or not you can have lube and toys available in your clinic, developing a good relationship with your local sex toy shop(s) is a great way to be more pleasure positive in your practice. In Minneapolis we are incredibly lucky to have The Smitten Kitten, which not only provides a welcoming atmosphere, educated staff, and sells only toys that are body friendly, but also frequently hosts trainings designed specifically for sexual health professionals. Another fabulous store, Self Serve in Albuquerque, New Mexico, offers "referral cards" to sexual health professionals so they can write down what they think their client, student, or patient would benefit from, such as "silicone-based lubricant," or "prostate massager." These are simple but powerful ways that sexual health professionals across various fields can work together.

While not everyone is lucky enough to have an educator-staffed, welcoming sex toy store near them, being familiar with online options for your students, clients, or patients to access can be very helpful. Many people are scared to look up sexual products on the Internet, worrying they will give their computer a virus or accidently stumble across porn they weren't looking for. Getting some suggestions about websites from a professional makes it more likely that they will feel confident enough seeking these options out. Professionals can treat this like giving their patients or clients referrals: Provide three options and the client can pick which feels like the best fit for them.

Advancing pleasure-positive culture may mean incorporating the word "pleasure" front and center in the way you advertise your work: in the language of your website, pamphlets, brochures, or class descriptions. This gives the people you work with permission to ask pleasure questions right from the start. It means understanding how to explain to confused clients (or other professionals) why pleasure is valuable and absolutely a professional topic. Use the information in this book to help form a mission statement about why your organization or practice values pleasure. Including questions about pleasure on your intake paperwork is another great way to welcome the conversation and can be as simple as, "Do you have any questions about pleasure, sexuality, orgasms, or the way your body works during sex for this visit?"

Pleasure-positive culture values consent. As sexual health professionals, we need to make sure we are giving the people we work with the power to consent (or decline) in their interactions with us. Forcing a cheery view of pleasure down the throat of someone who is terrified is not helpful and is dismissive of people's negative experiences. Being able to gently share information on the benefits of pleasure while understanding that pleasure still means danger for many people is a part of pleasure-positive culture. Informing classes of what topics might be included, and letting participants know they are welcome to take a break, leave the room, or participate passively (not expecting them to answer questions out loud or participate in discussions) if they wish to are ways to give your students the ability to consent to each part of class and to support their choice to leave or withdraw if needed.

Lindsey Says

Pleasure positivity can be a meaningful and liberating awakening for people who have struggled their whole life with feelings of guilt and shame. Claiming pride in your sexuality is life altering. This is something that, for some, doesn't even seem possible. When an educator, doctor, therapist, or someone else approaches sexuality from this viewpoint, the ripple effects of curiosity and confidence may lead to tremendous impact in one's ability to feel peace and joy in their life as it pertains to their body and relationships.

Perhaps one of the most powerful things that we can do as sexual health professionals is to stand proudly and confidently in front of our clients and classes as we talk about pleasure. We demonstrate pleasure-positive culture through our words and actions. As people see confident, knowledgeable professionals who believe in the power of pleasure, and who know there is always an appropriate and factual way to address pleasure issues, society's general perception of pleasure will shift and change. Each of us can be a gateway to a more positive relationship with pleasure for the people we work with. What an important responsibility. What an amazing gift.

Index

Note: Italicized page numbers indicate a figure on the corresponding page. Page numbers in bold indicate a table on the corresponding page.

abstinence-based sex education 6, 43
achievement language 85
active participation of sexual partners 68
adaptive equipment and pleasure 51
adults/elderly: consent and 154–6; pleasure awareness 93–6; pleasure education 5–6; pleasure timeline exercise 100; reproductive *vs.* pleasure anatomy in education 48
American Dialect Society 79
American Medical Association (AMA) 21
American Psychological Association 21
Anal Pleasure and Health (Moran) 146
anal sex: lack of knowledge about 44; oil-based lubricant 126; sex toys and 142–6
anatomy and function discussions 87–9
anus 88
arousal information 89
awareness between sexual partners 68

bacterial vaginosis 125
BDSM 5, 152, 169; toys 152
beautiful people myth 49
belief systems and guilty pleasure 108–13
binary gender expression 58
body expectations, clarification 88–9
boundary aggressions 155–7
boundary-breaking behavior 75
boundary-setting skills 74
breast forms 150

Centers for Disease Control (CDC) 22
childhood pleasure timeline exercise 99
chlamydia 131
cisgender men: gender expressions 45; gender stereotypes 58–9; pleasure-danger connection for 63–4; rape culture and 57–8

cisgender women: gender stereotypes 59–60; rape culture and 57; talking about pleasure 77, 165–6
clitoris: reproductive education and 40; stimulation of 42, 74; talking about 88
cock rings 139, 147–8
cognitive disabilities 47
collaborative decisions between sexual partners 68–9
communication: sexy sounds 171; sharing pleasure and 159–70; skills and exercises for 170–5; verbal communication 170–1; visual communication 171–2; written communication 173
community and pleasure 169
community centers 5
comprehensive sex education 21, 49
conception-friendly lube 130–1
condoms 29–30, 131–3
consensual nonmonogamy 169
consent: boundary aggressions 155–7; enthusiastic consent 155–6, 159; interested consent 158–9; non-consent 155–6; non-enthusiastic consent 155–6, 157–8; sharing pleasure and 153–9, *155*; *see also* rape culture and consent
couples therapists 4
cultural baggage and sharing pleasure 164–5

dangerous pleasure: case studies in pleasure 25–7; condom use 29–30; healthy and safety outcomes 28–9; introduction 19; reshaping sex education dialogue 27–8; sex education results 23–5; sex education *vs.* sexual health 20–2; sexual health professionals and fears 30–3
desire and rape culture 57–8

Made in the USA
Monee, IL
05 January 2023

24601473R00108